Botanical Painting

WITH THE

Society of Botanical Artists

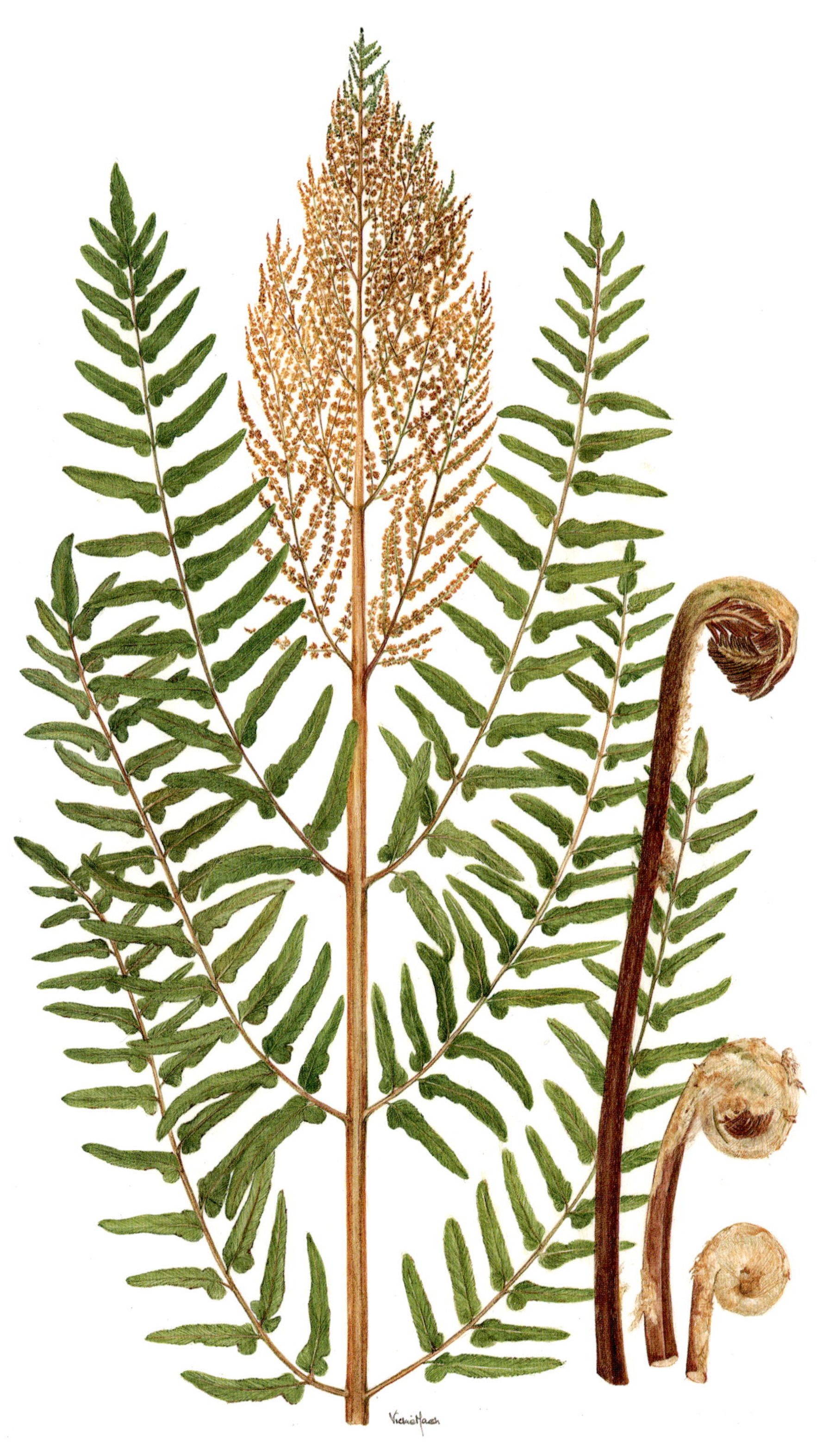

The *Osmunda regalis* (royal fern) is one of a series of paintings by Vickie Marsh (see page 84) and is an example of a plant which grew in Britain 9,000 years ago.

Botanical Painting

with the
Society of Botanical Artists

MARGARET STEVENS

BATSFORD

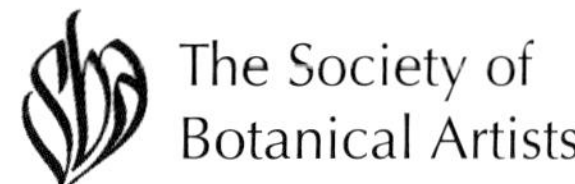

The Society of
Botanical Artists

First published in the United Kingdom in 2018 by
Batsford
43 Great Ormond Street
London
WC1N 3HZ

An imprint of Pavilion Books Company Ltd

ISBN 9781849944526

A CIP catalogue record for this book is available from the British Library.

10 9 8 7 6 5 4 3 2 1

Reproduction by Mission Productions Ltd, Hong Kong
Printed and bound by Toppan Leefung Printing Ltd, China

This book can be ordered direct from the publisher at
www.pavilionbooks.com

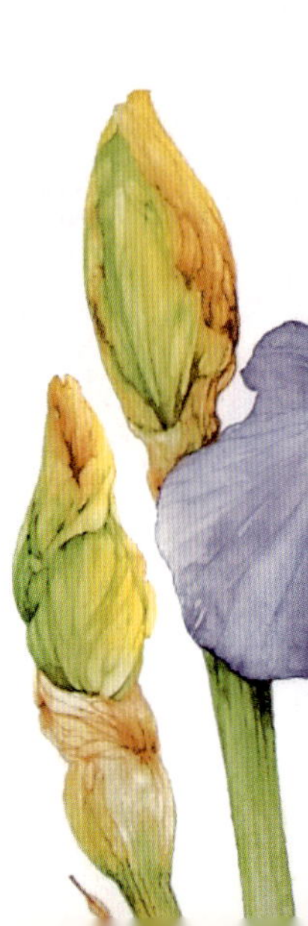

Iris | Jan Harbon | Watercolour on paper
Jan has developed a technique for working with
contrasting colours without them appearing harsh or
garish, of which this is a fine example.

Contents

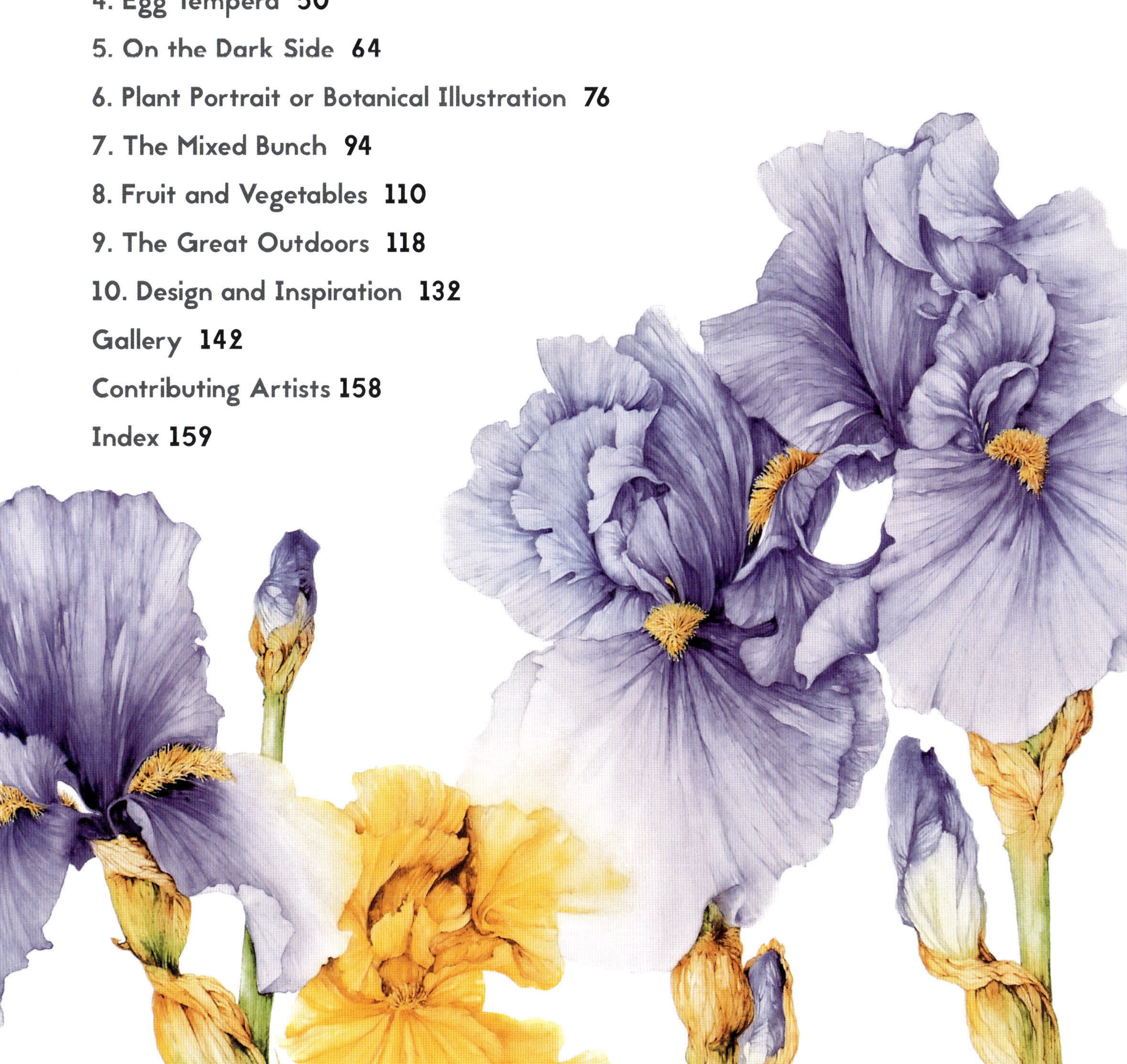

Introduction

The adjective 'botanical', from the noun 'botany', is applied to the study of the structure, genetics, ecology, distribution, classification and economic importance of plants or, secondly, the plant life of a particular area or period. Those of us who choose to paint plants must fit into that list somewhere as the creators of botanical art – the least regarded of the art forms and for centuries totally overlooked or viewed from a very narrow perspective.

About 35 years ago I was wandering around the RHS Chelsea Flower Show when Patricia Dale, an exhibiting artist whose stand always drew crowds of admirers and collectors, told me that an acquaintance called Suzanne Lucas was thinking of setting up a society exclusively for botanical painters. She wanted to gather a nucleus of founder members, and in order to ensure a very high standard, they should already have either Silver Gilt or Gold medals from the Royal Horticultural Society. For many years this august body was the only one that recognized the art form and each of the four winter shows in London included a section devoted to paintings. Named after the First World War Field Marshal Lord Grenville, the Grenville Bronze, Silver and Silver Gilt medals were eagerly sought and the RHS Gold, then as now, often reduced the recipient to tears of joy, as a mark of excellence equal to any awarded at the Olympics. Less frequently awarded, the Lindley medal, named for the first secretary of the RHS, was given for work of special educational or scientific interest.

At the time of my husband's death in 1982 I had returned to painting after a gap of some 20 years and that, together with gardening, helped to restore my equilibrium after a very difficult period. I had exhibited at the RHS on three occasions and had the required Silver Gilt Medal, so I left my address with Pat and thought no more about it. A few weeks later I received a letter from Suzanne that was to change my life and set me on a totally unforeseen path with some very interesting byways.

Suzanne recognized that the art of flower painting had bloomed and flourished with increasing vigour since the 17th century yet no one had thought to form a society where like-minded people could meet and exhibit. This might help to counterbalance the rather negative attitude to botanical art displayed by critics and those who consider themselves to be the arbiters of fashion and good taste. Regardless of them, the public who buy paintings to adorn their homes tend to choose natural beauty and colour, as many of us had found at our solo shows. Before the Society of Botanical Artists (SBA) was officially formed, a trial exhibition was held at the Mall Galleries in London that attracted many admiring visitors. Thanks to Suzanne's hard work and a dedicated council, within two years we had a functioning society with an established home in the new Westminster Gallery at Westminster Central Hall, where it has remained for the last 30 years. Now the SBA also holds a biannual exhibition at the Botanic Gardens in Frankfurt and as I write one is planned for 2018 in Madrid. With our international membership, it is fitting to show our work abroad.

So the SBA has flourished, in spite of fighting a continual battle against rising costs. As it is a registered charity it is incumbent upon us to show members' work as part of its educational function, but the visitors who gaze with delight at some glorious paintings would be horrified if they knew how much it cost to hang each one on the wall. Nevertheless, we have managed to survive so far, although artists rarely receive the true value of their labour, and many would earn more stocking shelves on the midnight shift in a supermarket. It was ever thus and even Pierre Redouté, that master of the art, died in poverty, so no one does it for the money. Many artists eke out a living by teaching or other part-time work. However, no matter what their circumstances one thing is shared: the desire to capture the beauty of the natural world on paper.

From the start Suzanne was determined that the SBA should not just represent botanical illustration – the more scientific plant studies, sometimes showing what she referred to as 'little soldiers' standing to attention on the paper. The SBA should be a broad church welcoming all those whose work was excellent within its field, true to form, size and colour for classic botanical illustration but allowing for enlargement or miniature portrayal, with only the rough and ready element of impressionism considered unsuitable.

This wider perspective makes for a more interesting exhibition, which is without doubt appreciated by the public. For example, one would expect a man who was at that time the Director of the Royal Botanic Gardens, Kew to pounce on a beautiful pure botanical study when he visited the exhibition, and there were plenty of those to choose from. Instead, his favourite painting was a large vase of white lilies embellished with gold leaf!

The publication of my book, *The Art of Botanical Painting* in 2004, prompted the setting up of the first Distance Learning Diploma Course (DLDC) in order to fulfil the SBA's educational responsibility. We had no idea if this would prove popular, but we were amazed how many people were prepared to commit to a programme lasting 27 months, completing 12 assignments plus an essay and three Diploma pieces in that time. We are currently in the middle of the 14th course and over the years we have been delighted to welcome students from all across the globe; of course the internet now plays a large part in introducing our overseas students. The tuition by SBA members is of a very high standard and on an individual basis. The final Diploma is now coveted in much the same way as the RHS Gold Medal.

Building on these foundations, this book is aimed at the more advanced student but will also be appreciated by anyone who likes to gaze upon examples of skill and beauty. My focus includes areas that are now coming to the fore, such as the use of vellum and egg tempera, both of which have been neglected over the years with very little guidance available for those wishing to expand their horizons. I am indebted to both Shevaun Doherty and Marion Perkins for sharing their expert knowledge in both these disciplines and indeed to all the SBA members who gave precious time and energy to satisfy the ongoing thirst for knowledge in this botanical field.

Finally, I have included many paintings by members and students past and present, as if leading you through an exhibition, pointing out salient features that should be useful. There may be a few surprises as we look deeper into what inspires some artists, but I think it is worth remembering that Picasso's harlequin came in many guises and van Gogh's sunflowers came from the same hand and eye coordination as the dark interior scene of *The Potato Eaters* painted only three years earlier, so sometimes 'little soldiers' morph into something very different.

A final word to all those who endeavour to capture such beauty: remember the makers of Persian carpets who intentionally weave a flaw into the design, recognizing that only Allah is perfect. This display of humility is commendable and the best work will always be turned out by those who recognize their earthly limitations.

Rosa 'Paddy Stephens'

MARGARET STEVENS | Watercolour on paper

This is purely a plant portrait without any attempt to show the 'workings' of the plant. I was captivated by the magnificence of the blooms and the splendid leaves. These are leathery and so shiny that they could almost be sprayed with varnish. This allows the venation to be clearly observed and provides a wonderful way to portray texture through highlights. The flowers are long-lasting and fade to pink and pale yellow with touches of crimson so that a later portrait would appear to be of a totally different variety of rose.

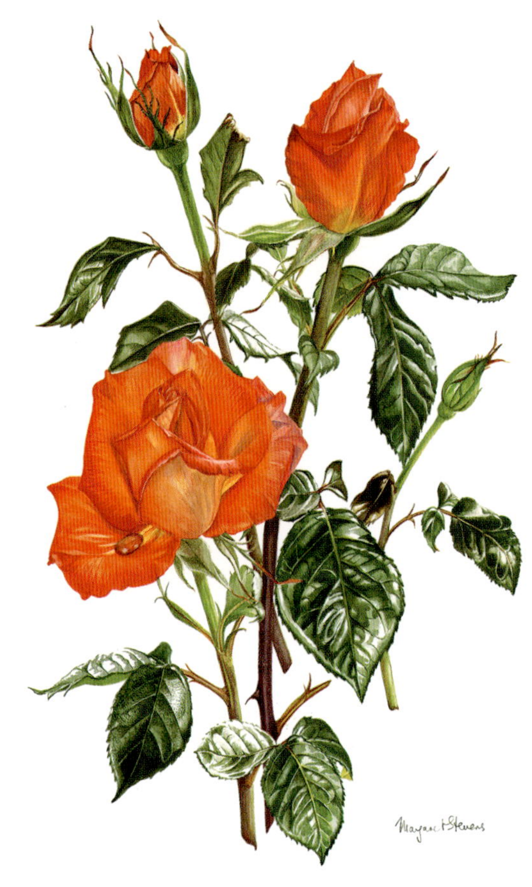

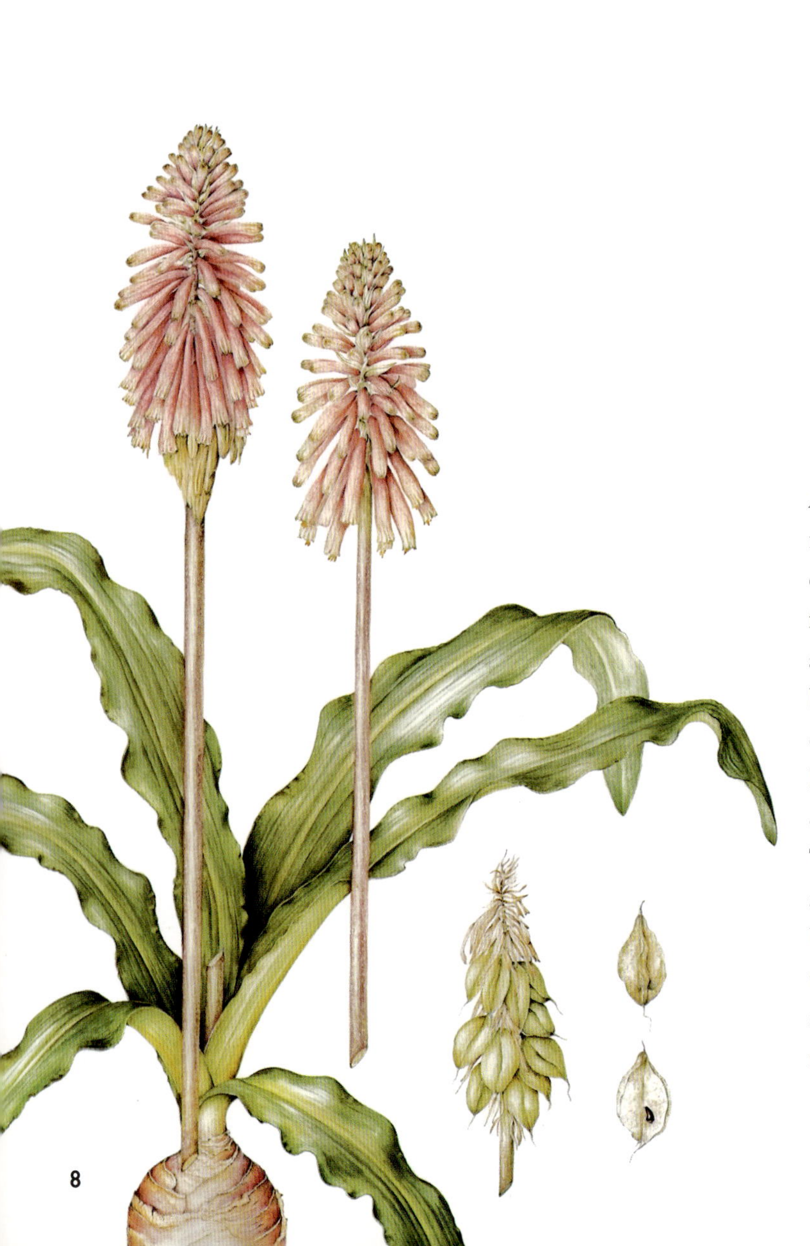

Veltheimia bracteata (Forest Lily)

SHEILA ETCHINGHAM | Watercolour on paper

A native of South Africa, this member of the lily family makes an excellent house plant. This is a true example of botanical illustration, which shows the life of the plant from bulb to seed in a pleasing manner, proving that a scientific approach need not detract from a painting's broader appeal. The composition is excellent and a good example of how to portray long-stemmed flower spikes. Placing the main stem in front of the bulb anchors the composition and allows the shorter stem to recede slightly. The seedhead echoes the shape of the other two stems and provides the third element, which helps to maintain balance, as odd numbers always will. The odd number theory is reinforced by the two brown seed capsules alongside the seedhead, showing that colour as well as form helps to create a harmonious composition.

Summer Garden 2

ELIZABETH SHERRAS CLARK | Watercolour on paper

This is the type of picture that many botanical painters find most
challenging; although happy to portray formal plant portraits or
botanical illustrations, they seem to take fright when confronted
with a mix of blooms to make a flower painting. Here Elizabeth
chose some of her favourite garden flowers and, working entirely
from life, created a sunny medley of blooms.

CHAPTER 1

Monochrome

Today we tend to think first of graphite pencils as the tool for the job when we wish to create a study in black and white, though they were unknown to Old Masters such as Leonardo da Vinci, who used materials such as ink, clay, charcoal and silverpoint. In the 16th century, the discovery of a large deposit of graphite at the head of the Borrowdale valley in the English Lake District introduced a new method of drawing and writing. As it could also be used in the production of cannonballs, graphite was regarded as a very high-value product, to the extent that miners were searched on leaving the mine in case they were sneaking lumps out in their pockets. A means of encasing graphite in wood to make a drawing tool was soon found, but it was only in the early 19th century that the first pencil factory opened in Keswick. The brand, named Derwent after the local river, is now known worldwide and a visit to Derwent's pencil museum at Keswick is worthwhile for any artist visiting the English Lakes.

The illustration opposite shows a beautiful iris by Guy William Eves, an experienced artist whose stunningly intricate work is much admired. Even as a child Guy preferred monochrome to colour, a passion that prevailed through his art school years, to the exasperation of his tutors. Inspired by the photography of Ansel Adams and Irving Penn, he developed his black and white films and made prints in his own darkroom at home, refining the appreciation of lighting direction, depth and contrast, which can be seen in his botanical drawings today.

RIGHT *Iris* | Guy William Eves | Graphite on paper

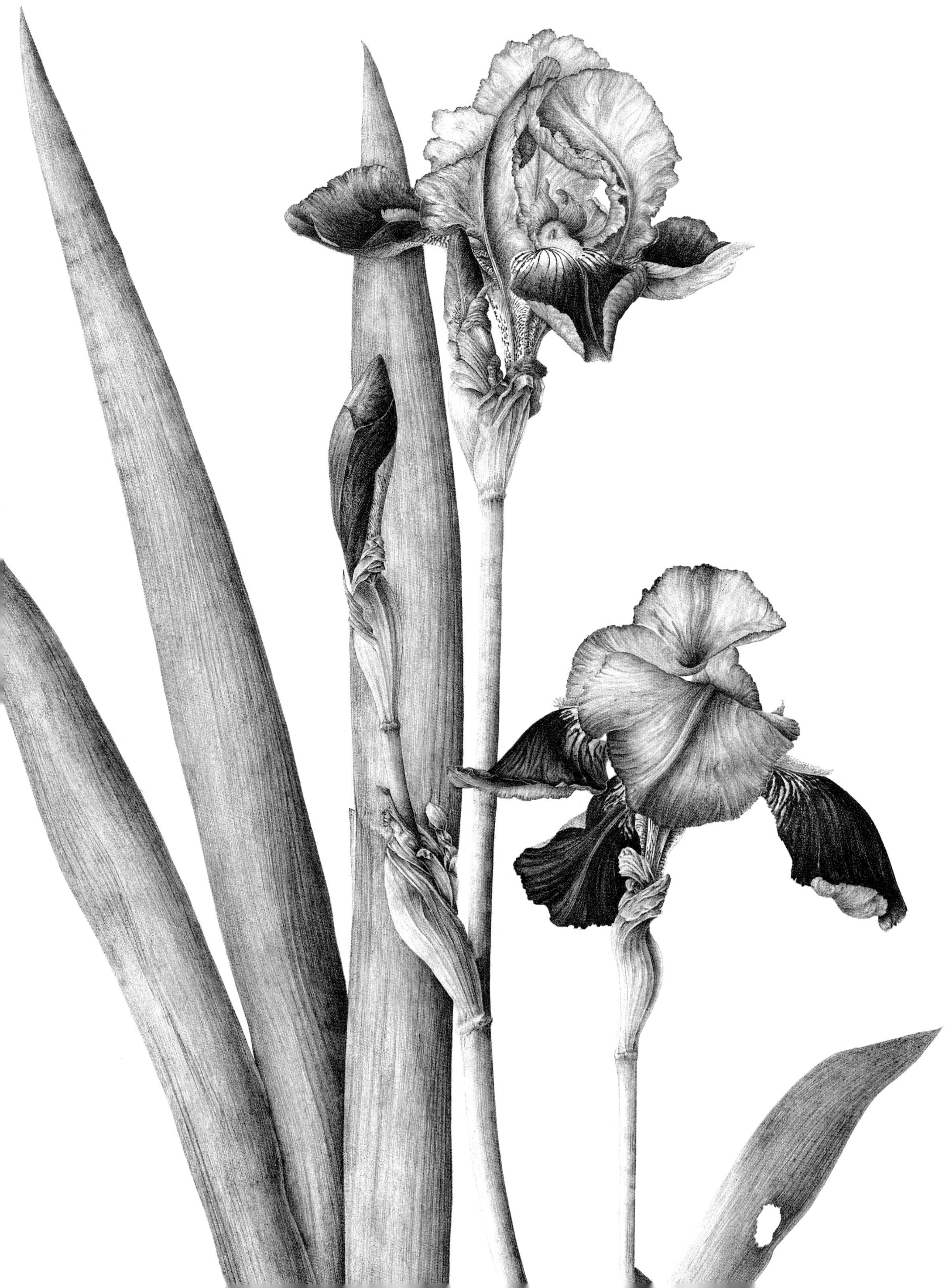

Step-by-Step

HYDRANGEA 'HORTENSIS', MOPHEAD, CULTIVAR UNKNOWN BY GUY WILLIAM EVES

Guy is always careful to choose a specimen that shows off the flowers, foliage and stem to their best advantage. In the case of this hydrangea the head of multiple bracts forms a sphere – the 'mophead' by which it is known. This required well-placed lighting in order to show off the rounded form. Lit from the front it would appear flat, so lighting from the left-hand side was important (a left-handed artist may prefer the light source to emanate from the right).

STEP 1

Using an old mount enabled Guy to frame his subject and plot its composition on paper, where it would be shown life size. He drew a simple outline using an F grade pencil as this stays sharp and leaves a line just dark enough to see without putting enough pressure on the pencil to make an indent on the paper. Such a line can easily be erased if necessary. Guy always tries to complete the outline drawing in one sitting in order to avoid having to reposition himself. If he does have to move he makes sure the chair stays in the same place and he keeps a fixed reference point in mind so that he can return to exactly the same position. This important point is often overlooked, which is the reason why so many artists/exhibitors present work that is out of line, as if seen from two or three different angles.

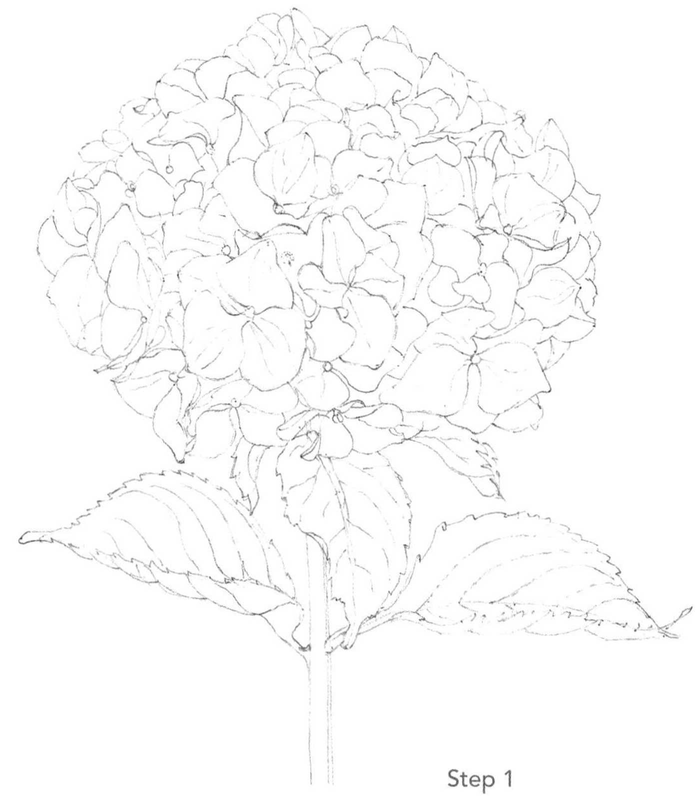

Step 1

STEP 2

Next Guy covered the drawing with a sheet of paper from which he had cut a small window through which to work, ensuring that his hand would not touch the drawing surface again – tracing paper is best for this purpose. He started with a hard 2H pencil and, using a series of light strokes, laid down a pale tint, leaving any veins or light areas as untouched paper. He added darker tone using a grade H or HB pencil to pick out subtle tonal changes, wrinkles and textures before adding further depth with a 2B. This may sound a short and simple process but in fact took many hours, going over and over again until the whole flower head had been worked up.

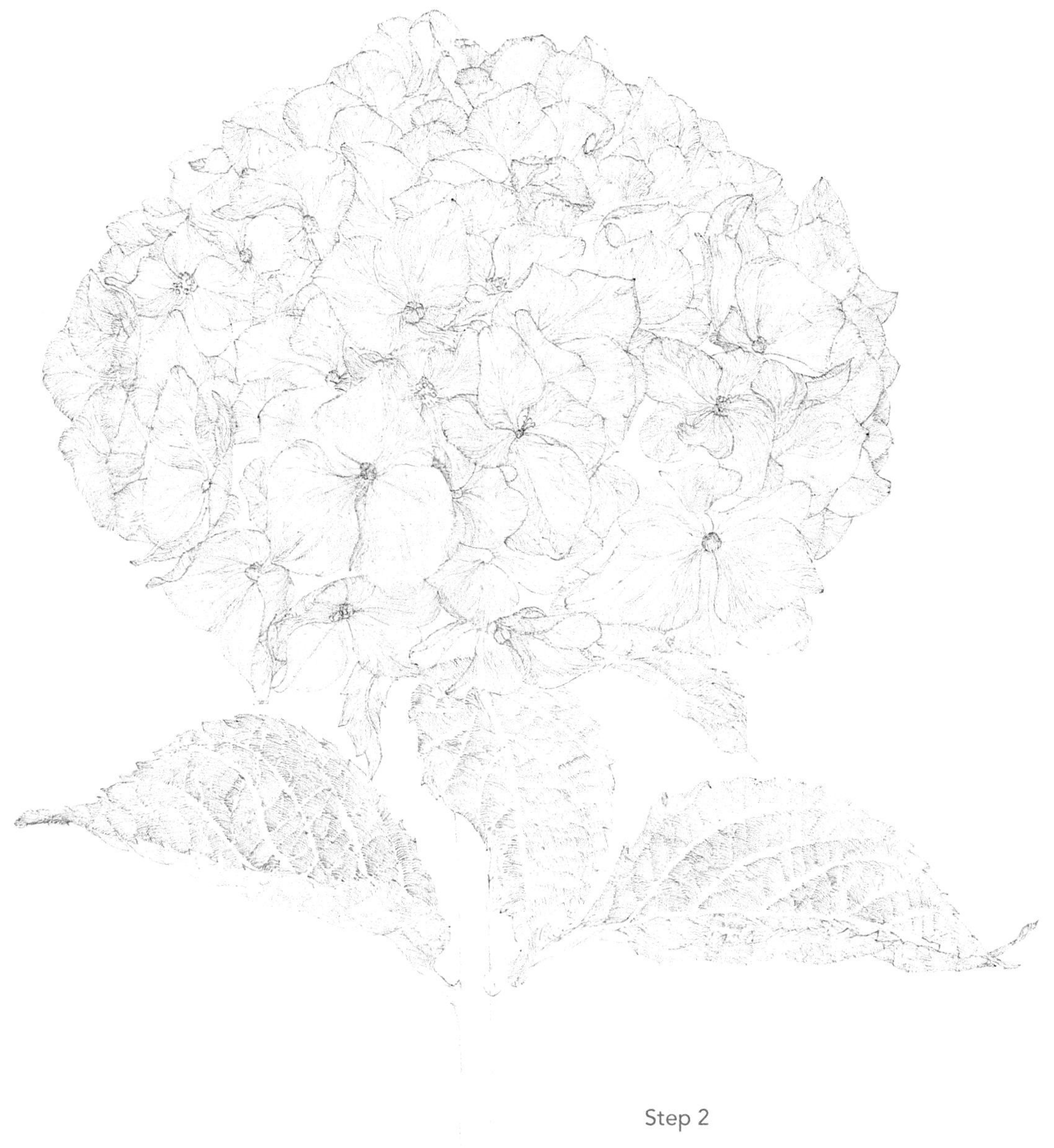

Step 2

With the flower head well underway Guy started on the
leaves, again with pale tone, and following the reference
lines of the main veins he drew initially. After using the
same grades of pencil from 2H to H or HB he finished
with the softer 2B to enhance the depth, thus creating the
three-dimensional appearance that was emphasized by
the light source. There was much fine detail to be added
to the bracts and tiny flower buds in the centres of each
cluster and for these a well-sharpened pencil was essential
– HB or F grades are ideal here.

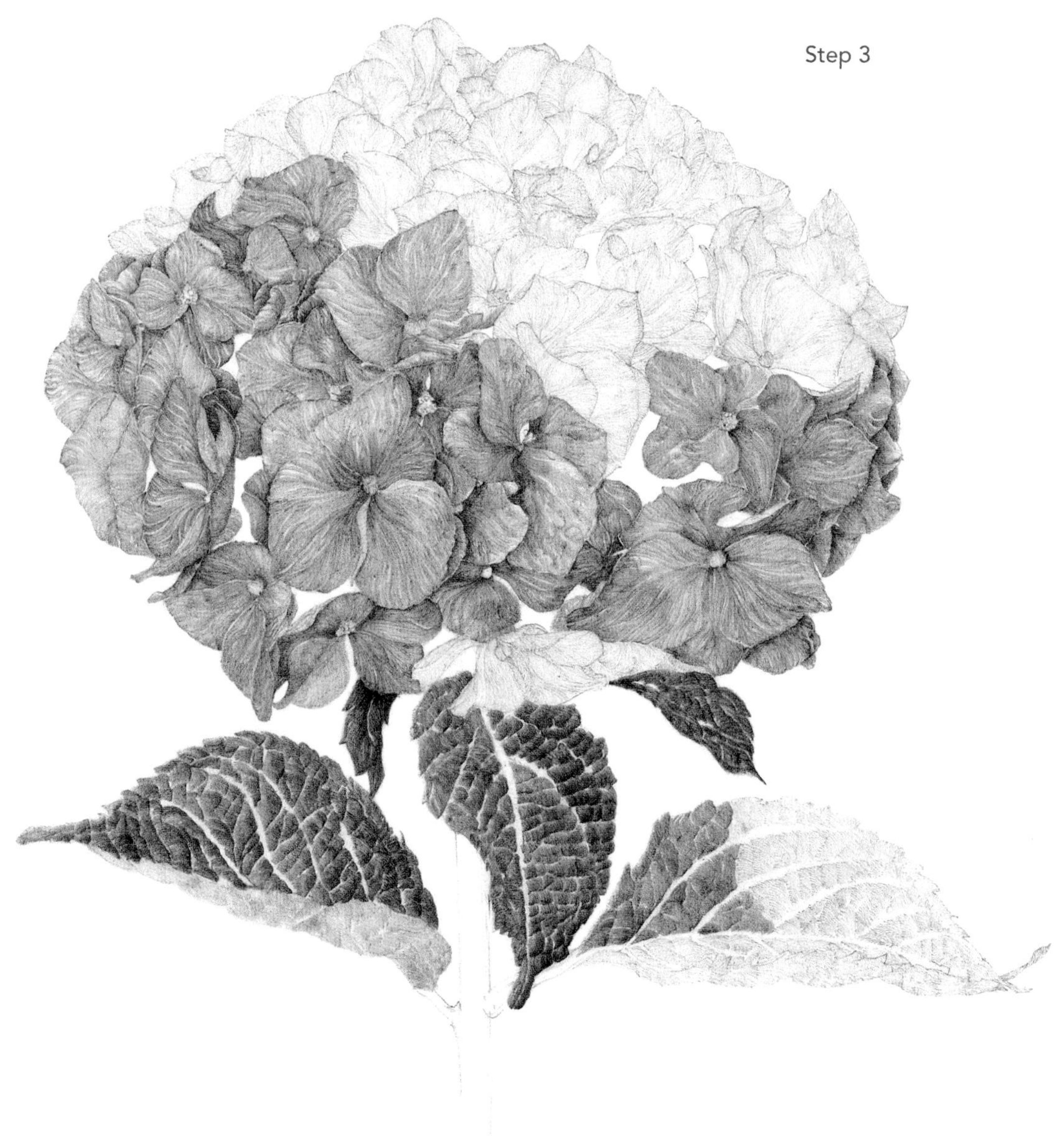

Step 3

STEP 4

The underside of the leaves was much paler so here Guy used only a mid-tone pencil to flatten and smooth the surface, adding a small shadow along the shaded edge of each vein with a 2B pencil. This increased the three-dimensional effect of the underside surface. Next he did further work on the mophead, adding more detail and tone on the shaded side to increase the spherical illusion.

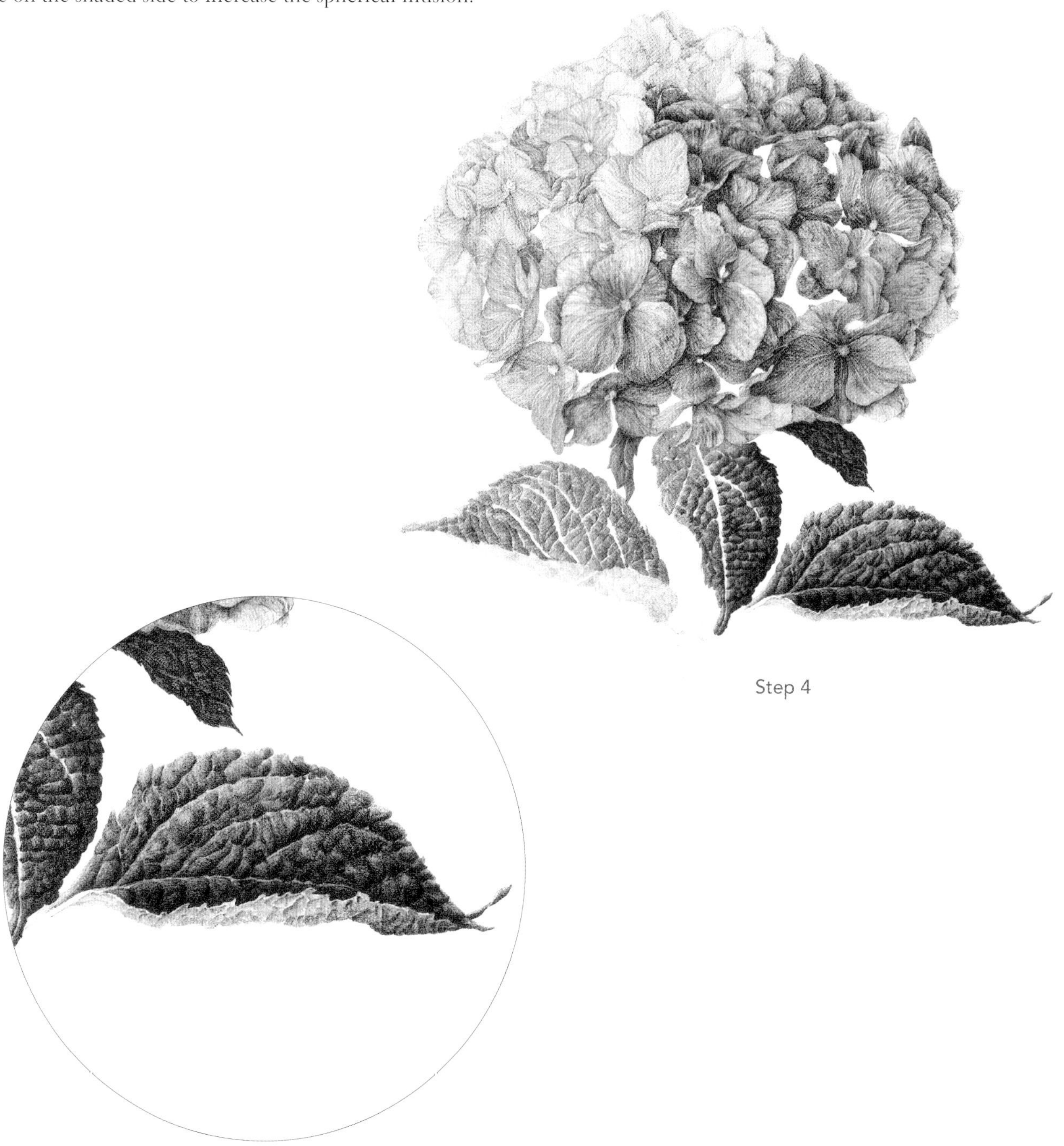

Step 4

Nearing completion, Guy gradually added still more tone to the darkest areas at the bottom right using grade 2B, 3B and 4B pencils. He worked the leaf joints and markings on the stem, which was well shaded to make it fully rounded.

Finally, Guy checked over the whole drawing and sharpened all the edges, using an F pencil to make them crisp and clear. However, where the edge caught the light on the left-hand side it was important to make sure the edge matched the tone of the flower bract, or leaf, so that it was not just a hard, dark outline overall, which would spoil the three-dimensional image completely.

Work that takes so much effort and dedication demands that care is taken right to the very end, so finally Guy used a very clean putty eraser to remove any unwanted background marks or graphite dust which might have found its way onto the paper.

Artist's Tips:

Guy starts with the flowers that will fade first and completes them as soon as possible. If a petal or bract withers completely he finds a similar one and uses that as a substitute. Leaves and stems are generally longer-lasting and can be left until later. If a root or bulb is involved, he lifts that out of the soil at the last minute to complete the study.

In the case of a specimen such as the hydrangea, which consists of so many bracts and shapes, Guy uses a magnifying glass to isolate the area on which he is working. Using Blu Tack, he sticks a pin to the glass and positions it to point at the part of the flower on which he is working. This makes it much easier to look up and down between paper and subject without the eye becoming confused. A third hand gadget, available from craft shops, is invaluable for holding the glass.

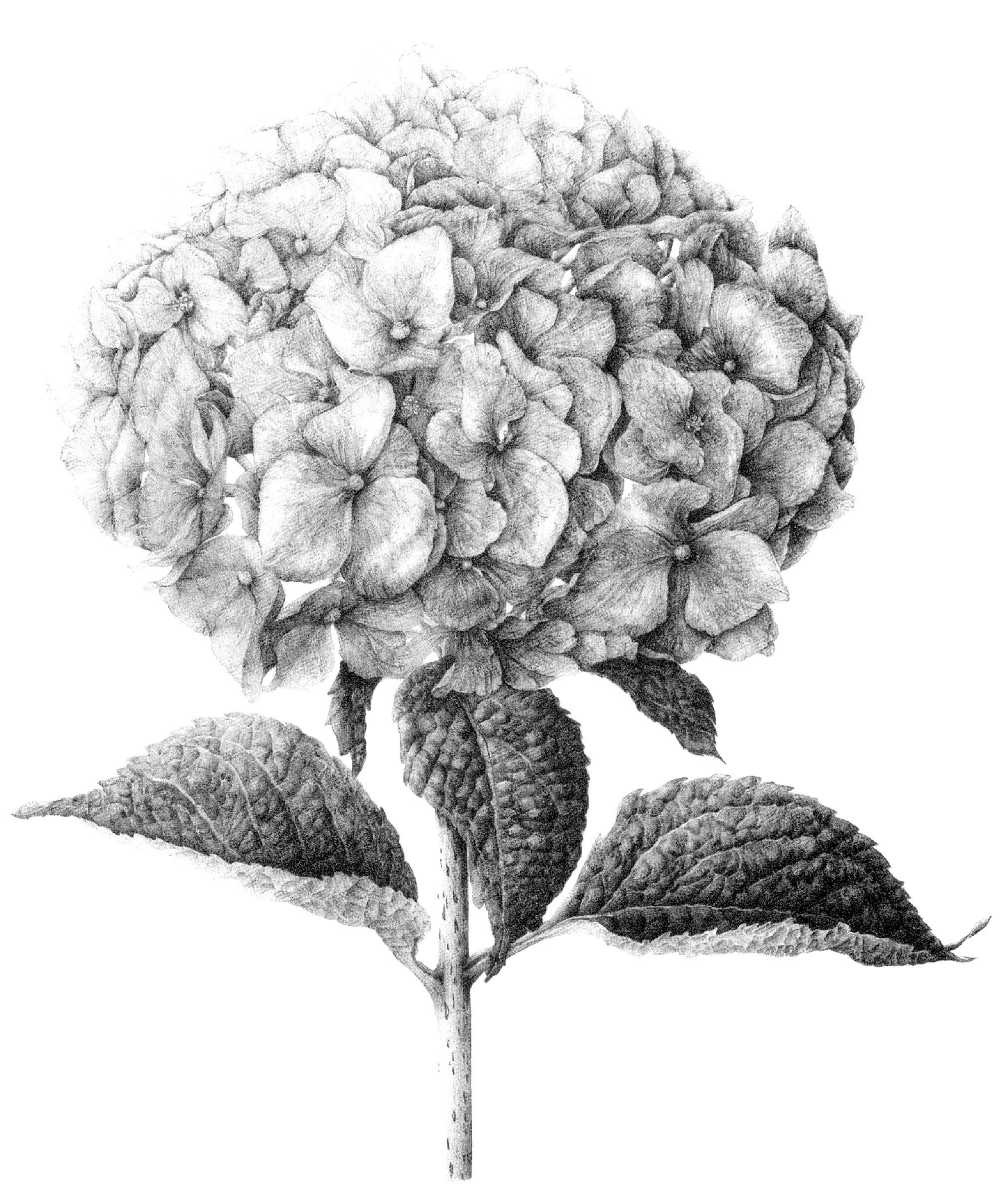

Cymbidium

DONA LEONARDI | Graphite on paper

This classic study of a familiar orchid is beautifully executed by Italian artist Dona Leonardi and shows a mature understanding of tonal values. No matter where you look you will see how each part, no matter how small, has been drawn and shaded in relation to its neighbour.

A darkened section of leaf throws a flower forward, thus helping to achieve a three-dimensional image. This attention to detail is essential when showing the form of the reproductive parts in the heart of each flower.

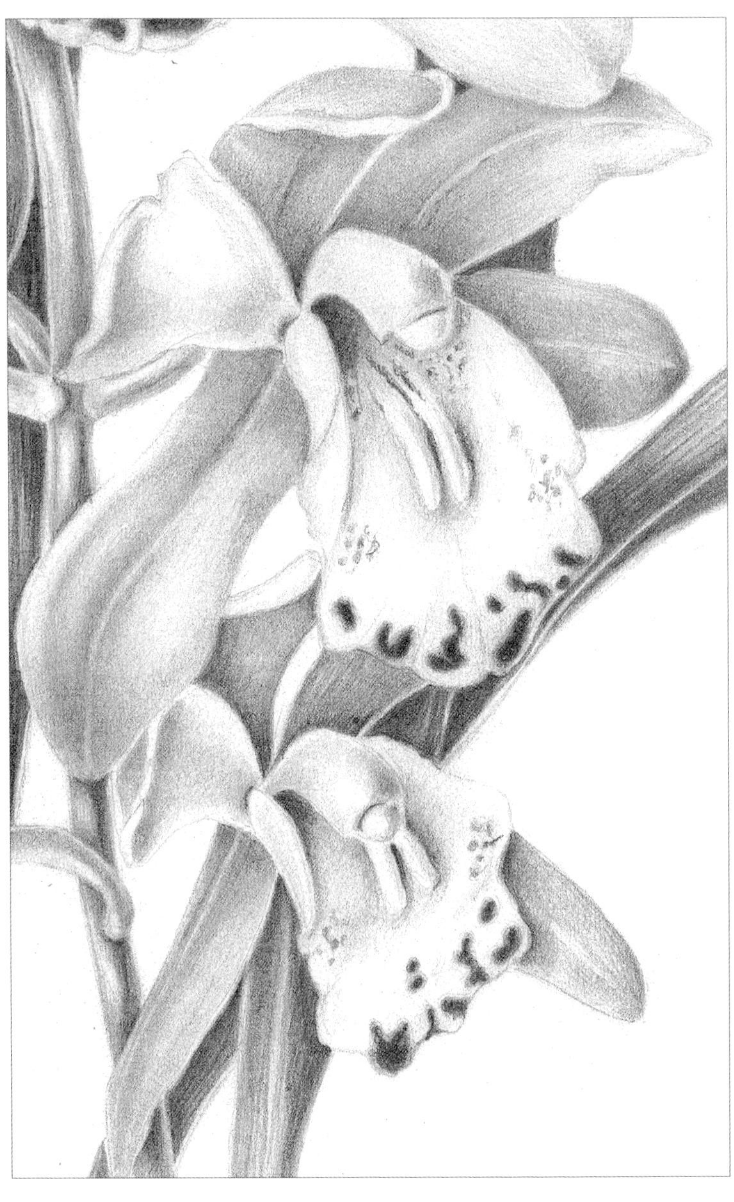

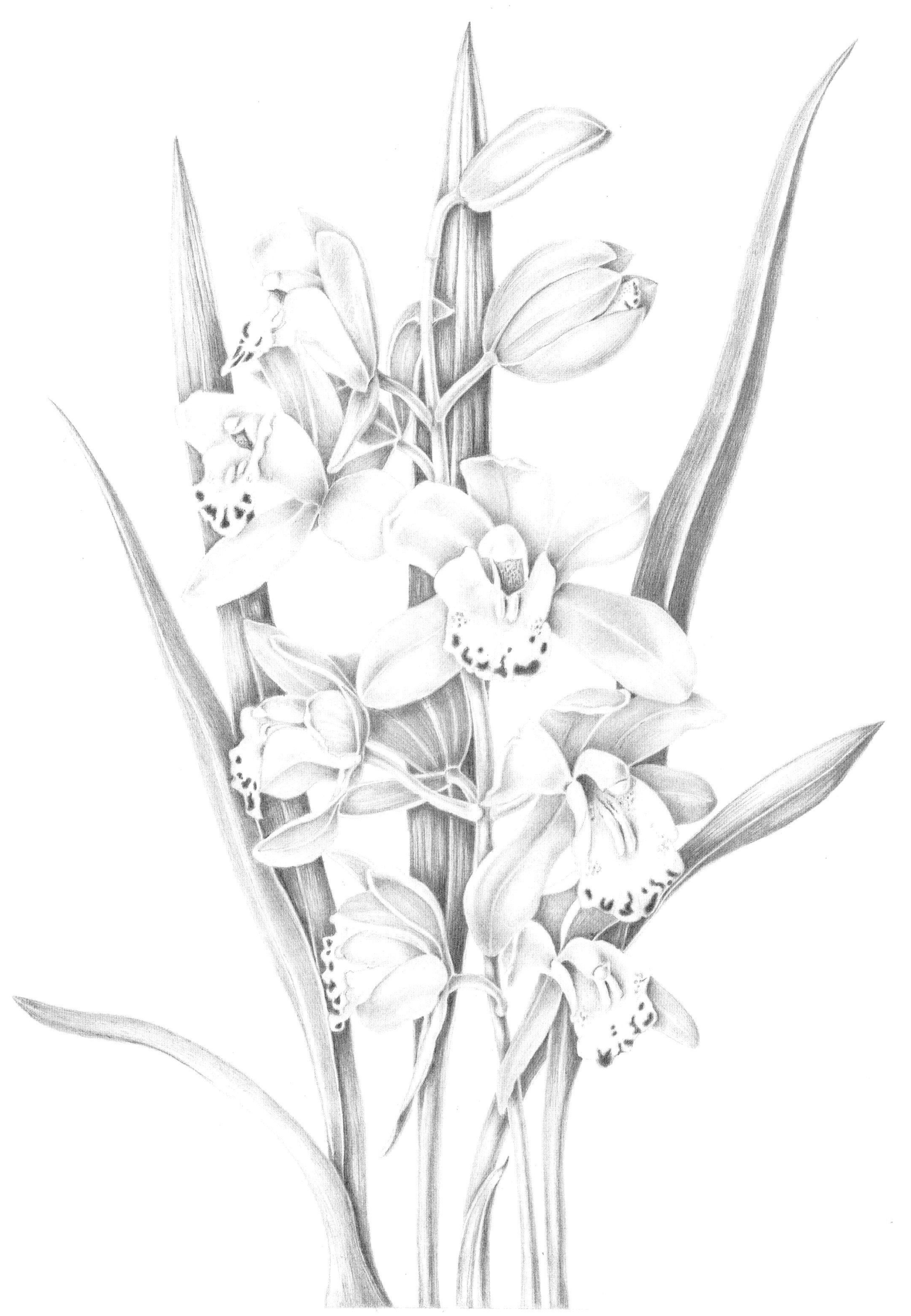

Celosia cristata (cockscomb)

DANIELLE CHOI | Graphite on paper

Here is more proof that one does not need colour in order to create a thing of beauty. Sometimes form and tone are all that is needed, especially when faced with something as complicated as *Celosia*. This native of tropical and sub-tropical Asia, Africa and America may grow up to 1m (3¼ ft) tall and has strikingly coloured flowers. Both enlargements show the level of observation required to depict the intricate markings on the stem and below the flower head. Danielle Choi, from South Korea, has arranged the lighting to emphasize the rounded shape, which adds to the beauty of the flower and gives surface texture to the leaves.

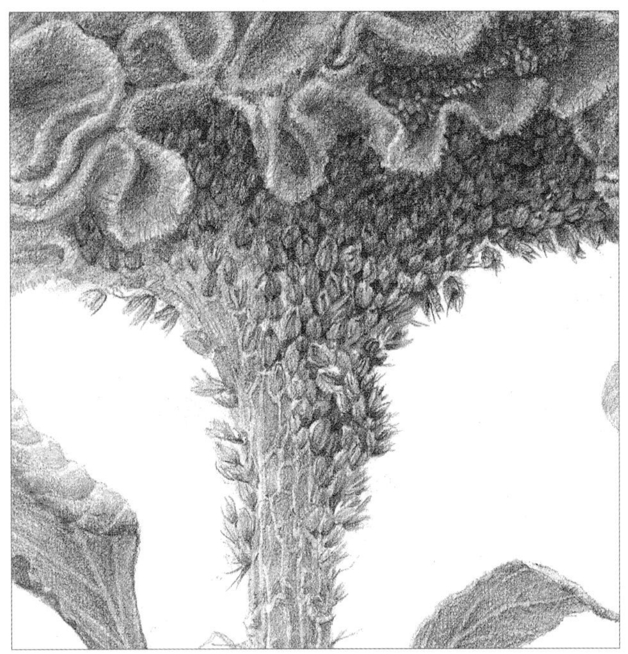

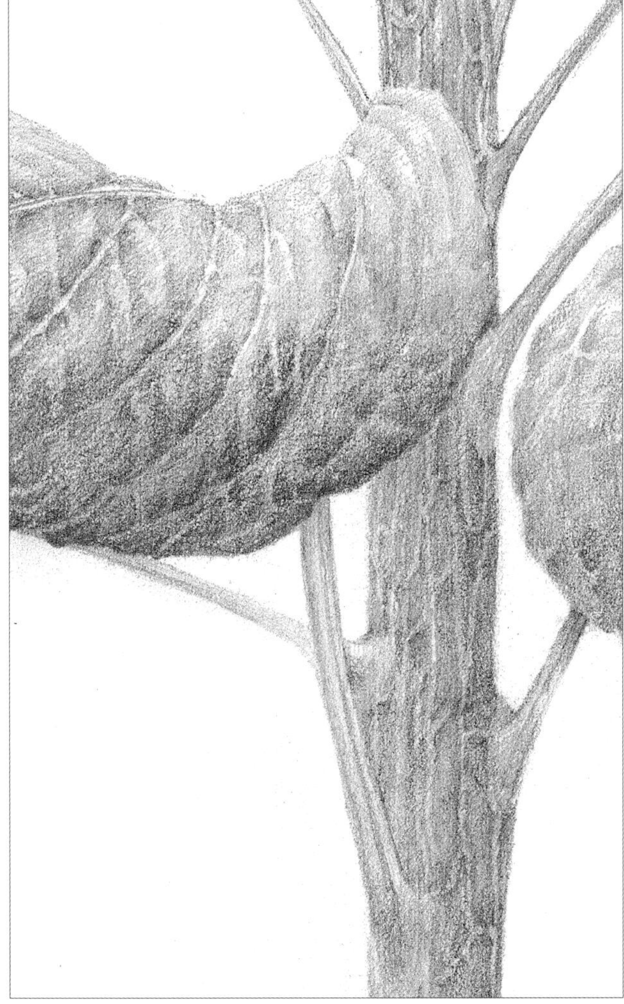

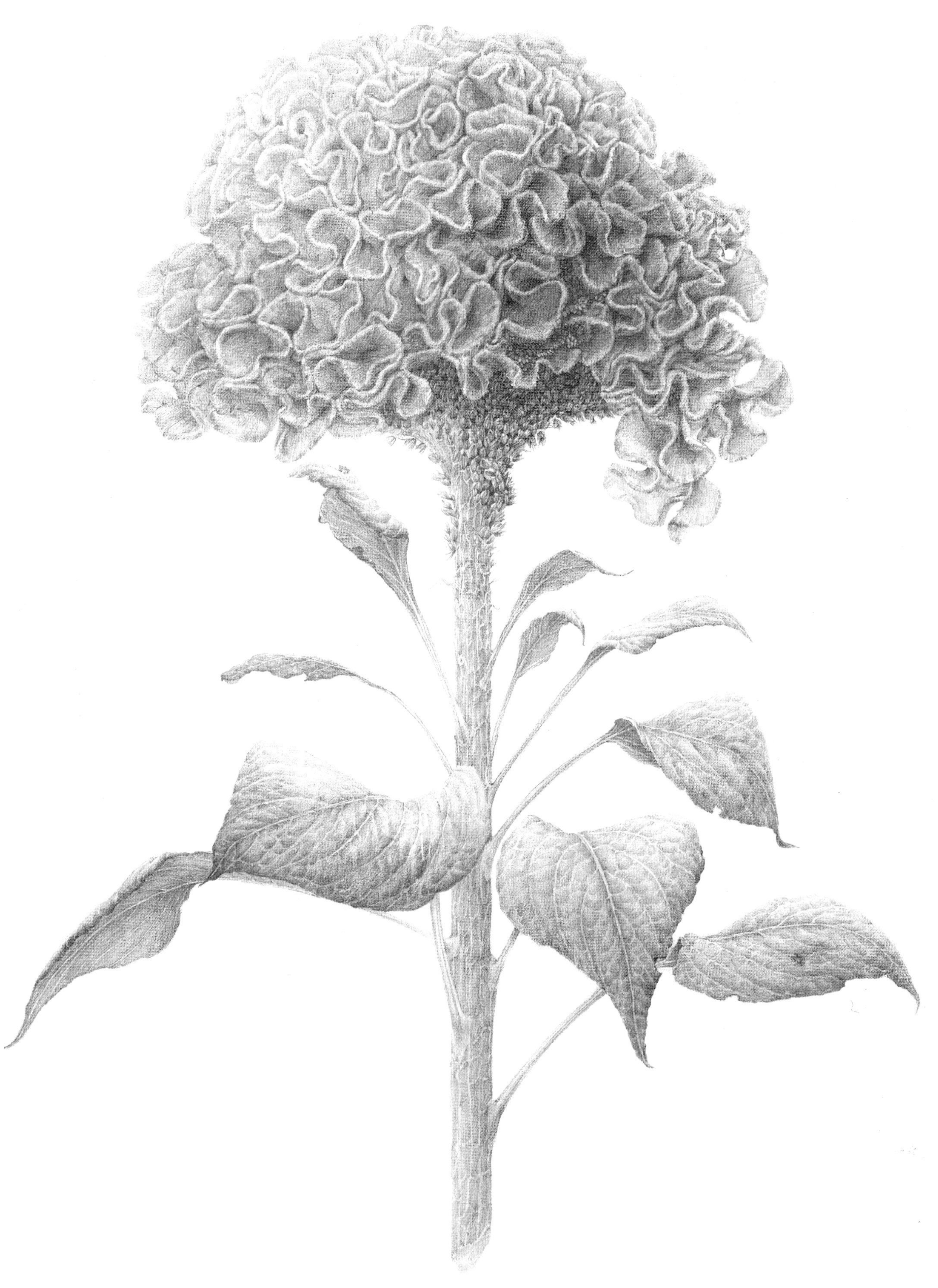

Cynara scolymus 'Violet Globe' (globe artichoke)

ROS PURKIS | Graphite on paper

There is a classical beauty to the form of this artichoke and one can almost imagine it sculpted in marble. The enlarged section shows how shading has created the corrugated effect on the stem; too often a student will think it is sufficient to just draw lines – a pinstripe effect – when in reality each line must be shaded away from the light source. This same shading must be applied to each leaf vein to create surface texture. Eventually the sepals will open to reveal the beautiful purple flower, which is a worthy subject for a painting.

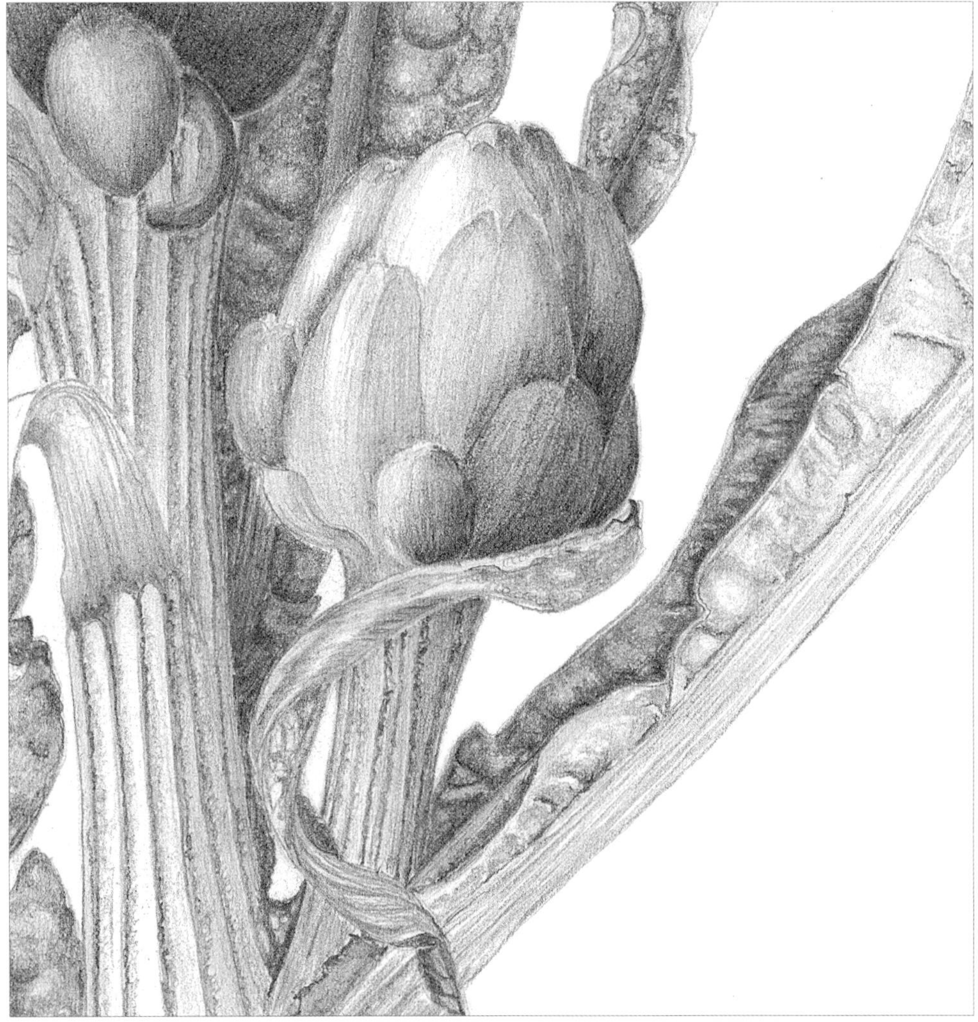

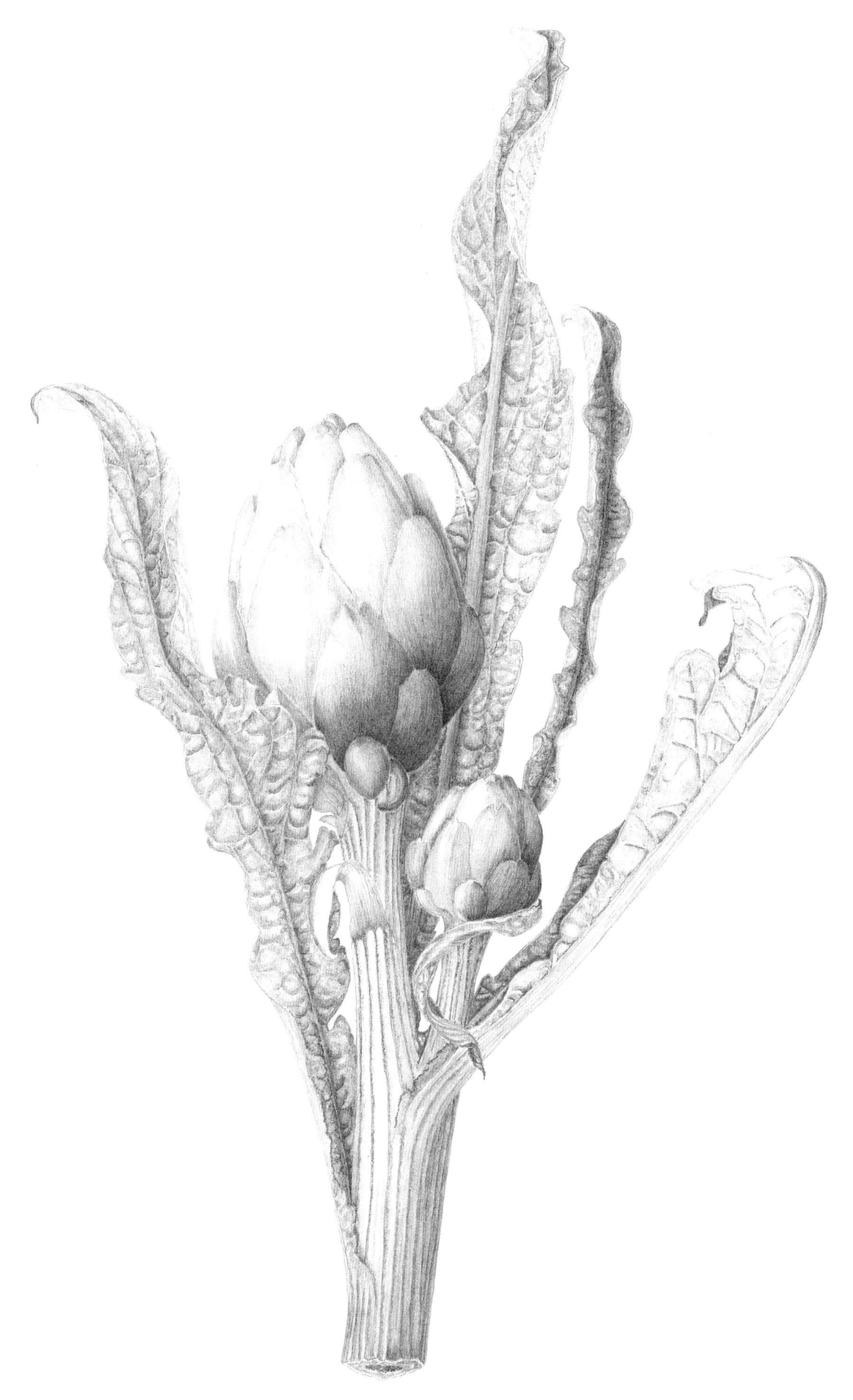

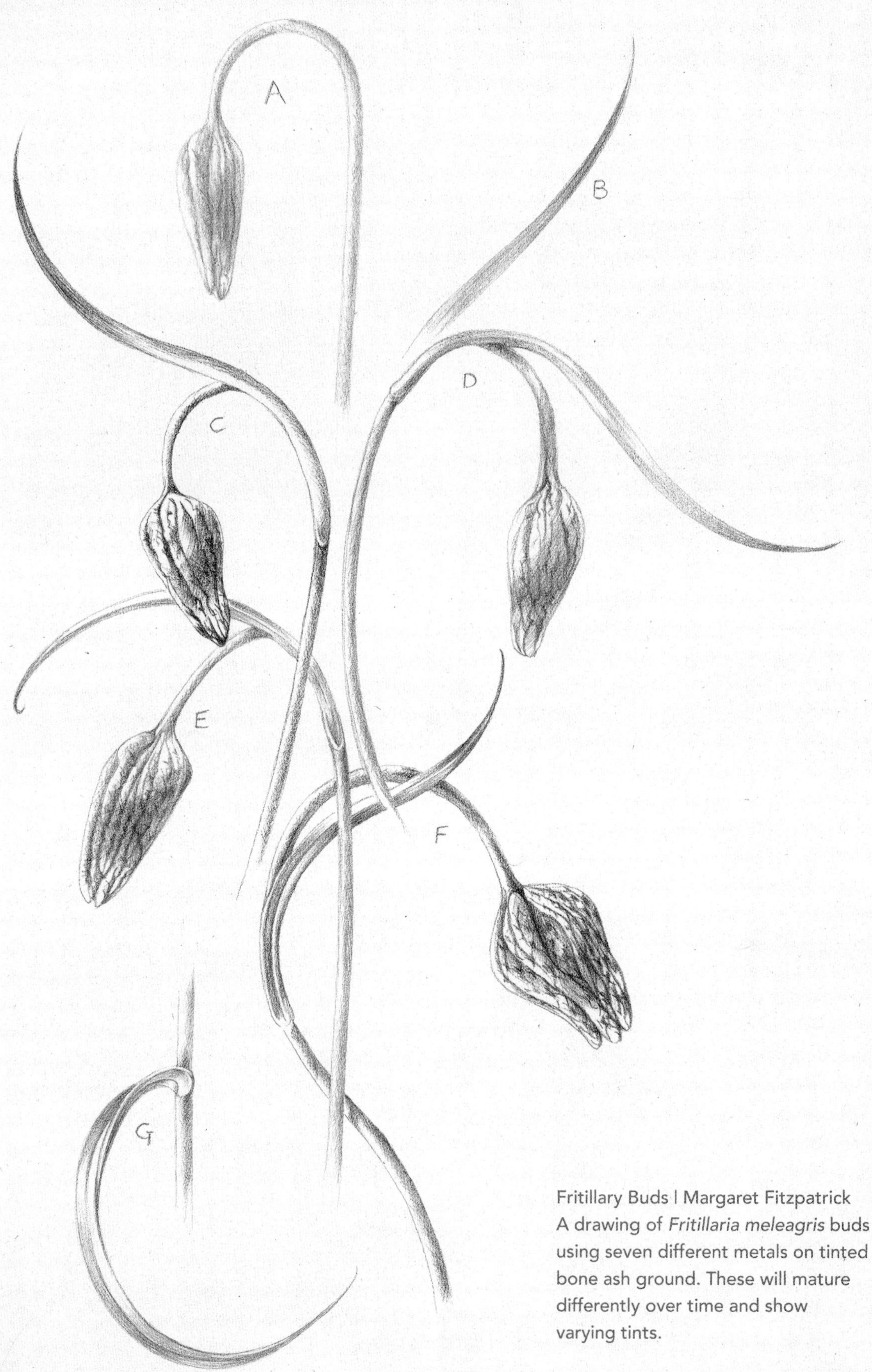

Fritillary Buds | Margaret Fitzpatrick
A drawing of *Fritillaria meleagris* buds
using seven different metals on tinted
bone ash ground. These will mature
differently over time and show
varying tints.

Metalpoint

An ancient method used to achieve a fine line drawing, silverpoint is more properly called metalpoint, since any metal capable of leaving a residue on a prepared surface may be used. This method is of truly historic interest as it was known to the ancient Egyptians and even the Sumerians, who are believed to be the earliest settlers of human civilization. While it is possible to see stunningly beautiful examples of classical figures by such masters as Leonardo, there is little to be found of botanical interest even though silverpoint lends itself to exquisite and delicate drawings, and is therefore well worth consideration for the genre.

A metal point or stylus, these days resembling a piece of wire, is fitted into a holder, not unlike one which may be used to hold charcoal. The surface to which it is applied needs to be abrasive in order for the metal to leave a residue – you can buy a ready-prepared surface from a good art supplier. The usual coating is made of bone ash from calcified bones. If you are a beginner with the technique you may like to experiment by coating paper with gouache, but in my experience it is just as well to use prepared paper as it is not expensive. It is so easy to be put off if your first attempts are less than brilliant, so it's worth using the most suitable ground.

Here Margaret Fitzpatrick discusses the metals which are used in her drawing of *Fritillaria meleagris* (opposite):

By using different metals you can achieve subtly different marks and tonal ranges. The drawing of fritillary buds and leaves shows seven different metal points on a traditional off-white bone ash ground. With time the metals oxidize, producing subtle and varying changes in colour. The time taken to oxidize depends on the atmospheric conditions to which the drawing is exposed – for example, if a drawing is framed and sealed this will limit its exposure to oxygen and the time for oxidization will be longer. The seven metals are as follows:

A. Nickel

This is quite a hard point to work with; it has a limited tonal range producing a soft grey mark which fades almost completely with time.

B. Brass

Though the mark is rather darker than nickel, the tonal range is still limited. Brass turns a yellowish-gold and fades with time.

C. Aluminium

This has a greater tonal range, produces a coarse line and does not blend well. Aluminium shows little colour change with time.

D. Gold

While the tonal range is quite narrow, gold offers a lovely soft grey mark, blends smoothly and does not change colour with time.

E. Copper

This blends quite well; it is a little coarser than gold but has a slightly better tonal range. Copper turns greenish with time.

F. Silver

The tonal range is good and silver blends well to produce beautiful soft greys. It turns to a warm brown and darkens with time.

G. Bronze

This has a limited tonal range. Bronze will turn greenish-yellow and lighten with time.

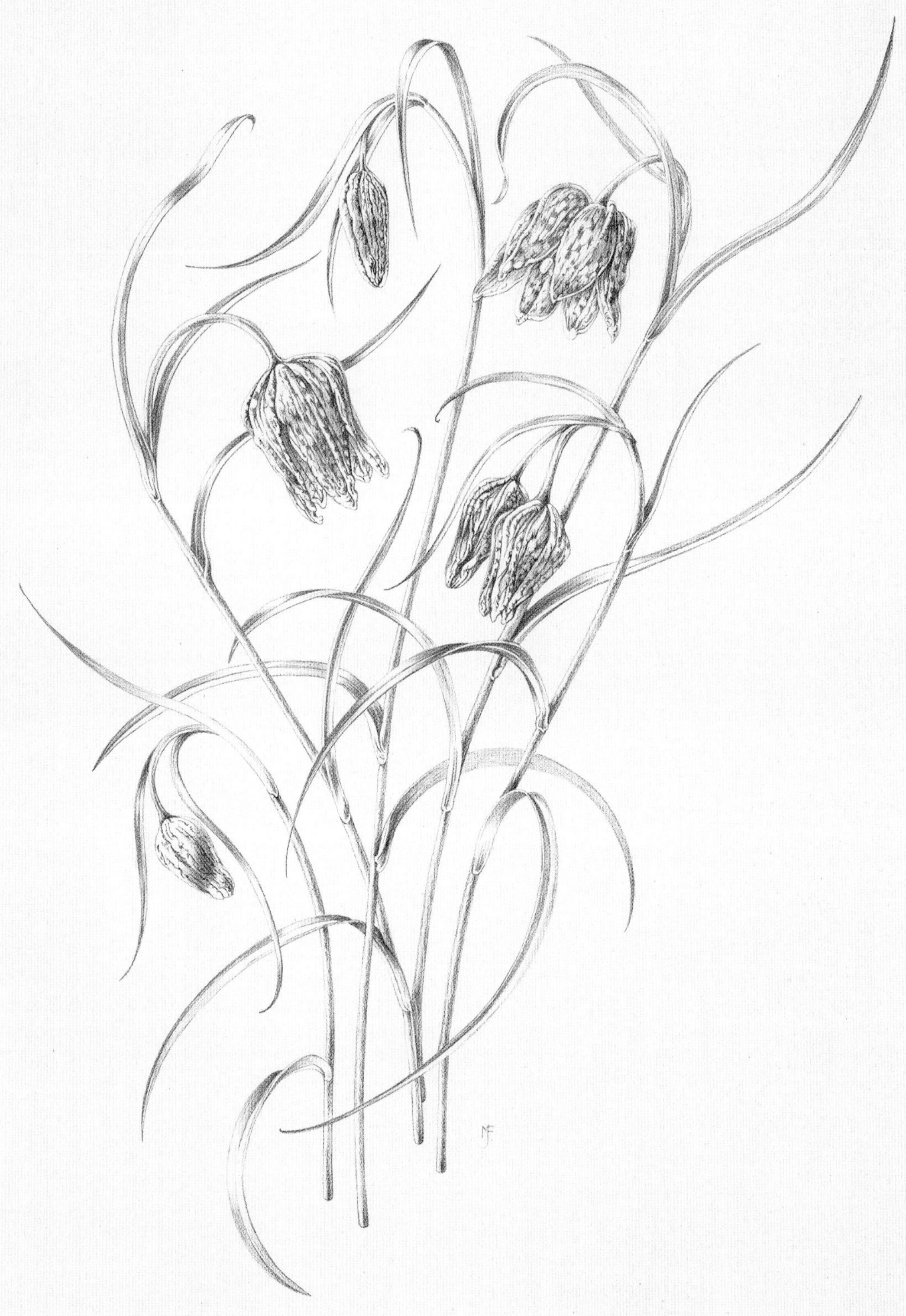

Fritillaria meleagris | Margaret Fitzpatrick |
Silverpoint drawing on tinted bone ash ground

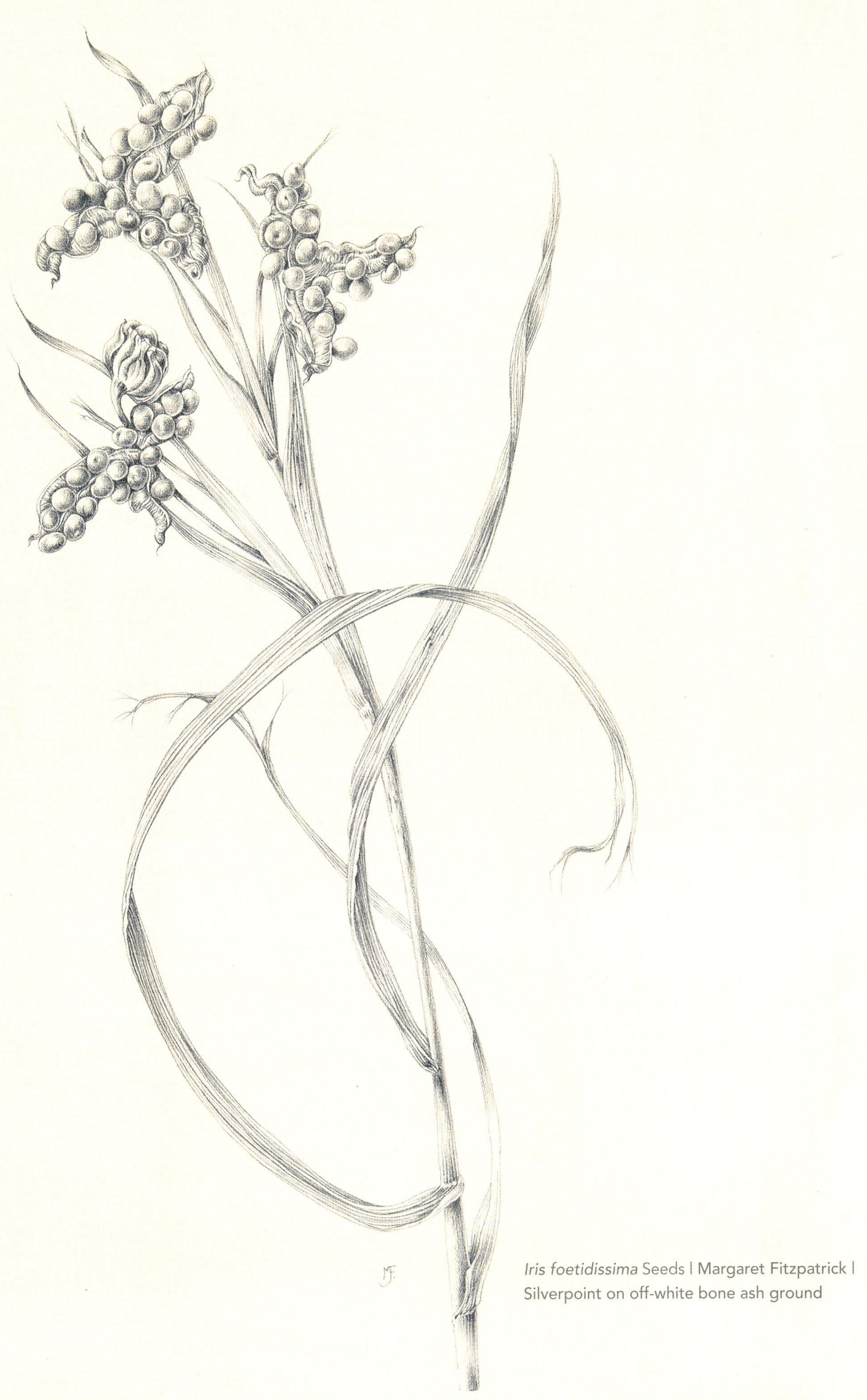

Iris foetidissima Seeds | Margaret Fitzpatrick |
Silverpoint on off-white bone ash ground

CHAPTER 2

Coloured Pencils

The introduction of high-quality pigment into pencils was a huge advance from the 'crayons' familiar to many of us from school days. Now, after a somewhat slow start, works of art produced with this medium are accorded the merit to which they are entitled. With lightfast pigments and framed with glass that will filter out harmful rays, these pictures represent the heirlooms of tomorrow.

There is no quick fix when you are setting out on a study in coloured pencil. It is quite a slow and painstaking process, but the same can be said of working with a dry brush on vellum, or indeed on paper. From my own past experience I know that time ceases to matter when I am painting the lace on a bridal gown in miniature and two or three hours' work results in just a square centimetre of fabric accomplished. So it is with fine botanical studies and in truth we botanical artists would not have it any other way.

RIGHT *Iris* 'Gay Trip' | Janie Pirie | Coloured pencil on paper
This study by renowned artist Janie Pirie captures the vibrant colours, exquisite detail and form of a bearded iris. Note the way shading is applied to give the frilled edge to the flags and falls also along the length of the leaf veins. Both rely on the direction of the light which, once fixed, must not vary. Working across the tonal range from light to dark, not just in monochrome but of equal importance in colour, will produce a three-dimensional image full of realism and life.

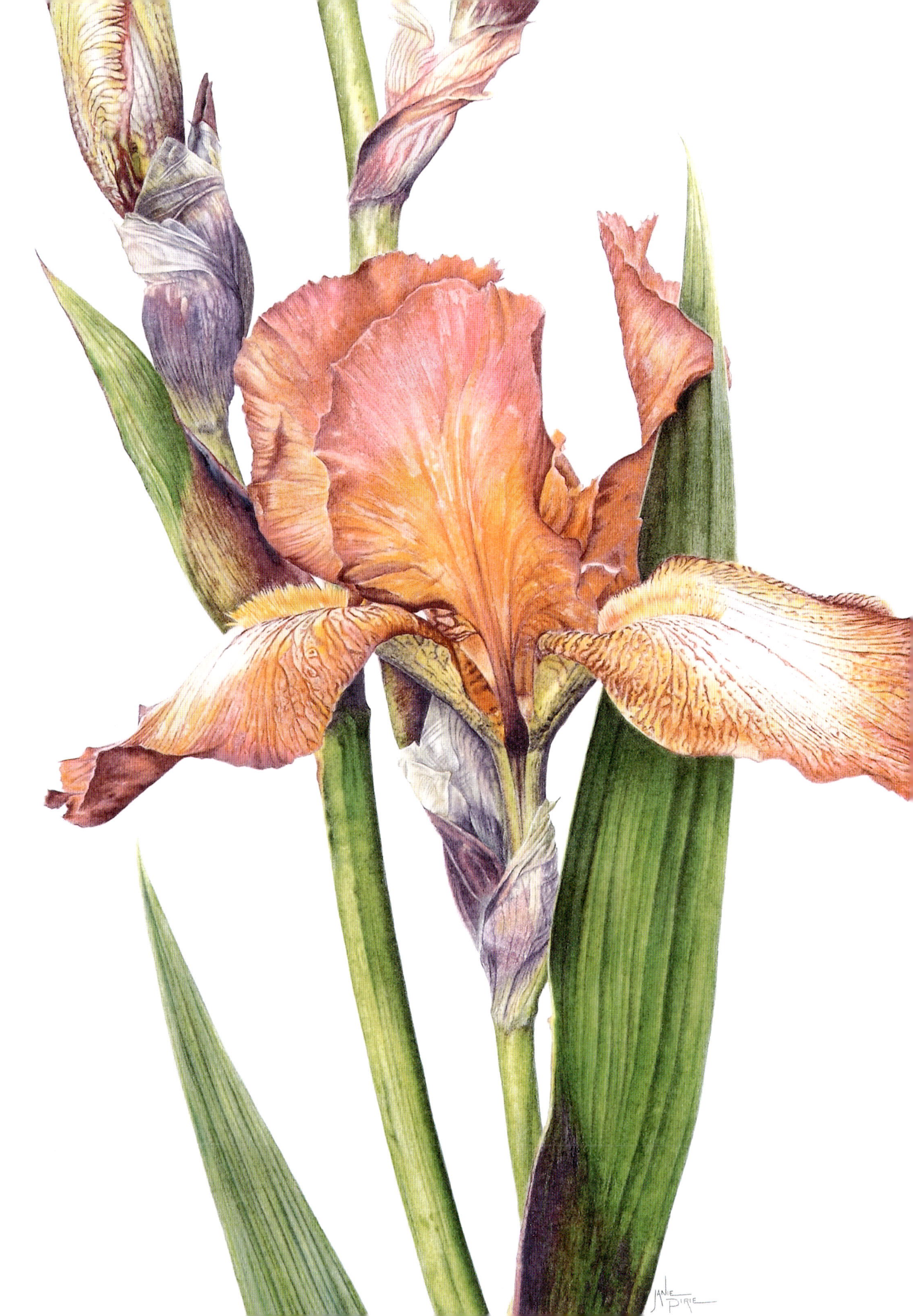

Janie
Pirie

Step-by-Step

CHERRIES BY JANIE PIRIE

Here Janie tells you how to copy her study of luscious cherries. This provides a wonderful introduction for someone new to the medium of coloured pencils. Each little fruit requires accurate colour and form with glossy highlights, while the leaves and stems need fine-detailed attention.

STEP 1

I prefer to draw everything from life, that is, with the subject in front of me at the time, as was the case when I drew these cherries. However, for you to re-create my drawing you will have to trace my image or have a go at drawing it freehand for yourself. To make the latter approach easier you could draw a grid to enable you to render the image any size you like. To do this, mark out equal-sized squares on the Step 1 drawing, and then draw the same number of squares onto your art paper at the size you want. Draw the image, matching the original square by square.

If you have access to a lightbox you can use this to trace the image on to good-quality art paper. Alternatively, use a sheet of Tracedown paper. Although the traditional tracing method takes longer I prefer it as I can achieve a really fine image on my art paper. For this illustration I have used Fabriano Classico 5 HP (Hot Pressed), but any HP paper would be suitable.

Trace my drawing, using the finest tracing paper you can find. I use 53g if I can obtain it, but up to 63g is more than acceptable. Work with an 0.3 HB propelling pencil as this will give you a really fine line when tracing. Turn your tracing paper upside down and go over your marks very carefully. Try not to make double or wobbly lines as they will not give you an accurate image once it is transferred to your art paper.

When you have redrawn your image on the reverse of your tracing, turn the paper over so that your image is

Materials required:

* Fine tracing paper and a light box, or Tracedown paper
* A piece of good-quality Hot Pressed (HP) paper
* Graphite pencil
* Colourless blender

FABER-CASTELL POLYCHROMOS:
* Deep Red (223)
* Pink Carmine (127)
* Pale Geranium Lake (121)
* Permanent Carmine (126)
* Pink Madder Lake (129)
* Dark Sepia (175)
* Caput Mortuum Violet (263)
* Caput Mortuum (169)
* Burnt Umber (280)
* Burnt Carmine (193)
* Brown Ochre (182)
* Dark Indigo (157)
* Chrome Oxide Green (278)
* Earth Green Yellowish (168)
* Warm Grey III (272)
* Chromium Green Opaque (174

PRISMACOLOR:
* Black Cherry (P.1078)
* Raspberry (P.1030)
* Poppy Red (922)
* Beige (997)
* Olive Green (911)
* French Grey 50% (1072)
* Pale Sage (1089)
* Rosy Beige (1019)
* Yellow Chartreuse (1004)
* Beige Sienna (1080)
* Lime Peel (1005)
* Ivory (103)

the same as mine. Place it on your art paper and, using masking tape, secure it at the top only. The next step is to transfer the tracing to make a very clear and clean image on your art paper. To do this, I use a Dresden decoupage tool, which resembles a tiny hockey stick, but the back of a small teaspoon will suffice. Rub gently over the graphite, starting with a tiny bit at the top, then lifting the tracing paper to see if your image is showing clearly. If it isn't then you need to use more pressure, but avoid pressing so hard you are left with an indent in your art paper – check every now and then to make sure your image is appearing on the paper without any damage to the surface.

STEP 2

Using Black Cherry, begin by colouring all the shadow areas, making tiny elliptical movements. Try to keep your pencils really sharp because you need to make crisp, clean edges. I use my pencil almost upright, at just a little less than 90 degrees to the paper. This ensures I get pigment from the pencils into the whole surface of the paper rather than just picking up the top fibres. It is very important that you fade out the Black Cherry so that the colours you put on top will have a gentle gradation of colour; if you just stop the Black Cherry at full saturation there will be a visible line and this will show when the reds are used. It is this layer, more than any other, that will make your cherries look amazingly three-dimensional and therefore realistic.

STEP 3

Now, with Raspberry and the same small elliptical movements, colour over the Black Cherry to take the colour further. Look constantly at the fruit to make sure you are colouring all the areas that are a very rich red. Follow this with a layer of Deep Red. At this stage you will be working right up to the areas that are catching the light on most of the cherries. Again you need to use the Deep Red over all the areas coloured so far and then extend it to the areas where this shade is required. Just keep looking at my

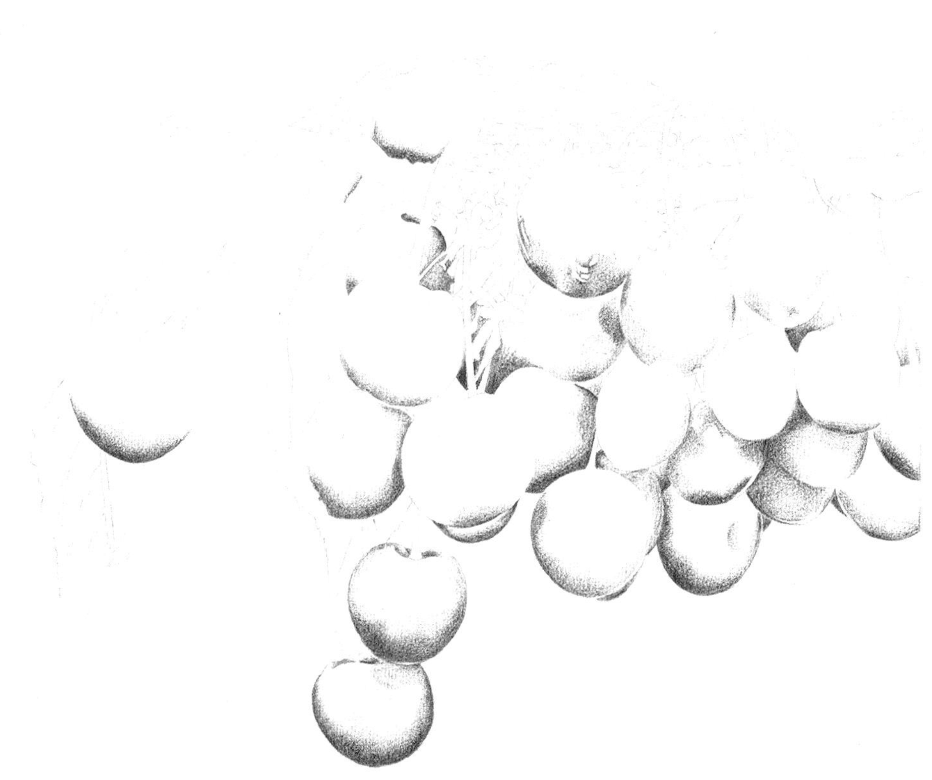

Step 1

drawing and you will see where you need to take this layer.
The last colour for Step 3 is Pink Carmine. Adding this will
give your fruit the rich pink/red shade they actually are.
When adding this layer you will again be working right up
to the areas that are catching the light on the remainder
of the cherries. Look carefully as you progress since some
of the light areas have quite sharp edges while others fade
gently into the white. Taking the time to do these edges
accurately will make all the difference to your finished
illustration as it is this attention to detail that will make your
work look real.

STEP 4

At this stage the cherries can be finished using a selection of
rich pinks and reds. I have used Deep Red, Pale Geranium
Lake, Permanent Carmine, Pink Carmine, Poppy Red and
Pink Madder Lake. There is no particular order in which to
use these colours – it's up to you to finish each cherry using
some or all of them. I applied Pink Madder Lake in the
areas I had left white – not all over, just in the area where
there was a degree of light rather than bright light.

It is very important at this stage of an illustration to note
that not all fruits are exactly the same colour. Some of
my cherries were quite dark, some were a very bright red
while others were just a lovely rich pink/red. If you feel
some of your fruits require extra rich red at this point, use
more Raspberry. It's all a matter of balance, so stand back
and look at your work – and be honest with yourself! If
your cherries all look alike, make a few minor changes so
you have a variation of reds, otherwise your finished piece
will look as if you found a formula for colouring cherries
that you have applied to each one in more or less the
same way. Be sure to put in blemishes, too, because these
will also add to the reality of your finished work.

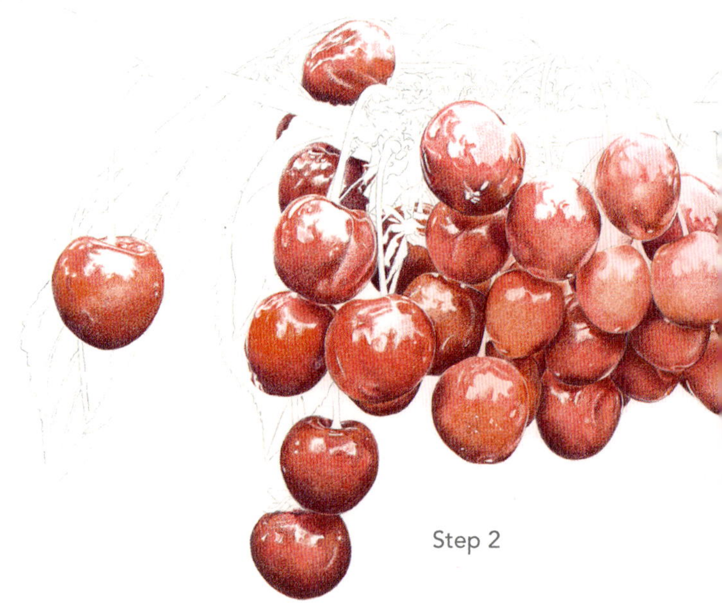

Step 2

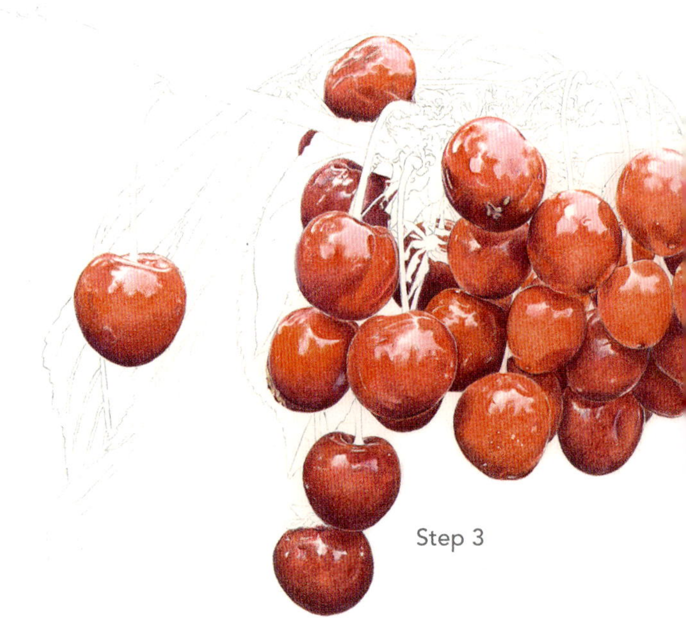

Step 3

STEP 4

It's now time to get to work on the leaves, the nodes, the dried remains of the petals and sepals and the branch itself. If you have ever seen cherries hanging on a branch you will know how complex the nodes are where the bunches of fruit attach themselves to the branch. In all botanical illustration it is imperative to get these areas accurate. On many occasions I have seen beautifully drawn or painted flowers and fruit but the stems and leaves have been treated like the poor relation! Obviously this can spoil the piece, so please treat these areas as lovingly as you have treated the main attraction – the cherries themselves. It takes time, but it's worth it.

As I can only show you how I have worked on my illustration in just a few stages, this one will incorporate all the first layers of the leaves, the branch, the nodes and the dried remains of the sepals and petals.

Using Dark Sepia, pick out all the very dark areas on the underside of the branch and where the stems join the nodes that are attached to the branch. This helps to define the intricate shapes in these areas and therefore makes them easier to follow. Next, use a mixture of Caput Mortuum Violet, Caput Mortuum and Burnt Umber to colour the remaining dark areas of the nodes.

Then use Burnt Carmine on the fruit stems at top left – just a light hint of the colour, given a very soft gradation as it has meet up with a light green later. Finish the nodes using a combination of Brown Ochre and Beige.

Moving onto the leaves, use Dark Indigo to shade the very dark leaf in shadow, taking care to leave the veins only just visible. Then colour in the shadows on the really long leaf on the left using Chrome Oxide Green and Olive Green. It is really important to ensure these shadows fade out very gently rather than suddenly stopping otherwise subsequent layers will not look natural. For the last colour in this stage, apply French Grey 50% over the Dark Sepia on the branch and extend it before fading it out.

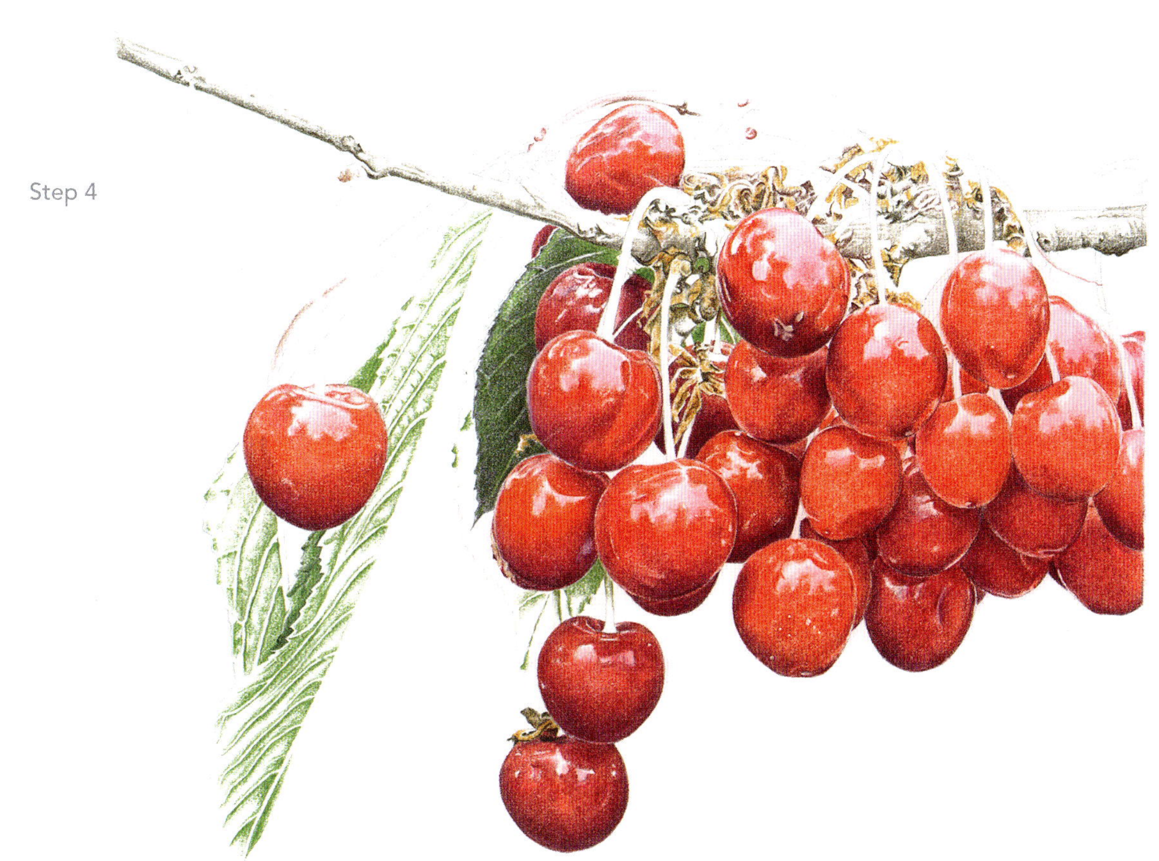

Step 4

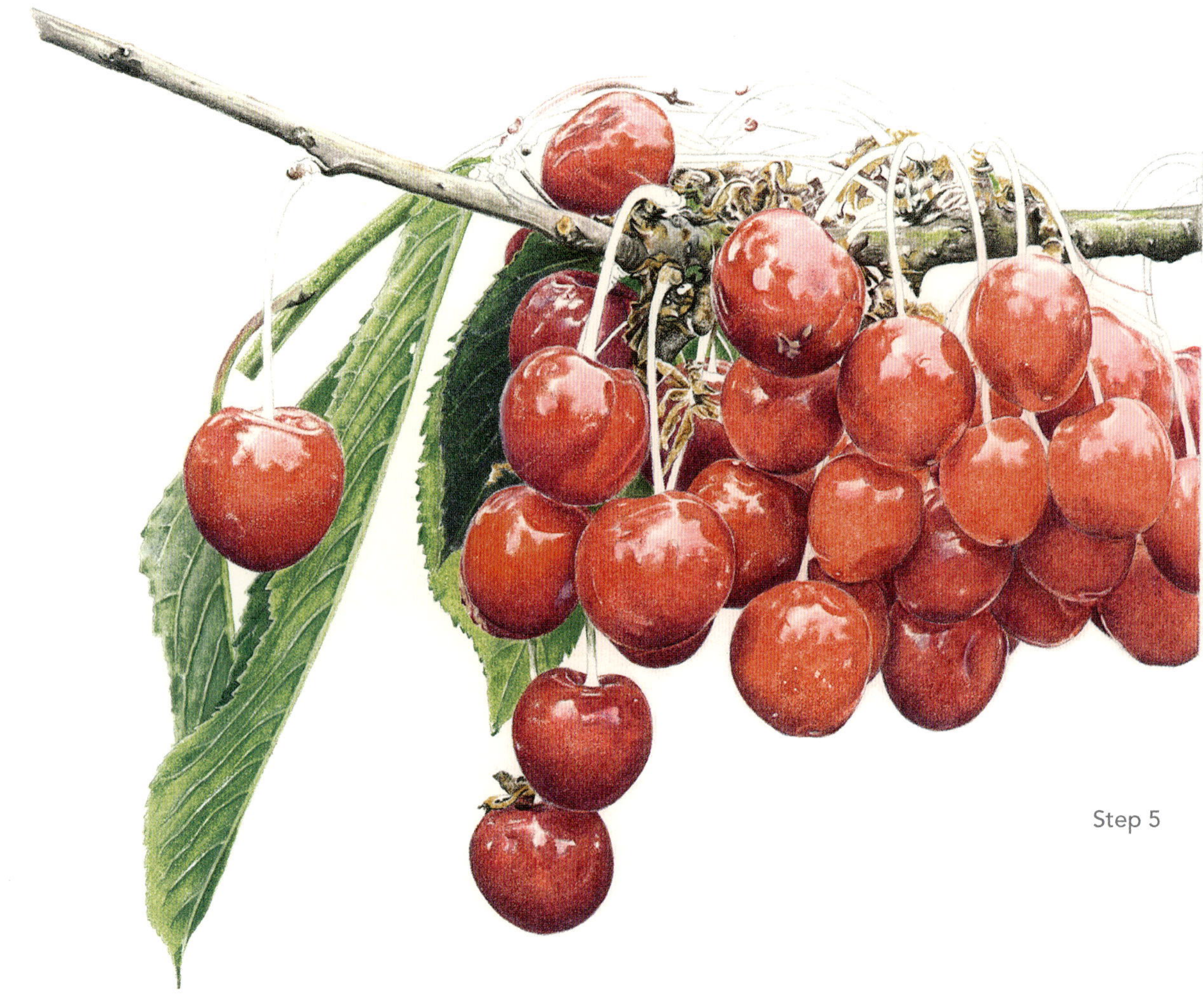

STEP 5

Now the leaves can be completed. Beginning with Earth Green Yellowish, colour over the shadow areas already completed and then continue over the rest of the leaves, taking care to change the pressure depending on whether the green is in the light or not. At this stage you should also look carefully at the lighter edges of the leaves and leave a tiny edge of white paper. To colour the veins use Pale Sage and then work across the backs of the leaves with the same pencil. Note that the two leaves on the far left are mostly showing the back of the leaf while the two in the centre are showing the front, so they will not require Pale Sage except for the veins. With Earth Green Yellowish, finish a little extra shading on the central veins on the left-hand leaves. Next, tackle the branch. There are so many colours in branches and twigs it's not surprising that you will require several pencils to compete this stage. I have used the following: Warm Grey III, Rosy Beige, Beige Sienna, Earth Green Yellowish and Burnt Umber. Just follow my picture and use all or some of these where you see you need them. Sharpen up the edges on the underside of the branch using more Dark Sepia if needed.

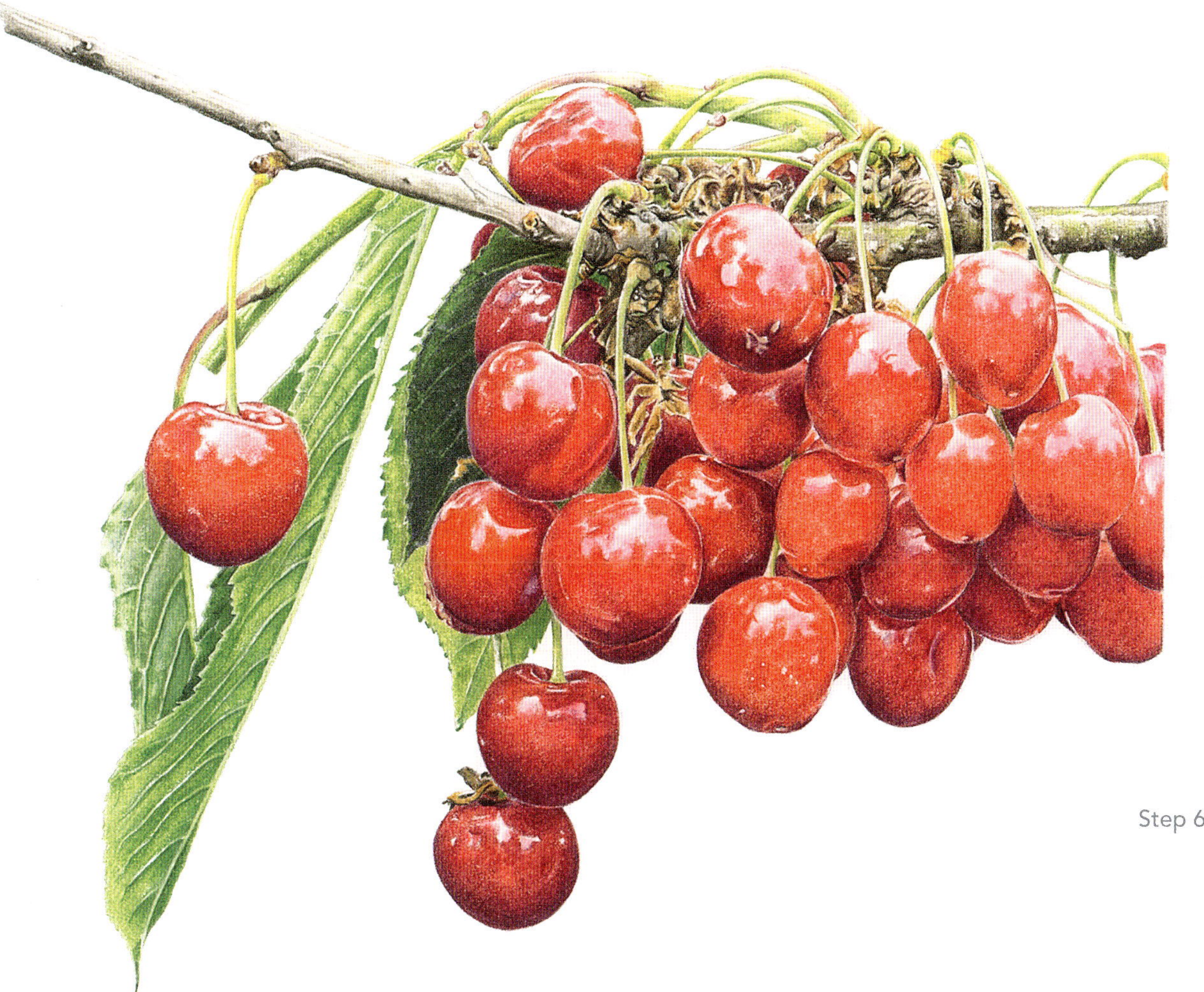

Step 6

STEP 6

The illustration can now be completed by colouring the stems of the cherries and tidying up the nodes and so on if necessary. Start by putting in any areas of stem that are in shadow using Chrome Green Opaque. Look carefully at the tiny bits of stem that are showing between the darker cherries at the bottom and in the centre. After this you will need to colour the remainder of the shadows but this time the lighter ones, using Earth Green Yellowish. Now use a mixture of Lime Peel, Yellow Chartreuse and Pale Sage for the lighter shadows. You will see there are some stems that appear not to have colour at all because they are curling at the very top of the branch and catching the full force of the light. It's best to leave these white and finish them off with just a touch of Ivory. On one or two stems there are some touches of warmth and for these you can use Burnt

Carmine, but be very careful with this colour as you will only need the lightest of touches.

Look carefully at the nodes and if you feel it necessary add little extra touches of colour to finish them off. At this final stage you can also darken any distinct shaded areas to give the illustration extra depth. Finish your work by using a colourless blender to blend all your layers of colour and push them into the surface of the paper. This will also enrich the colours. Note that colourless blenders drag colour, so do one colour at a time, clean the tip of the pencil and then move on. If you go from the deep red of the cherry to the lighter part where it is catching the light you will drag red into the pink or white areas, so be extra careful not to let this happen or you will spoil your work.

Savoy Cabbage

JANIE PIRIE

Looking at this remarkable study, photographic in its accuracy and encouraging the viewer to study and appreciate its miraculous structure, one can only marvel at so much intricacy of design and beauty in the creation of a humble cabbage. Janie has captured the colours so well, from the slightly glaucous outer leaves to the spring green heart, that the crisp cut of a knife almost seems possible. For anyone who struggles with leaves and venation it might be an idea to take just one Savoy cabbage leaf and work on that, in coloured pencil or watercolour, as it would make a challenging practice piece.

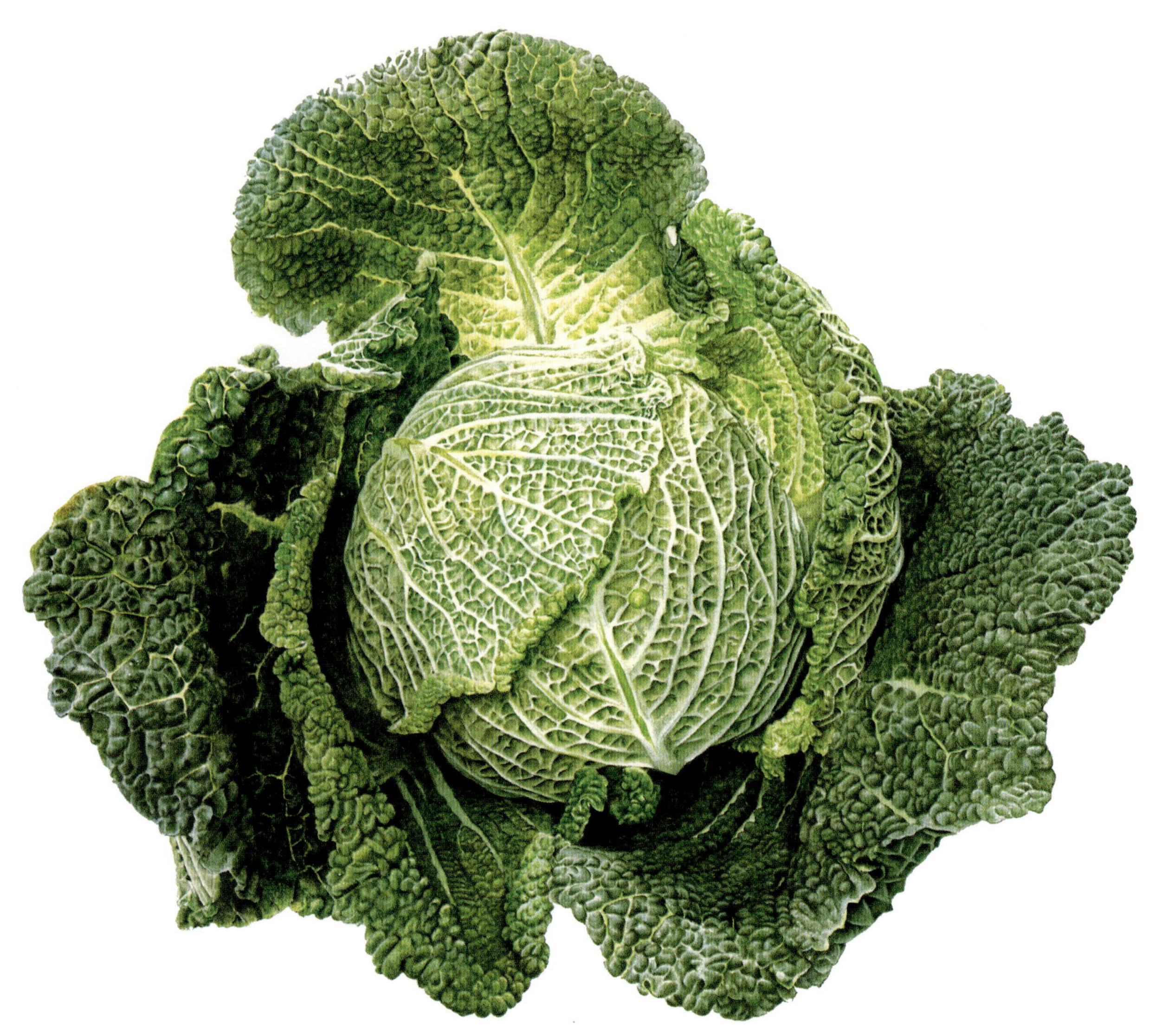

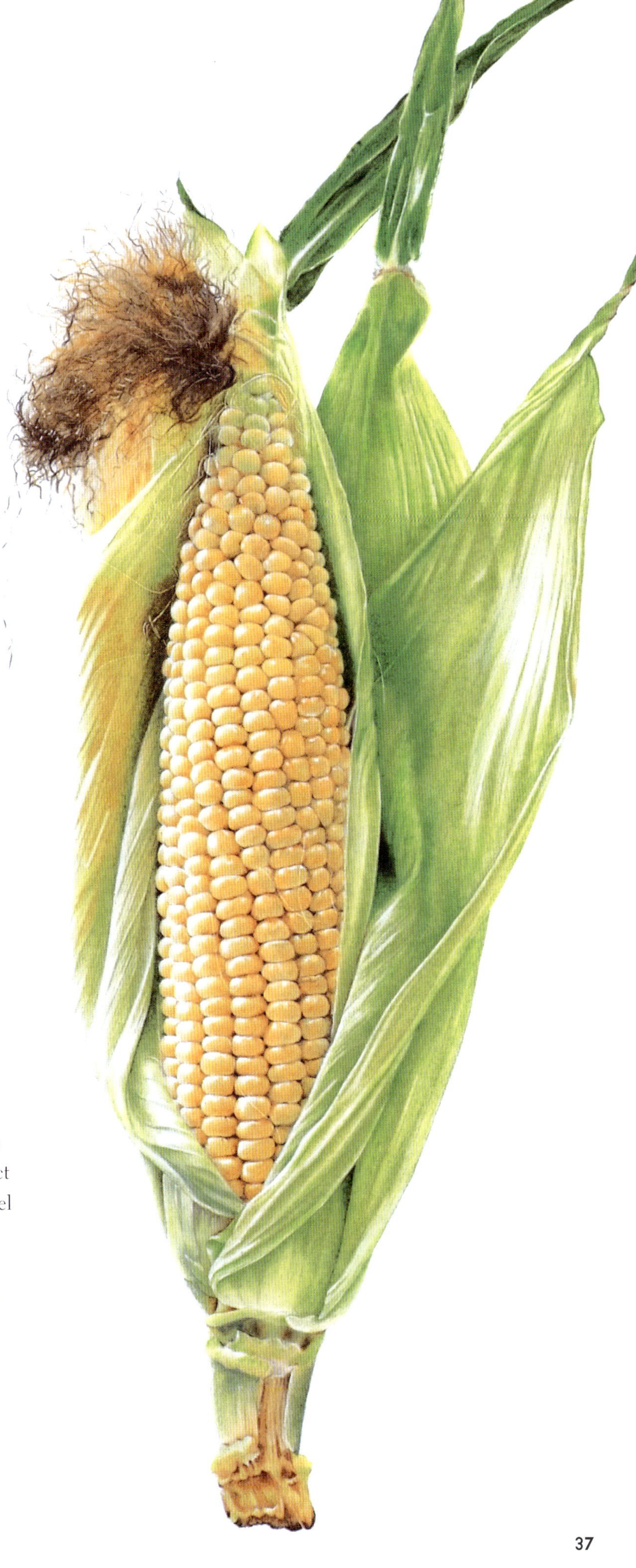

Zea mays (Sweetcorn)

JANIE PIRIE

This is another of Janie's highly realistic portrayals of a familiar subject more commonly found in the kitchen than the artist's studio. Look closely at the way the edges of the highlights are carefully blended to give a soft effect which helps to convey the texture of the husks. The tassel also suggests the fuzzy heart with silky strands escaping at the edge, and if you look carefully you will see where one or two are dangling down in front of the seeds. This shows the level of observation and fine detail that Janie has employed here.

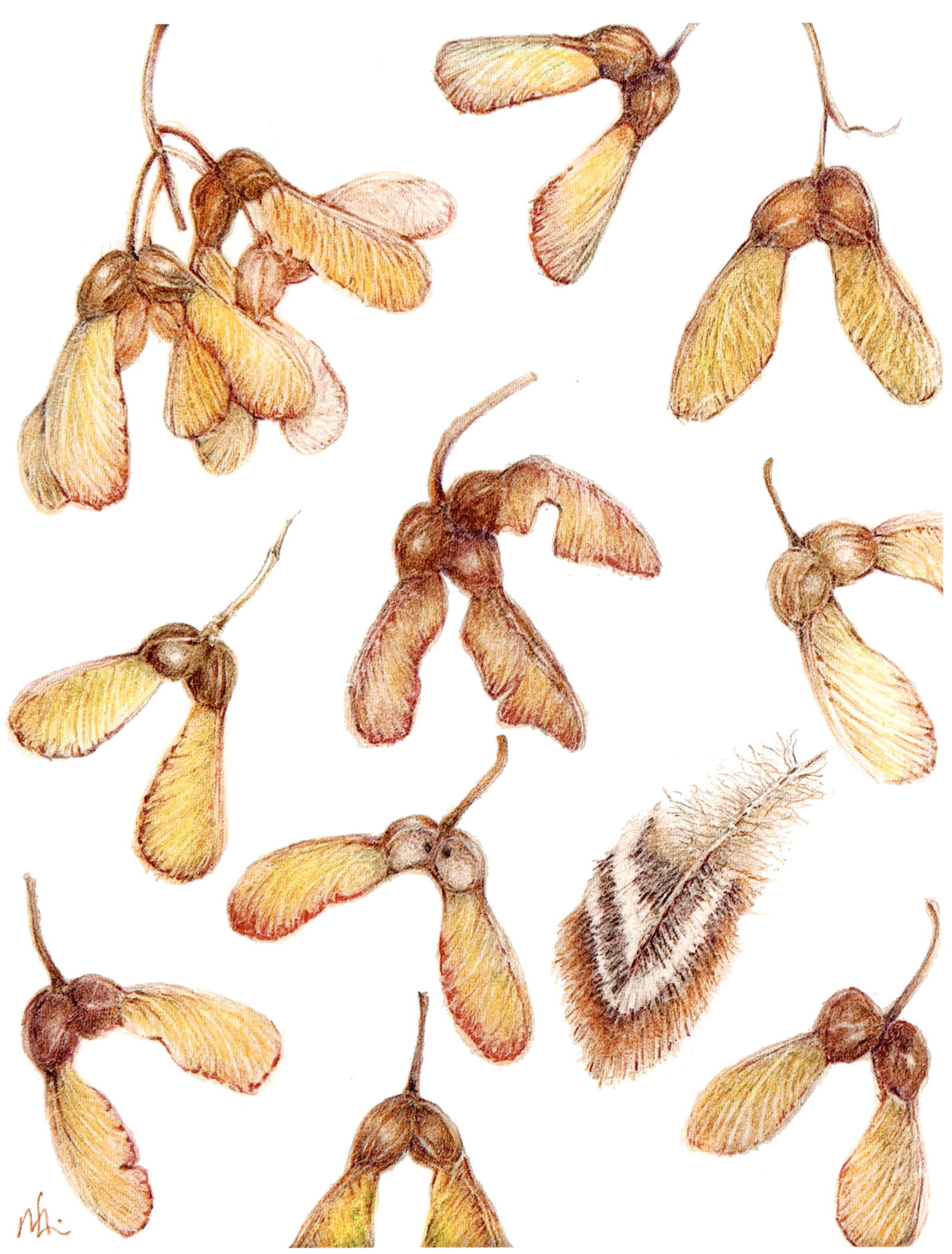

Sycamore Seeds

MARY LASSERSON

Mary was fortunate enough to find a feather whose colours perfectly replicated the shades of the sycamore keys, a reminder that it is always worth while keeping an eye open for any found object which may come in handy in the future – feathers, snail shells, broken eggshells thrown out by a houseproud bird tidying up her nest, a broken twig with a pretty clump of lichen and so on.

Lavender and Bees

MARY LASSERSON

A popular subject for artists, whether in the fields of Provence or smothered with bees in a domestic garden, lavender evokes a summery sense of well-being. The calming scent and the gentle hum of bees is all that one could wish for as an antidote to life's often harsh realities. When choosing subject matter it is useful to consider the effect your work might have on viewers when it is exhibited – the buyer is likely to be someone with whom it strikes a chord, not necessarily because of the technique or colour.

Mary's fluffy-tailed bees with their gossamer wings create a romantic and timeless image. She likes to work on Bockingford Rough paper using Derwent Artist's and Studio Pencils. She finds the surface excellent for conveying textures including smooth ones rendered with sharp-pointed pencils.

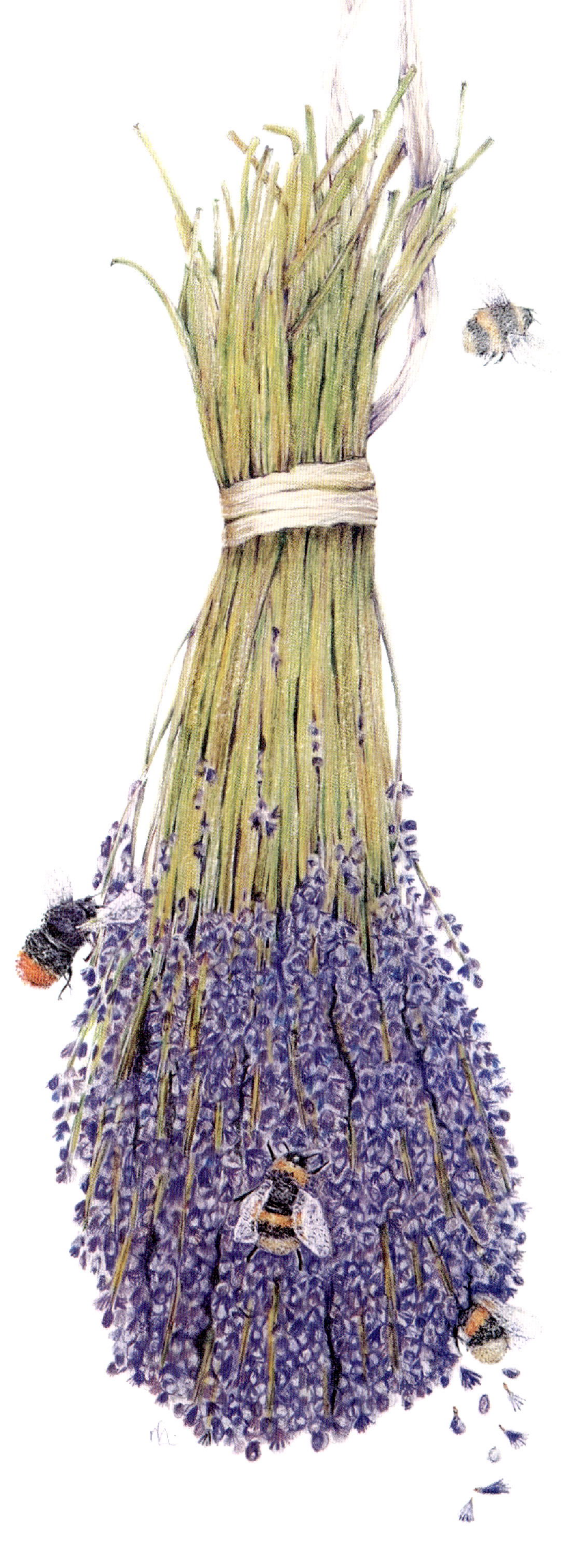

CHAPTER 3

Painting on Vellum

In recent years there has been a resurgence of interest among artists in the use of vellum as a support. Vellum rolls dating from medieval times record much of human history, so if you write or paint on vellum you can truly feel you are producing something for posterity. Traditionally, the pin feather of a snipe was used by miniature painters and others seeking to record the finest detail, but such a thing can only be acquired from someone who has shot a snipe; I have one carefully guarded specimen and can vouch for its efficiency.

At the moment there is not a lot written to help the student who wants to explore this option, so I hope this chapter will clarify the method and encourage others to have a go. Vellum is more expensive than paper but worth every penny for the reward of seeing colours glow almost as if they are lit from within. It is advisable to start small, as it will take time to become accustomed to working slowly and with quite a dry brush – anyone who is fluent with the wet-on-wet technique may struggle to adapt. As always, patience is the watchword.

If you feel confident you may like to draw directly onto your vellum using a fine pointed brush and a pale wash of whatever the main colours are – green for leaves, brown for twigs and so on. It is easily wiped clean with damp kitchen paper in case of error or painted over if all goes well.

RIGHT *Laburnum anagyroides* (Golden Chain) | Shevaun Doherty | Watercolour on vellum
It would be difficult to make a bad composition when working with this plant. Like those of wisteria, the racemes drape themselves elegantly down the page and the yellow flowers glow against the mottled surface of the vellum. Anyone lucky enough to visit Bodnant Gardens in North Wales when the laburnum pergola is in full dress knows that as you walk beneath it the light itself is golden, which coupled with the heady perfume, makes for an unforgettable experience.

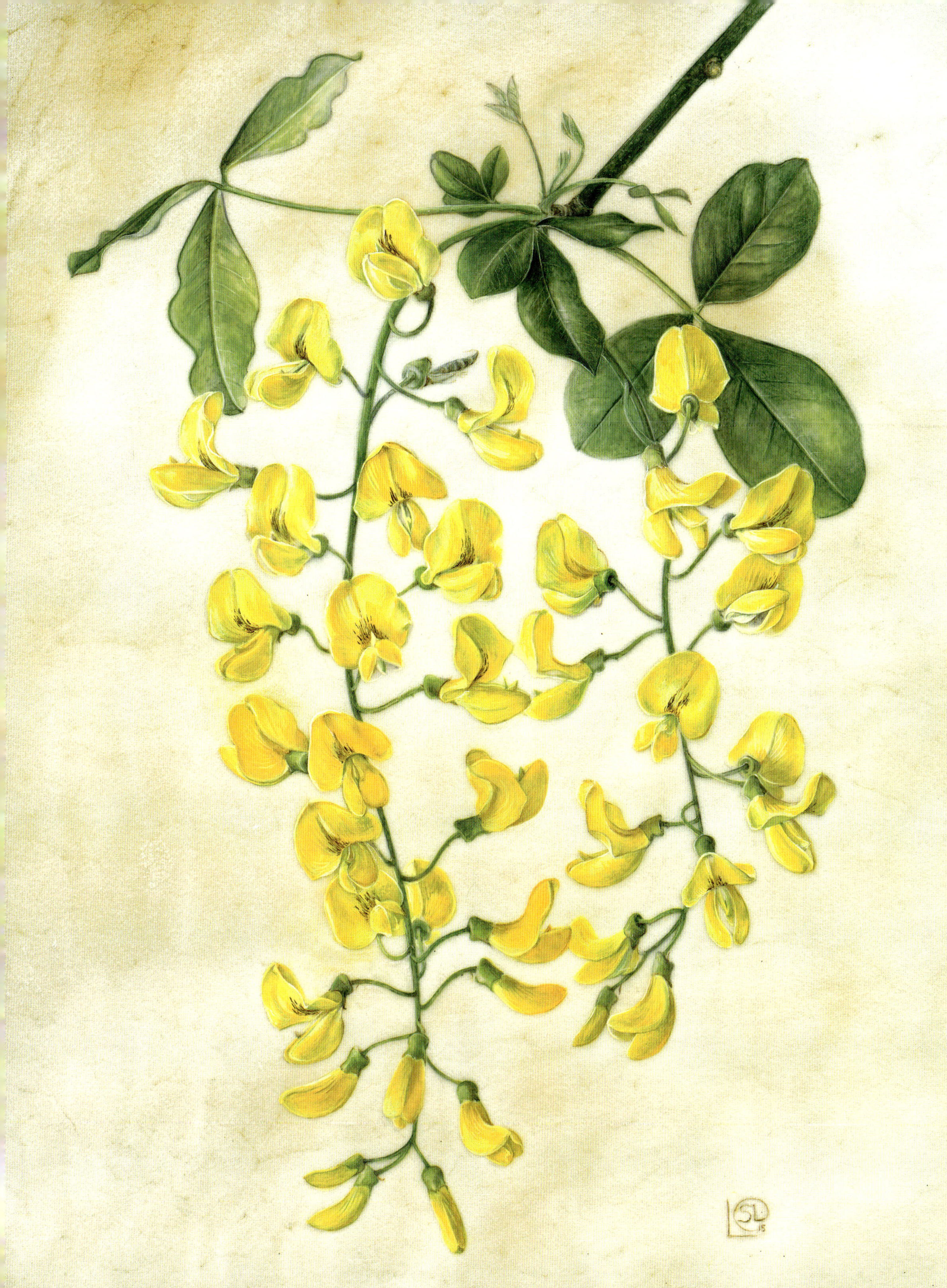

Step-by-Step

PRUNUS DOMESTICA 'VICTORIA' BY SHEVAUN DOHERTY

Step-by-step guides are usually very formally structured, showing the work in progress from drawing to completion. For her painting of Victoria plums, Shevaun has managed to give a crash course on the use of vellum so the usual sequence has not been upheld. Also, because it is a slower process, new leaves had to be brought in as the original ones withered and furled. This is normal for the artist who chooses to paint from life and who does not rely on photographs to complete their work. I hope many more people will be tempted to try vellum and Shevaun has given you all the basic knowledge required to work on this beautiful material.

Painting on vellum is a different experience to painting on paper and rather exciting as the organic markings make each piece truly unique. Kelmscott vellum is considered to be the very finest surface for an artist to paint on as the calfskin is repeatedly dipped in a 'broth' to give a chalky and velvety smooth surface which holds paint well – though my preference is for the markings and coloration of natural calfskin vellum as I find this often suggests the subject matter. For this painting I chose a piece of well-veined calfskin with a rich honey tone and mottled markings which reminded me of the dappled light beneath leaves.

PREPARATION

Preparing the vellum is relatively easy. I tape it to a piece of foam board stiff enough to hold the vellum flat, but light enough to move around and be pinned to my easel. The vellum must be taped down because it is an organic substance and therefore highly sensitive to humidity and capable of cockling in what appears to be an alarming manner – but if this should happen simply place it in a dry warm place, such as an airing cupboard, and it will soon revert to its flattened state. I recommend blue painters' tape, available from most hardware shops, as it is easy to remove and more effective than brown gummed paper or masking tape.

Next, and most importantly, all traces of grease must be removed from the surface of the vellum. To do this I place a tablespoonful of artists' quality pumice powder into the foot of an old nylon stocking then, allowing some of the powder to fall onto the vellum, I gently rub with the powder-filled stocking using circular movements (Fig. 1). This will not only remove any grease spots but also the slightly abrasive nature of the pumice helps to polish and smooth the surface, allowing for greater detail when painting. Afterwards I gently brush the powder off and wipe the vellum with a soft, clean cloth.

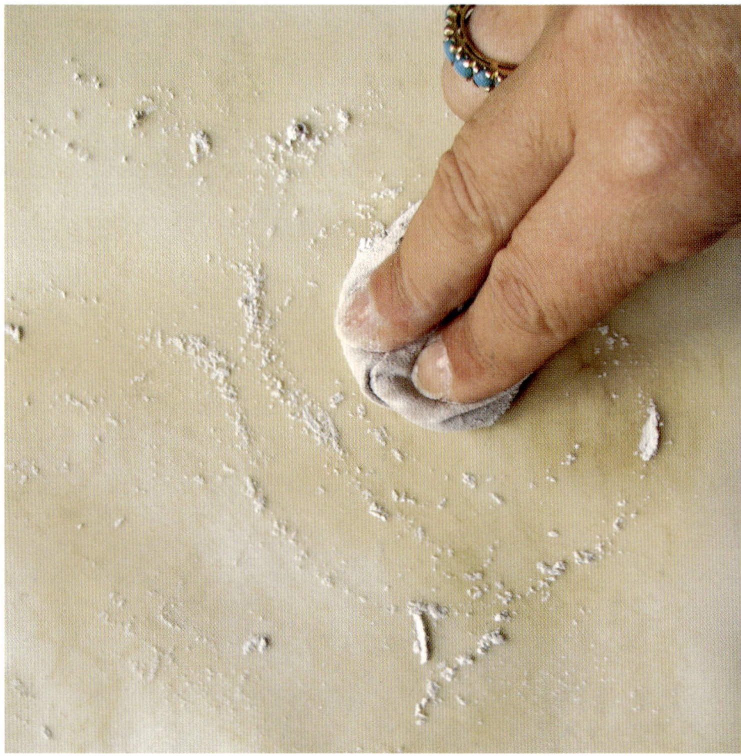

1. Shevaun uses pumice powder to ensure the vellum surface is clean and free from grease.

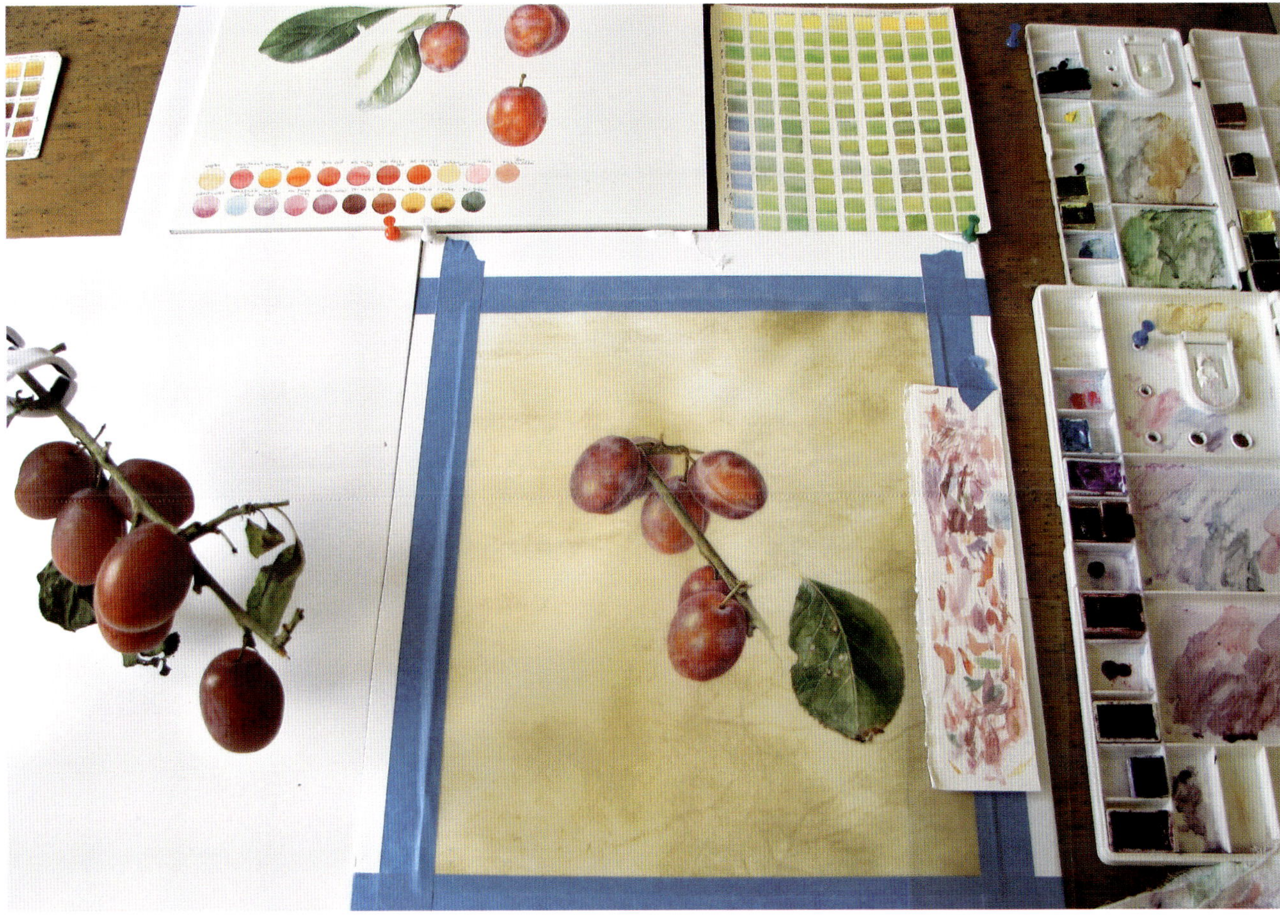

2. She works methodically, using charts to ensure accurate colour matching,
and paints a trial study on paper before working on the vellum.

COMPOSITION

Finding a suitable branch to fit the size of the vellum was
quite a challenge, for although I had a good supply to
choose from, none had just the right number of plums and
leaves to give balance. I settled for a branch which had a
pleasing selection of ripe plums but few leaves as the basis
of the composition; I could add leaves from other branches
in order to create an aesthetically pleasing picture, while
still keeping it botanically correct. It is always important to
understand how the plant grows and how its parts connect,
for although artistic licence is permissible it should never
be at the expense of botanical accuracy.

Having selected the branch I placed a piece of
tracing paper over the vellum and drew out my basic
composition, including the leaves from other branches,
balancing and tweaking the composition design. This
design was used as a blueprint throughout the painting
process.

Painting on vellum is a slow exercise – the paint goes on
lighter than it does on paper and because of vellum's non-
absorbent nature big washes of colour are not feasible.
The painting has to be built up using layer upon layer of
dry brushwork, which takes time. As the fruit was already
ripe I needed to paint it first before it dropped off the
branch, so I placed the leaves on kitchen towel and stored
them in an airtight container in the fridge until required.

COLOUR MATCHING

I always begin every painting by doing careful colour studies on paper. This helps me to work out my colour palette and become familiar with my subject. Here I selected which pigments to use by placing the plums and leaves on colour charts I had made previously. These are mainly painted from pure unmixed paints, but the green colour chart is always a mix of blues and greens. I tend to work with a wide range of pigments rather than a limited palette, though I do use a few basic colours to help create harmony. Blue pigments affect the tones of the painting so I generally use one light-value blue (Manganese Hue) and one mid-value blue (Indanthrene Blue) throughout. Both are transparent and easy to use. I also include Cobalt Violet in all my paintings as I find it is the perfect colour for reflected lights and soft shadows.

I made my initial studies on Fabriano Artistico Hot Point Traditional White paper, which is creamy-white. It is important to bear in mind that the pigments behave slightly differently on the darker tones of the vellum and may need adjusting. For example, I found that Permanent Rose was perfect on the paper but on the vellum it appeared slightly lurid, so I changed it for the more subdued Rose Madder (Fig. 2).

BRUSHES

Painting on vellum requires a lot of dry brushing, particularly in the later layers, which can wear out brushes quickly. To paint in the dry brush style, short-haired brushes work best; long-haired ones can disturb the layers of paint beneath and lift the pigment, leaving 'holes' which are very hard to smooth out. Spotters and miniature brushes work best on vellum and my favourite brush is Winsor & Newton Series 7 Miniature Sable. I also use Rosemary & Co spotters, which have short hairs and a slightly fatter body. I have a very fine brush for the tiny details, but do most of the work with a number 2 or 3.

It is easy to lift paint off vellum and I find Billy Showell's Eradicator Brush is ideal for this, or any stiff chisel-shaped acrylic brush. It is as well to be prepared for the occasional error!

The trick to painting bloom on fruit lies in the blending. For this I use a filbert brush, perfect for laying glazes in wide light strokes or for building form, particularly on fruit. I also use a fan brush to soften the glazes. There is a knack to using a fan brush as the paint must be damp but not wet or it will disturb the preceding layers. The brush must be used lightly and quickly in multiple directions to feather and soften the glazes, taking care not to go over the edges. It is a very effective technique which has long been used in marbling, but one that needs practice first.

TECHNIQUES

Painting on vellum is very different to painting on paper as it is non-absorbent and the paint sits on the surface rather than sinking in. This means the edges are crisp, whereas on paper there is always a slight bleed. The nature of the edges helps to give a distinctive three-dimensional aspect to a vellum painting.

Paint also goes on light, so more layers or glazes are required in order to build up depth of colour. Because the paint sits on the surface, each layer must be applied carefully in order not to disturb the previous one – a vital point, since success or failure will be decided by the artist's delicacy of touch. I keep a spare sheet of paper beside my vellum and always wipe the brush on this to remove any excess water before applying it to my painting. The final layers of pigment are almost as dry as coloured pencil. Graphite also sits on the surface, so you need to remove it carefully before you start painting. If left it will muddy the paint.

I began by drawing out the leaf onto tracing paper and then went over the lines on the reverse side using an HB pencil – softer B pencils leave too much graphite residue on vellum.

Using the composition template, I transferred the line drawing on to tracing paper to help me determine where to place the leaf (Fig. 3). After transferring the drawing I removed the graphite with pumice powder until only a faint line remained. I made sure to gently brush off the excess pumice before painting.

Next I painted over the lines of graphite using a fine brush and Raw Umber and Raw Sienna. These earth pigments blend into the vellum, so they work well in establishing those first lines. As the vellum is quite dark in tone I painted the edges which caught the light in Naples Yellow. This is an opaque pigment, so it appears brighter on the vellum. Once the lines were painted I started on the form of the leaf by establishing the areas of shadow and light. I used a wash of Manganese Hue mixed with a little Cobalt Violet in the highlighted areas and a darker wash of Indanthrene Blue mixed with my green mix of Payne's Grey and Transparent Yellow. The first washes can be quite wet but not as wet as on paper. Once the wash is laid it is essential to resist the temptation to fiddle with it or it will become patchy. Next I painted around the veins on the leaf.

Once the form was established I applied green glazes of Payne's Grey and Transparent Yellow that became progressively dryer with each layer. For the paler green glazes I added Winsor Yellow to the Payne's Grey and Transparent Yellow mix. A final thin glaze of Transparent Yellow was applied to areas where the sun shone through the leaf. For dry brushing the paint is diluted to the required thin consistency on the palette, picked up on the tip of the brush and any excess wiped off on kitchen paper. Application to the vellum resembles working with coloured pencil, partly because of the dry 'feel' and also because of the tiny stippled or hatched strokes one uses to establish detail.

The holes and spots on the leaf gave it character. I painted around the holes and gave the edges a highlight and a shadow to create definition. Finally I added the spots.

The enlarged leaf (Fig. 4) shows the result of working in the manner described. I always follow the same procedure: line, form, then colour. Because the vellum is quite dark in tone I picked out a few of the brighter highlights along the edges using a little white gouache, blending in places with the watercolour. This should be done at the very end as gouache will quickly deaden transparent watercolour if not used with care. Such paintings should be described as 'watercolour with some bodycolour'.

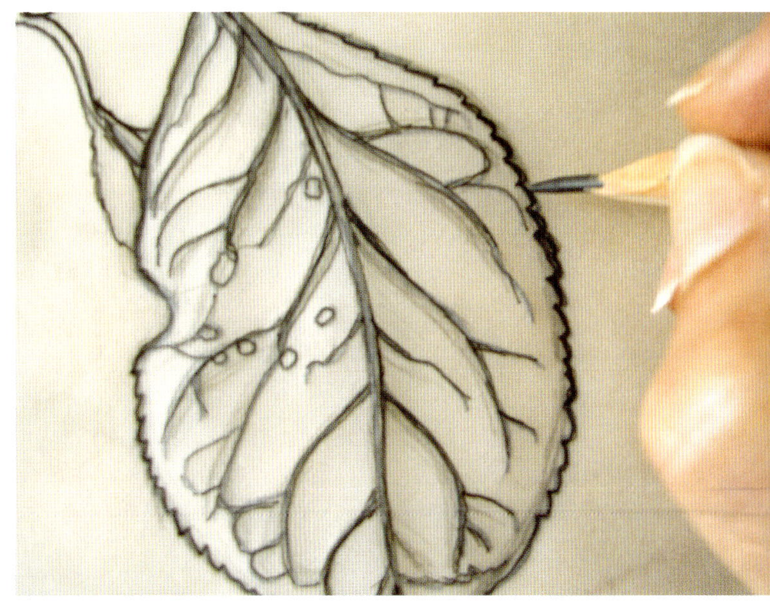

3. A leaf is carefully traced onto the vellum in the knowledge these will wither first and it is wise to establish form and colour at the outset.

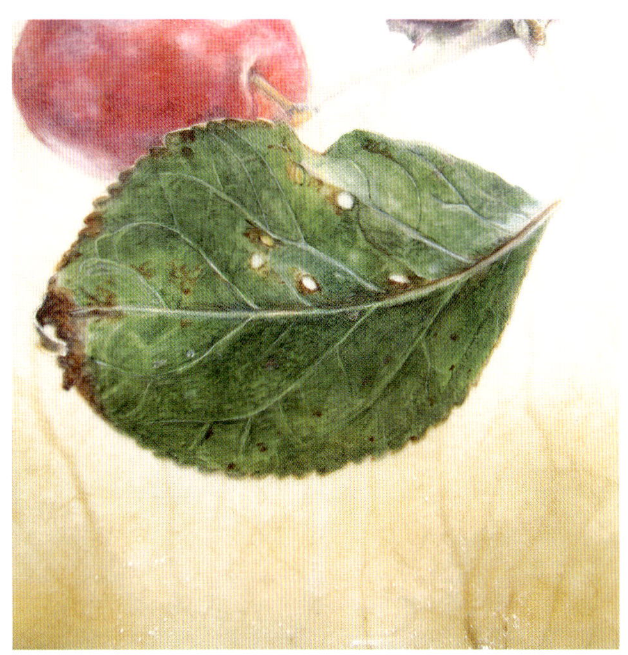

4. Enlarged leaf showing blended colours, detail and brush strokes.

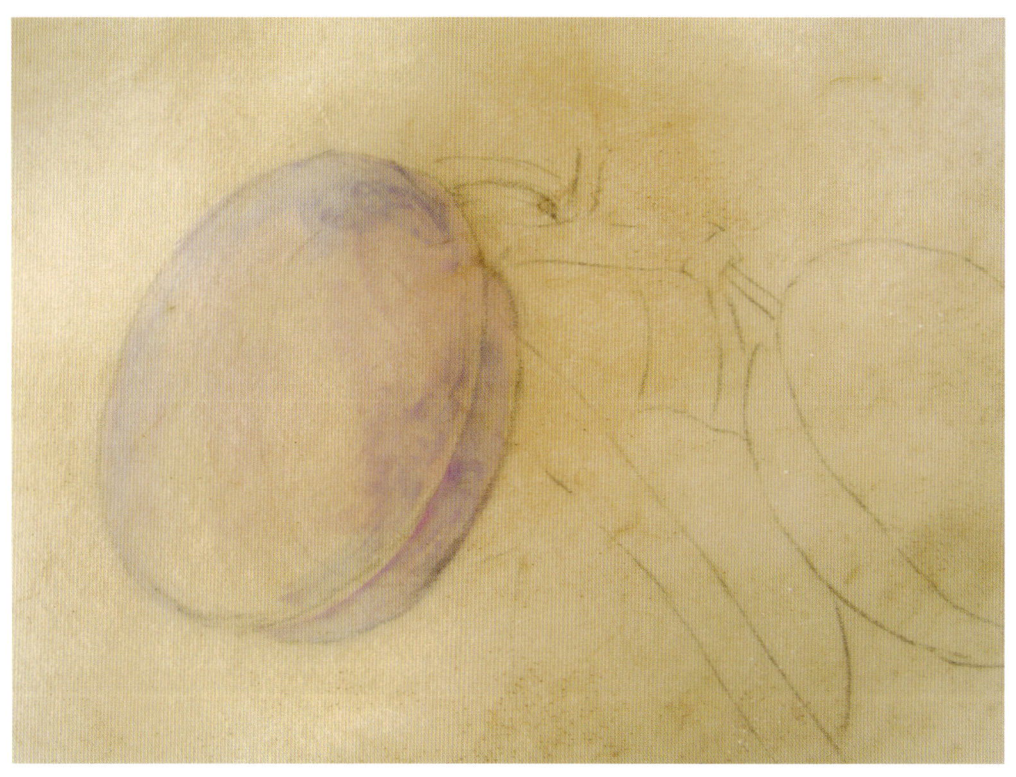

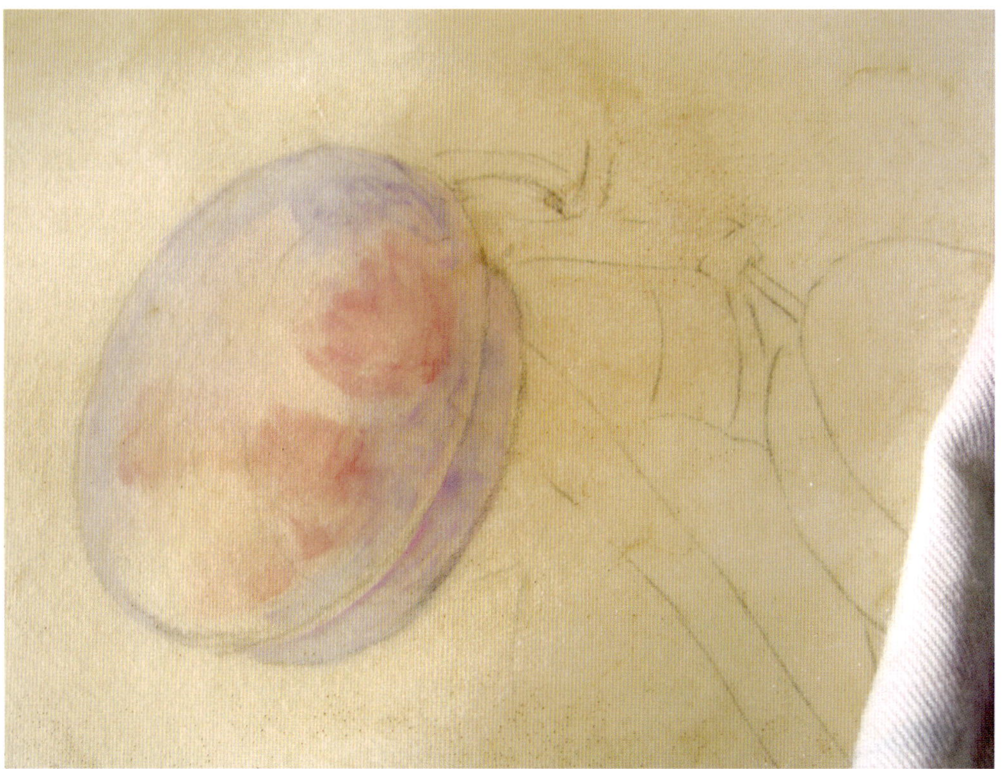

5. and 6. Enlarged plums show the build-up of bloom and skin tones which give form to the fruit.

PLUMS

With the leaf colours established I moved hastily on to the very ripe plums, which were in danger of falling off the branch. Bloom – the semi-transparent waxy layer produced by plants to protect the surface of fruit and leaves from water, dirt and insects – must be painted first. More noticeable on some plants than on others, it can be very important in making a painting look convincing. Because of its transparency the colour depends on what lies beneath – for example on green or yellow fruit the bloom will have a pale bluish tinge, while on purple or red fruit it has more of a purple bias.

I started painting the plums with Manganese Hue, which is a light-value blue, plus Cobalt Violet. Victoria plums are a beautiful rich pink so the bloom has more of the latter than the former. I used this bloom mix to help establish form. Keeping the highlights clear, I used more blue in the mix for the areas in shadow. Once the first layer was completed I started on the skin of the fruit, leaving areas of the waxy bloom untouched. I used thin washes of Rose Madder and Orange Red, blending as I went to create the impression of a smooth round skin, then applied a thin wash of Naples Yellow around the highlighted area to provide a warm base. This helped to pull the centre of the fruit forward while pushing the cooler shadow areas back, accentuating the roundness of the fruit (Figs 5, 6 and 7).

I continued to build up layers of colour, using shades of pink to create the subtle colour transitions from the warm orange areas around the highlights to the purples of the shadows, while leaving some areas of bloom unpainted. The important thing was to keep blending as this is a smooth, round surface despite the variations in colour. I use a wide range of pigments when I paint, keeping a colour chart of all the colours next to the painting to help me with colour choices. I always make notes of which colours I use and the order in which I use them so that there is a consistency throughout the painting.

The plum palette consists of Winsor & Newton Cobalt Violet, Manganese Blue Hue, Naples Yellow, Winsor Orange (Red Shade), Rose Madder, Quinacridone Violet, Perylene Violet, Perylene Maroon, Schmincke Ruby Red,

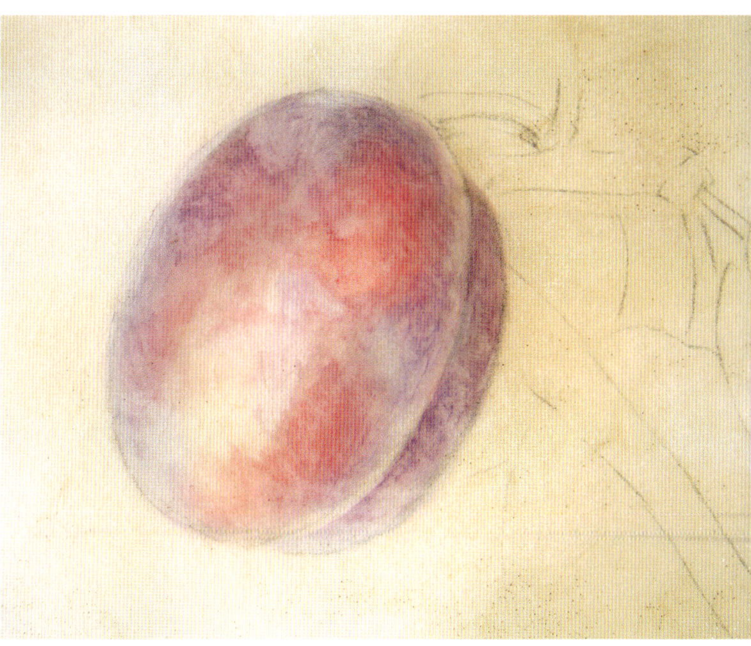

7. Adding white gouache to Cobalt Violet helps to intensify the bloom.

Schmincke Dark Red, Schmincke Manganese Violet, Schmincke Purple Magenta and Rembrandt Permanent Blue Violet. I also used mixes of Schmincke Dark Red plus Winsor & Newton Quinacridone Violet and Schmincke Dark Red plus Rembrandt Permanent Blue Violet. To give the plums a final warm burst of colour I applied very thin glazes of Daniel Smith Rhodonite Genuine or Indian Yellow, using a dry brush, to the centre of the fruit, which helps to bring the centre forward while pushing the edges away from the viewer.

I added a little white gouache mixed with Cobalt Violet simply because the vellum was so dark and I felt that the bloom was not bright enough. I applied it with a very fine brush using hatching strokes so as not to lift the underlying paint. On paper this would not have been necessary as the reflective surface would have been sufficiently bright. Again the gouache should only be used at the very end and with great care (Fig. 8).

Adding the stalk and a bit of the branch helped to bring the painting together. In places I allowed the natural markings on the vellum to show through. Once the plums were completed I turned my attention back to the leaves. I blocked in the branch quickly, taking care to note where the leaves would be attached. By this time I had to find

fresh ones that would fit into the composition and make
sense botanically. These were worked in the manner
previously described for the trial leaf (Fig. 9).

Finally I added the detail to the branch using pigments
from both the fruit and leaves to pull everything together.
At this stage a painting comes to life and when I feel it is
as good as I can make it I go over it with a magnifier for
one last check.

Compare the finished painting with the rough blueprint
shown in Fig. 2 and you will see how it was built up by
adding leaves and another stem.

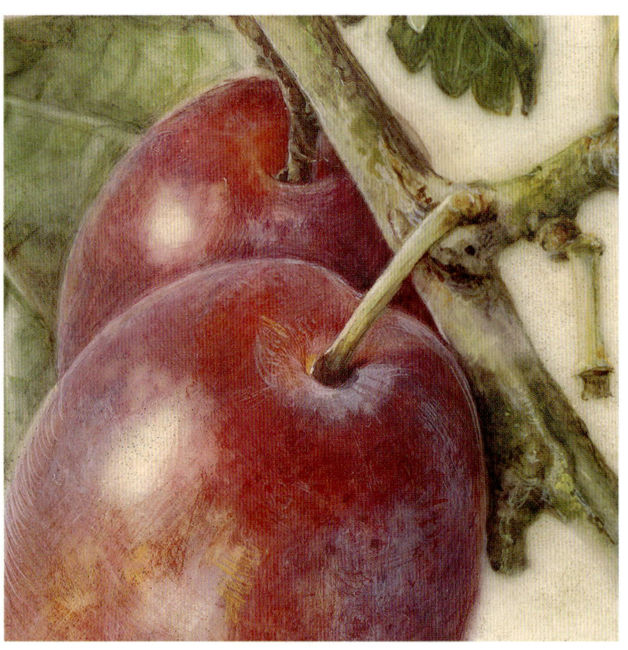

9. Tiny blemishes, the stalk and branch complete these
fruits and show the texture admirably.

Artist's Tips:

One advantage to working on vellum is that the
paint can easily be wiped off. Rather than battle on
with a section that has become muddy or patchy,
simply take a damp cloth and remove it completely,
then start again. I accidentally applied paint that
was too wet to one of the plums and ended up lifting
the paint, which made it patchy and uneven. After
removing the paint I allowed the area to dry and
then gave that section a quick rub down with some
pumice powder. After carefully brushing off excess
powder I began again with more success!

Smaller areas can be lifted off using a dampened
cotton bud. You can also remove layers of colour by
rubbing gently with pumice powder, which then
allows you to build up new layers of colour. Another
handy tool is a nail-buffing block intended for use in
manicures – it will gently remove patchy paint without
damaging the surface.

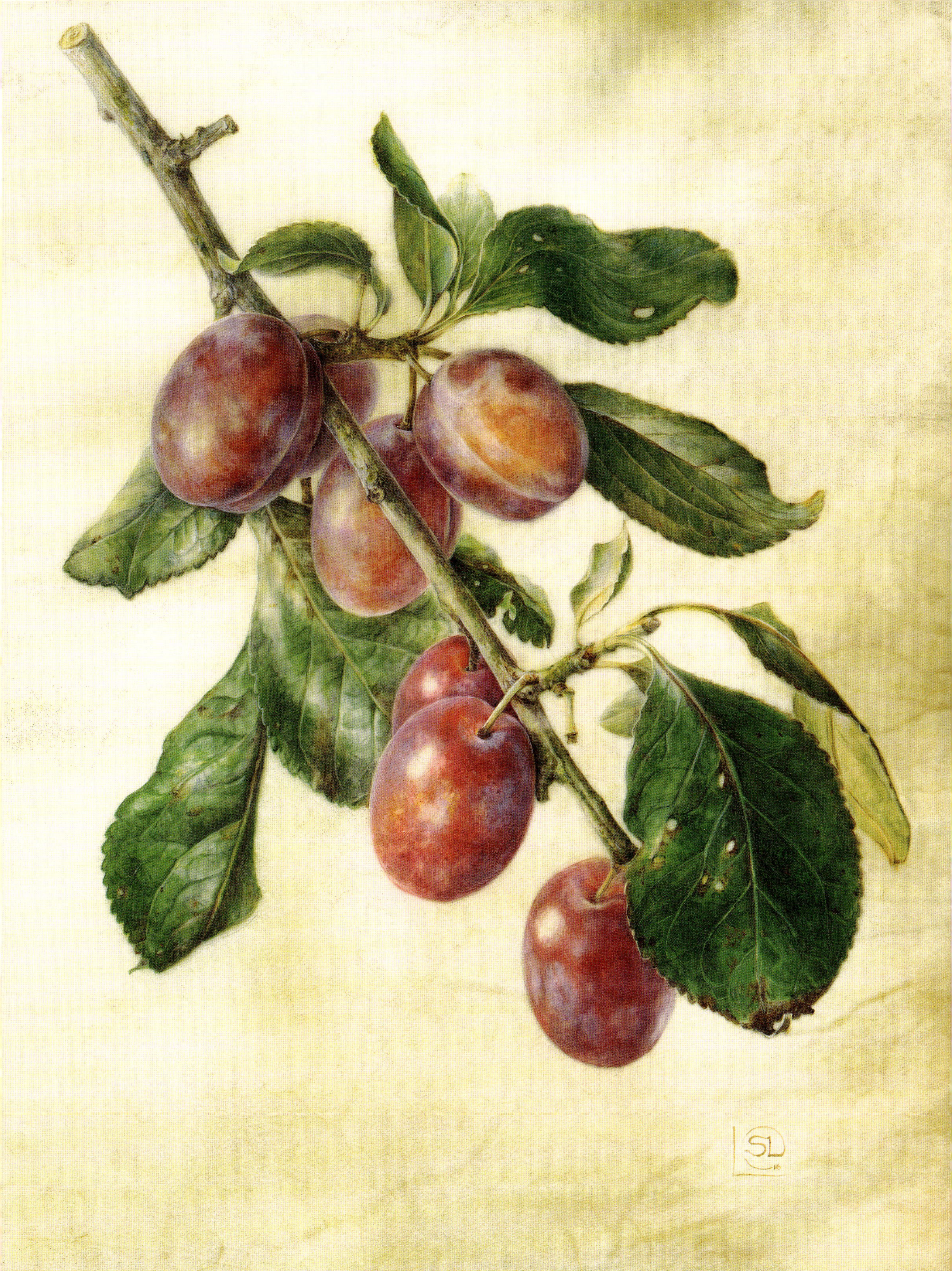

CHAPTER 4

Egg Tempera

It gives me a great deal of pleasure to include an historic but nowadays rather overlooked medium, since acrylic and ready-made gouache have rather taken over for artists seeking a change from watercolour. Also, I suspect that egg tempera is often associated with the soft, faded colours seen in frescos which are usually many centuries old, giving little hint of the vibrancy they would once have displayed.

We are lucky to include Marion Perkins among the membership of the SBA and here she offers readers the benefit of her knowledge and talent. From the examples of her work both in this chapter and later in the book you will see that beautifully bright and modern work can be achieved but, as with vellum, the method requires some skill and patient application.

As there seems to be little available to guide beginners wishing to make a start with egg tempera I hope the following may help to inspire more people to try something both historic and satisfying, as the effort put into the work will be rewarded with vibrant, fresh paintings perfectly at home in the 21st century.

RIGHT Joy of Winter | Marion Perkins | Egg tempera on gesso panel
Certain colours seem to predominate in each season and in the dark days of winter, shades of rich red lift the spirits. This is one of a set of four seasonal flower mug paintings.

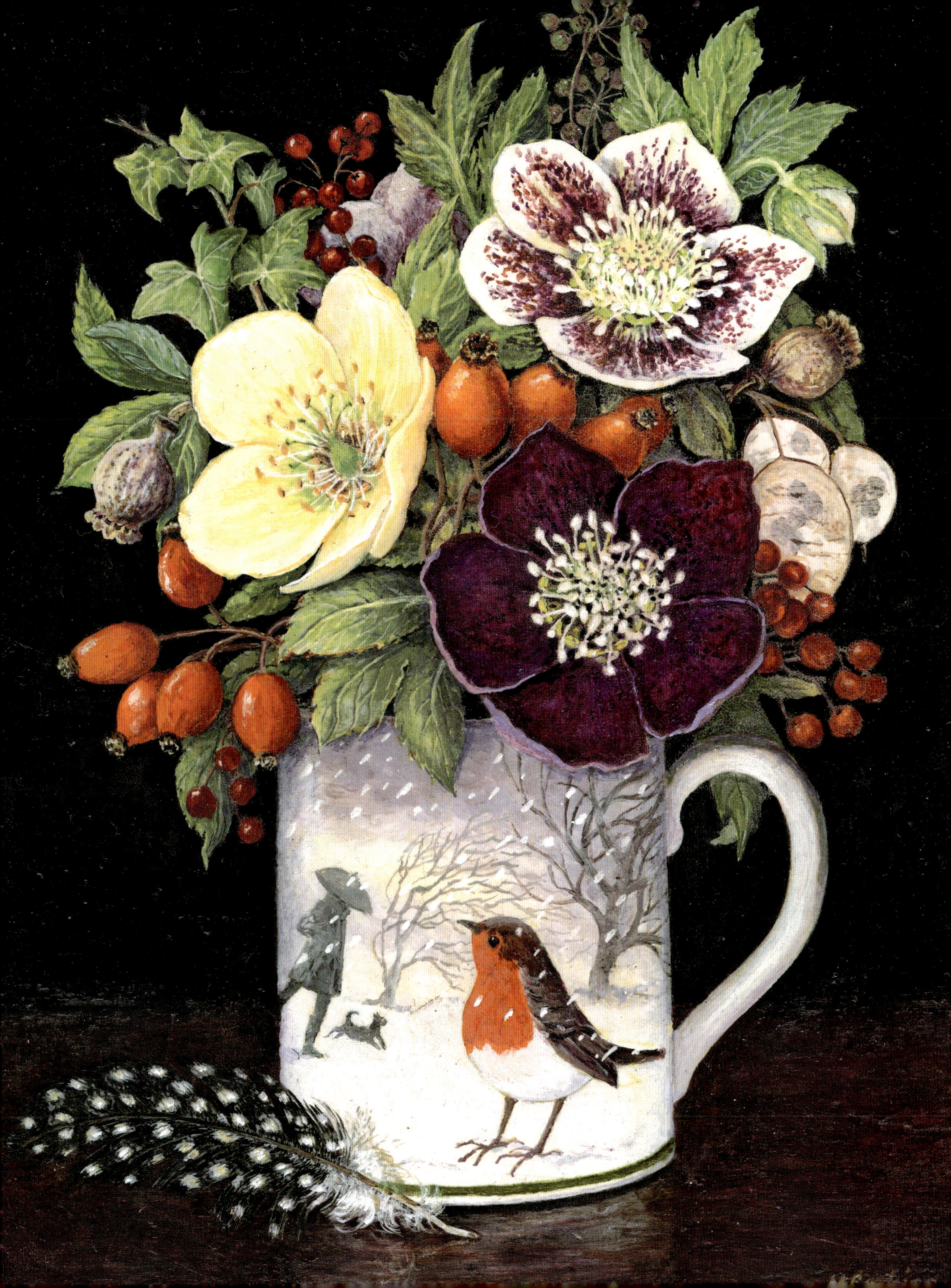

Egg tempera for the 21st century

By Marion Perkins

Egg tempera is not the first medium that springs to mind for botanical illustration, yet more than any other medium it responds to the careful, contemplative approach that is required for painting fine detail. Patience, dedication and faith in the process are essential, for only after several applications of paint with tiny brushstrokes or thin glazes can this translucent medium work its magic.

The use of egg yolk as a binder with ground pigment probably began around the 1st century AD or even earlier. The Ancient Roman writer Pliny the Elder wrote of this method being used then for wall paintings. It is a durable and stable medium and there still exist many well-preserved Egyptian funerary paintings showing the linear brushwork of egg tempera.

In the 15th century the painters of the Early Renaissance favoured a method of applying the egg tempera paint in layers, with tiny brushstrokes put down as cross-hatching, a method still used today. The quality of the medium dictates a method of this type as each brushstroke begins to dry straight away with a hard line, precluding blending or covering large areas – although the medium does allow for very thin glazes of colour with very little pigment.

With the increased use of oils as binders for ground pigments the popularity of egg tempera painting began to wane, and it is now a rather forgotten skill. However, the technique of proceeding in a deliberate, mindful and unhurried fashion allows considered development of shade, tone and hue. Similar to watercolour's dry brush technique, it is a skill to be learned with trial and error, coping with the disadvantages and delighting in the advantages. It is well suited to artists who are wary of free expression, fast wet-into-wet watercolour techniques and large-scale work, but are happy exploring detail with every brushstroke. It has the reward of allowing rich and deep colour effects, translucence, subtle change and the tiniest detail. For this reason it is ideal for botanical painting.

Method and materials

Very fresh egg yolks are essential as their binding qualities are then at their best. Pale yolks are easier to use as the currently popular reddish-orange yolk initially alters the colour of the pigment, although the colour of the yolk fades as the paint dries. It is curious to learn that in 1437 the Tuscan artist Cennino Cennini wrote in his book *Il libro dell'arte* that town eggs were paler and more suited to young faces, while country eggs had a reddish hue better for portraits of old men.

The egg yolk in its sac is separated and washed carefully in the hand under a gentle stream of cold water to remove the white; if the yolk breaks at this point it is probably not very fresh and is difficult to rescue. The yolk is placed on a strong paper towel and gently dried, then pierced and poured into a clean glass jar with a lid, leaving the sac or membrane to be discarded. A teaspoon of pure water is added and half a teaspoon of white vinegar. It seems the latter prevents bloom or mould appearing on any dark areas of a painting and it also helps the later mixing of the pigment with the yolk. With the lid on the jar, the egg-yolk mix will keep satisfactorily in a refrigerator for up to three days.

Colours are widely available in pigment form, sold in pots or bags of varying quantities, and as only very little at a time is needed they last for ages. The choice of pigments is a matter of the artist's preference and experience. Some are very toxic; some can be grainy and need grinding down with a glass muller; some are very fine and need just a drop of white spirit to dissolve them.

Traditionally, gesso panels are used for egg tempera as a rigid surface is needed or the painting could crack. Wooden boards are cut to a preferred size and prepared with a gesso made from rabbit skin glue or gelatine and whiting. Well-seasoned wood or MDF (medium density fibreboard) are less likely to absorb moisture and warp. The board is sized with rabbit-skin glue and, when dry, tightly covered with muslin soaked in the glue. The gesso is then prepared by mixing rabbit skin glue, water and whiting, strained through a paint strainer with air bubbles eliminated. The gesso is applied very thinly at first, and left to dry between coats, of which 10–12 are necessary. After 24 hours' drying time, the gesso is rubbed down to achieve a fine smooth white surface, finishing with a wet-and-dry sandpaper. Now the surface is perfect for egg tempera.

Prepared acrylic gesso will not do to save time as it renders a non-absorbent surface which the egg tempera resists, but a gesso for egg tempera is available at cornelissen.com. Fortunately gesso panels such as Ampersand's Clayboard are available in several sizes, so it is tempting to abandon the traditional methods and take advantage of today's ready-prepared panels, available from www.jacksonsart.com.

The initial drawing is transferred very lightly onto the board using tracing paper. That drawing is then emphasized in either diluted ink or a thin mix of tempera paint. A small quantity of colour pigment is mixed with a little water with a small watercolour brush and then an equal amount of egg yolk is added. This is the method for creating and using egg tempera paint.

At this stage corrections can easily be made by simply wiping off the drawing lines. When starting the painting it is best to use only a few pigments at a time, remixing frequently. Too many colours are confusing, whereas working with two or three pigments and moving on to areas that require the same colours is easier. The method is to build up colour slowly, allowing areas to dry before applying as many coats as required. The medium allows for continual adjustment of hue and form and the depth and glow of colour will intensify with each layer of paint – though the desired effect may be to allow the white of the gesso board to shine through.

A finished painting will take at least six months to 'cure' and extra care should be taken in this time not to scratch the surface. Occasionally burnishing the surface with a clean silk cloth will help to keep the lustrous finish and the brilliance of the colours should last forever.

Step-by-Step

It is always a rose that stops me in my tracks in my garden and this one is no exception. Darkening from rich magenta to plum black as it develops, with the light stripes fading from palest yellow to cream, each bloom looks unique and tantalizingly magical.

Painting roses is a delight for me as every detail enthrals, from velvety textures and dusty bloom on the petals to the intriguing centres and intricate buds. Roses allow the egg tempera painter time to work slowly before they change shape too dramatically and a short spell in the refrigerator works wonders for keeping them fresh.

STEP 1

I drew the rose on paper and transferred a line drawing of it on tracing paper to the board.

Pigments used:

* From www.cornelissen.com: Raw Sienna, Titanium White, Quinacridone Magenta, Quinacridone Scarlet, Cobalt Blue and C. Roberson & Co Bronze Powder Gold 2.5.
* From www.greenandstone.com: Primary Red, Alizarin Violet and Naples Yellow.
* From Sennelier: Quinacridone Red, Ivory Black and Yellow Ochre.

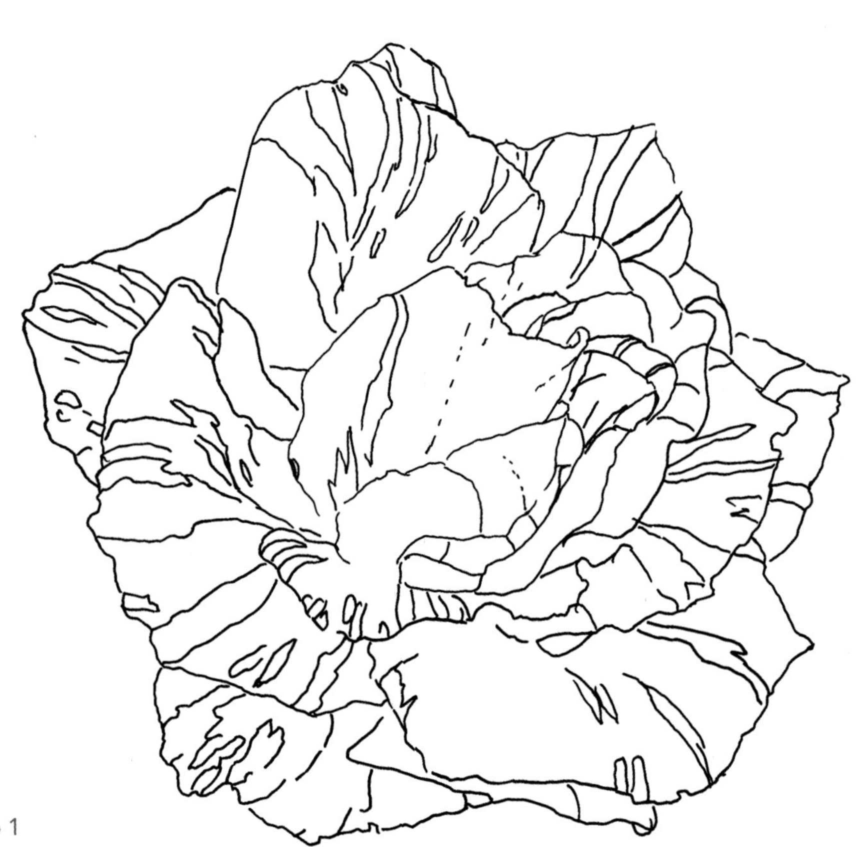

Step 1

STEP 2

I then applied a very thin layer of egg mixture all over the
rose drawing to give tooth to the surface and soften the
stark whiteness. I ignored the background as I was unsure
whether to leave it white or colour it. I then mixed some
puddles of pigment with a little water and with a size
0 brush took up some egg and, a little at a time, made
a mix on the palette of the required colours: Primary
Red, Quinacridone Magenta and Quinacridone Scarlet.
Starting on the red stripes, I glazed a thin undercoat of
colour of varying hue, then working slowly with a size
00 brush I cross-hatched and dotted more colour on
the red petals in a controlled way, leaving tiny specks of
undercoat here and there where the light stripes were
only slightly red. Egg tempera paint dries very quickly so
constant mixing is required.

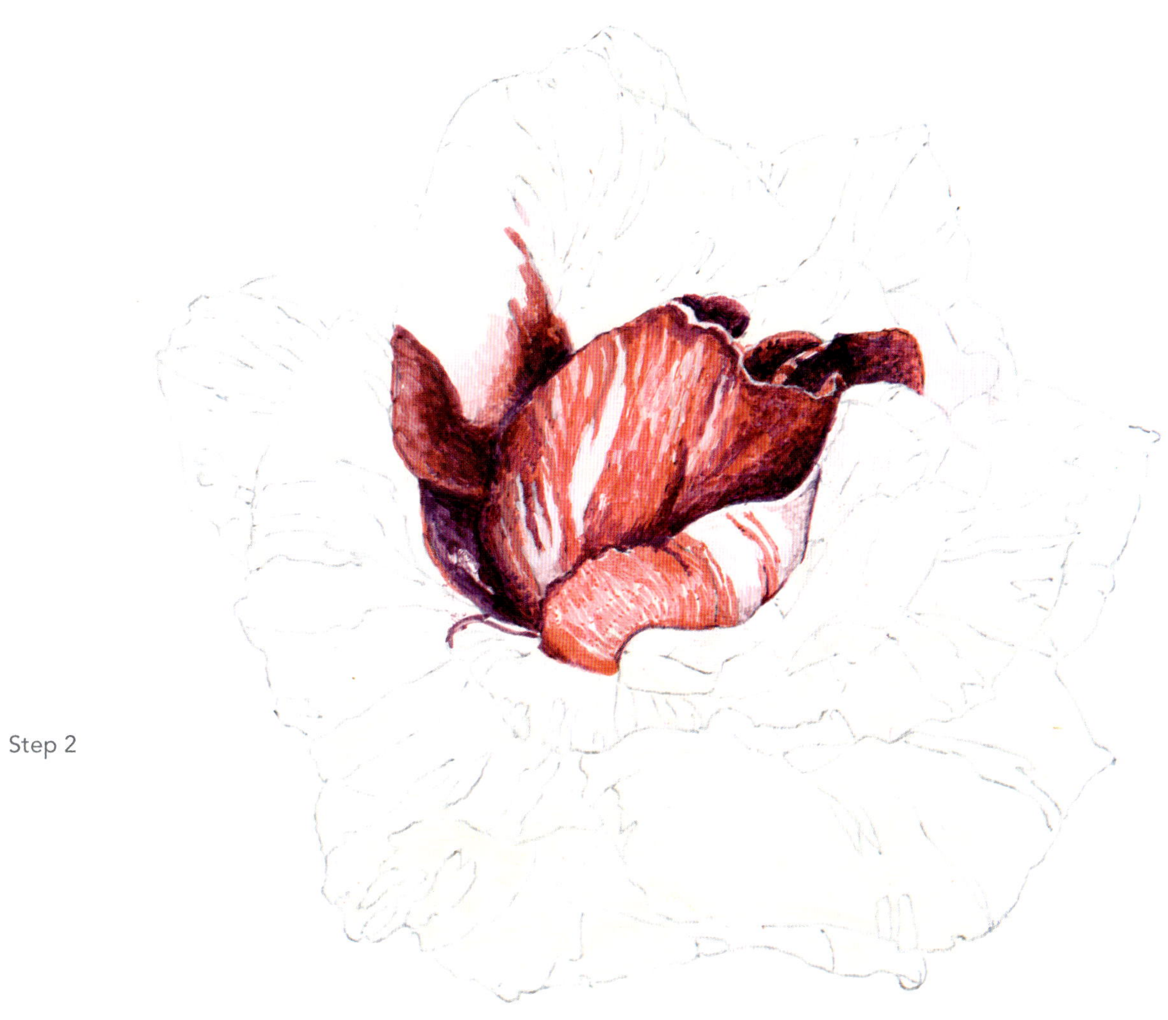

Step 2

Next I applied layer on layer of paint with the same linear or hatching techniques, intensifying the colours with subtle changes of pigment: Quinacridone Red, Alizarin Violet and Cobalt Blue. I added the dusty velvet bloom last with the same pigments in different proportions with the addition of the tiniest amount of Titanium White and Ivory Black, applied with the tip of a size 000 brush. Next I addressed the light areas of the rose with Naples Yellow, Titanium White, Yellow Ochre, Cobalt Blue and Primary Red, depending on the depth of shadow and reflected colour.

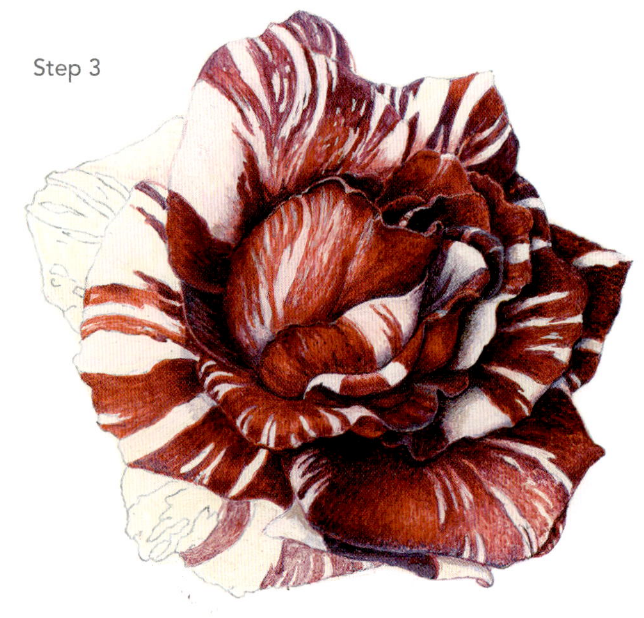

Step 3

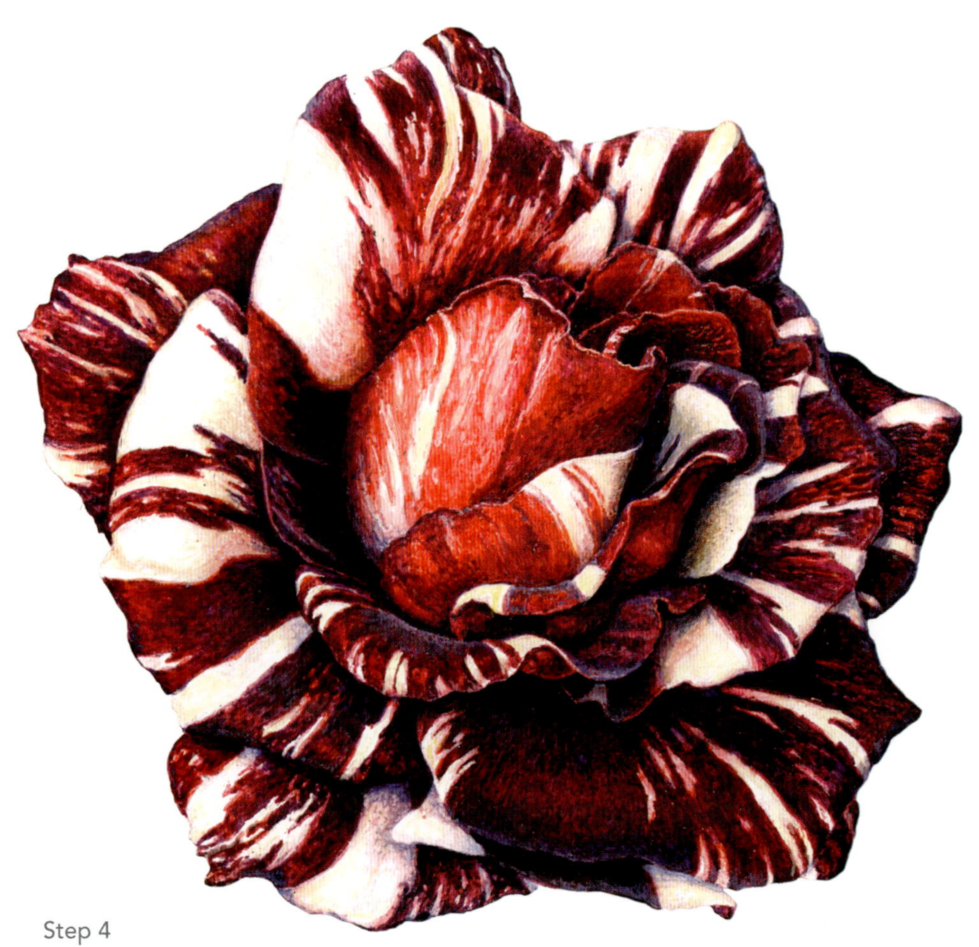

Step 4

STEP 4

I decided I could create a more mystical effect by complementing the rose with a dark background, a dramatic entrance for my 'Abracadabra' rose. I worked all around the flower with a thin glaze of Quinacridone Magenta as an undercoat and to link the background to the colour of the rose. I then proceeded in fine dots and lines to build up the background with Ivory Black and some Cobalt Blue, subtly graduating from dark to darker to add interest.

STEP 5

To bring in a traditional icon theme I added a narrow gold border using the same method of paint application with C. Roberson & Co. Bronze Powder, colour Gold 2.5. Several layers of this pigment are required to give a gold appearance. (Sometimes I use gold leaf, but this is another delightful skill to be learned.) When the painting was very dry I applied a glaze of egg mixture without pigment to restore lustre and glow where the dark, intense colours had lost some depth of hue.

Step 5 Detail

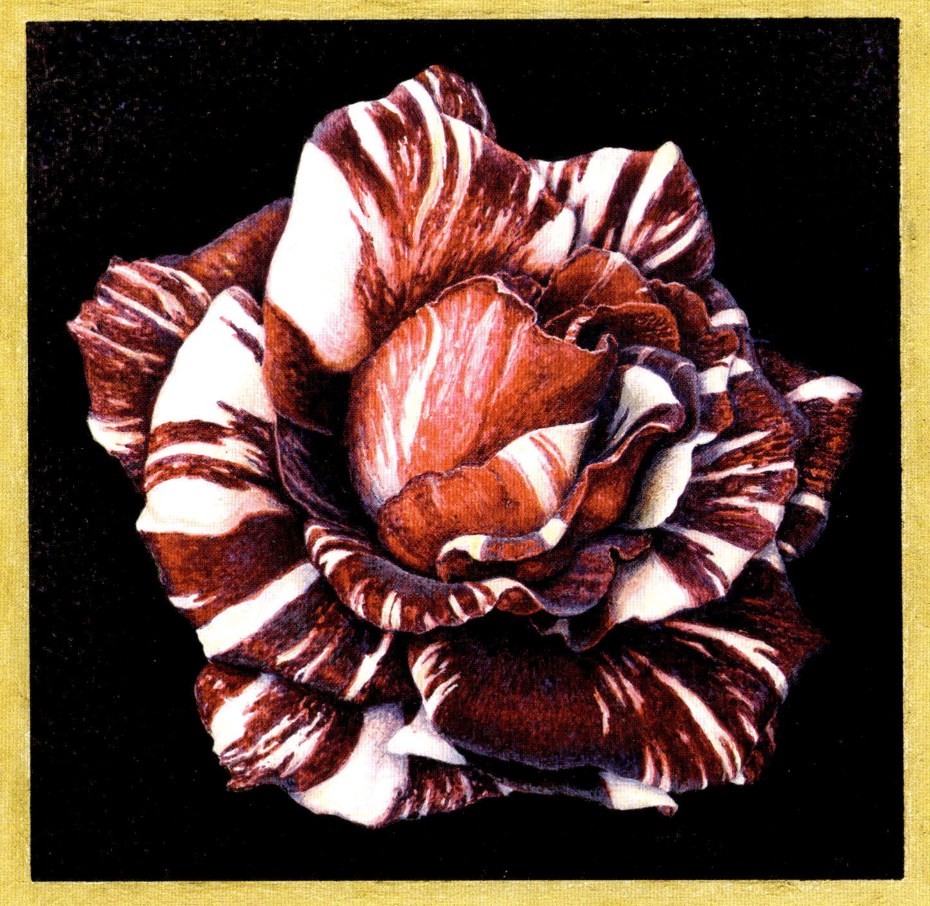

Frosted Leaves

MARION PERKINS | Egg tempera on board

Finding inspiration is not hard for the botanical artist. A stroll around a garden or park at any time of year will provide material to impassion us and drive us to creativity. One November morning a heavy frost transformed the garden into a magical scene and a jumbled collection of frosted fallen autumn leaves around some heuchera plants caught my attention.

I took a photo to record the frost and by chance a winter moth rested on a leaf, so he was photographed too for inclusion in the intended painting. I then collected a selection of the most interesting leaves of varied colours and picked some heuchera leaves to use for the focal point.

I decided watercolour on paper would be impracticable in this instance as leaving white paper to indicate all the frosty areas would not work, but applying white paint on top of painted leaves using egg tempera would create the required effect. I selected the leaves two or three at a time and painted them in detail on gesso board with layer upon layer of egg tempera in autumnal colors. Then I applied translucent white tempera in tiny brushstrokes to build up the appearance of frost, rather like nature had done, thinner here, thicker there. Finally, when the gesso board was covered with frosty leaves, I adjusted the depth of colour between the leaves, added a few strands of spider web and painted the delicate winter moth in the corner, flying into the picture.

1. A work in progress; note the tiny miniaturist's brush and consider the time and patience required to produce a work of any size.

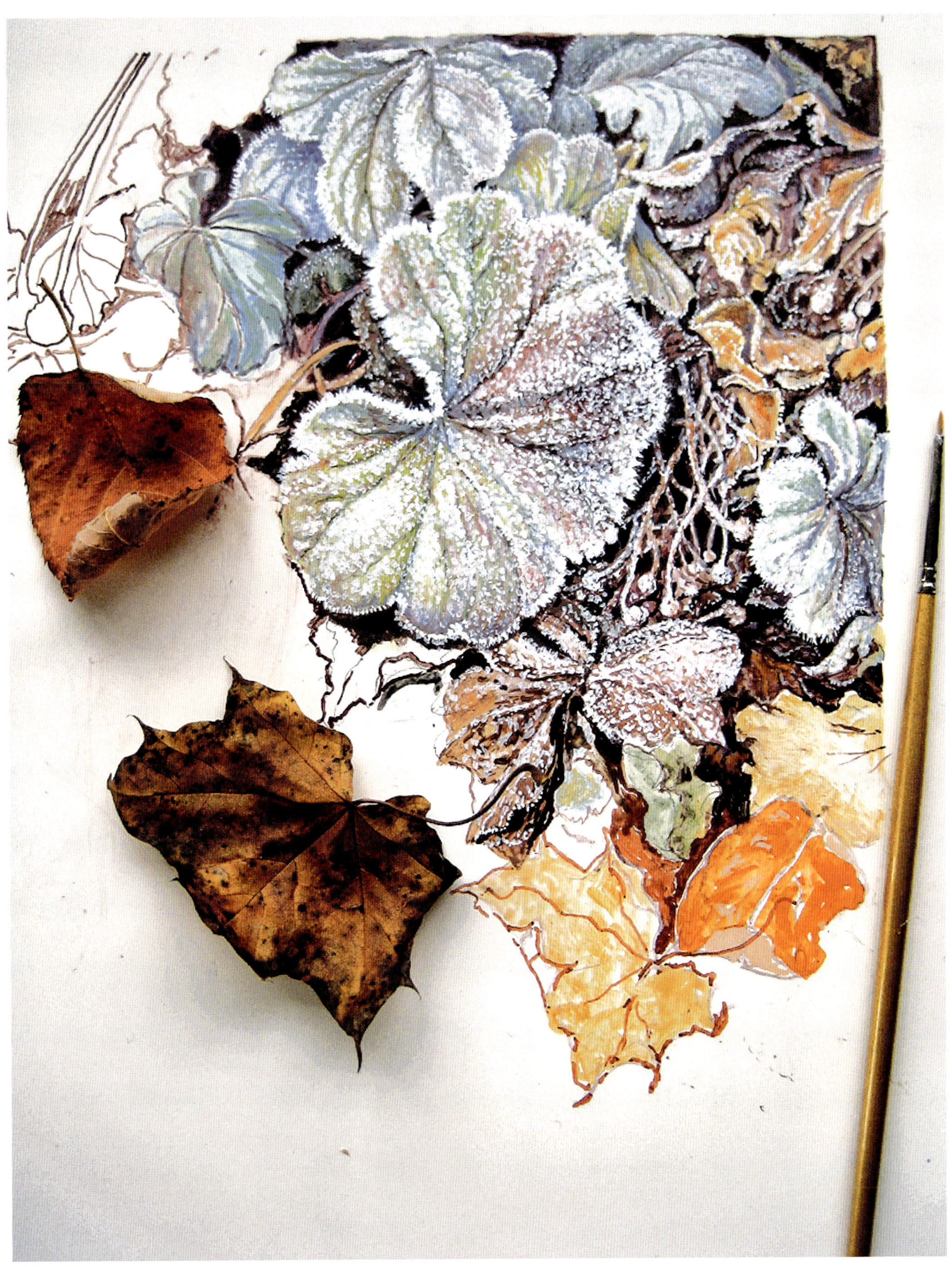

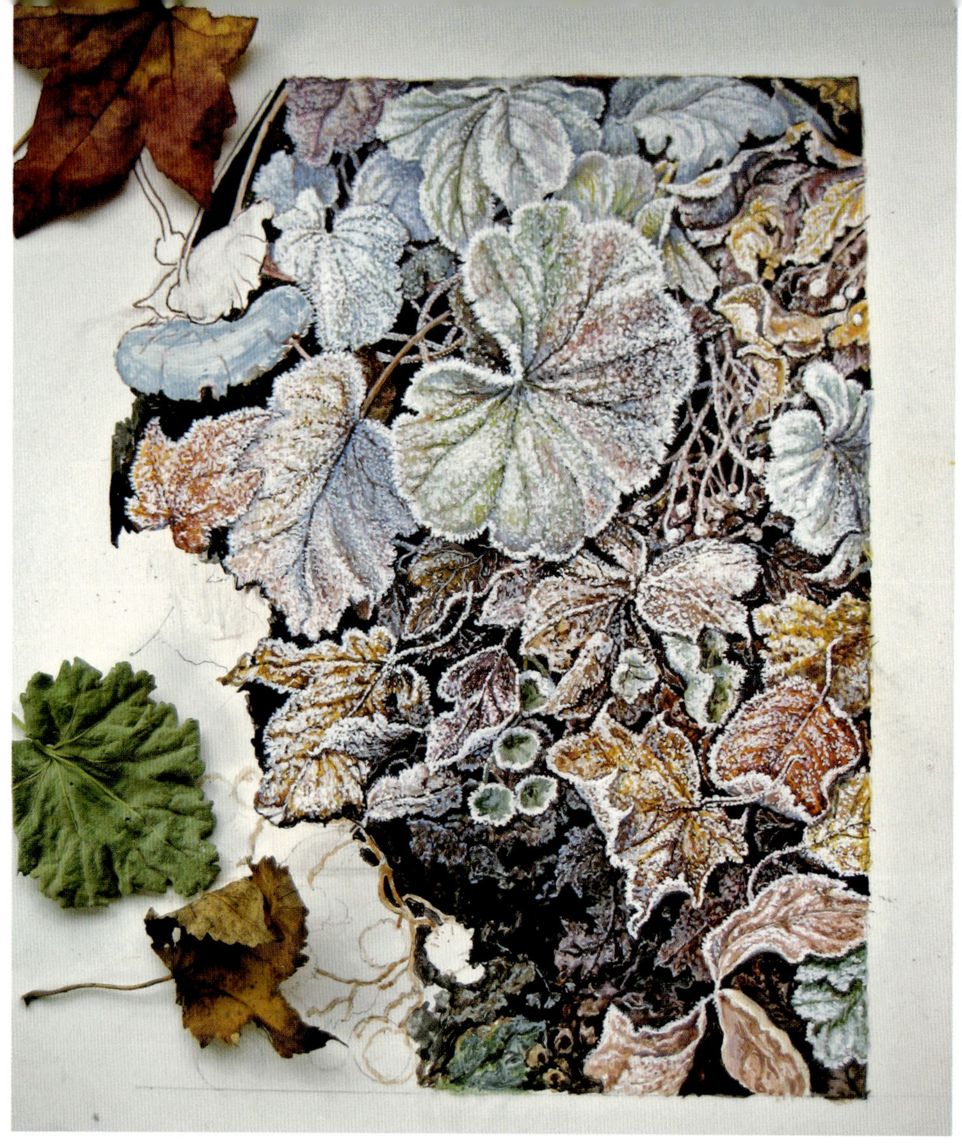

2. An enlargement focusing on a heuchera leaf which clearly demonstrates the build-up of frost.

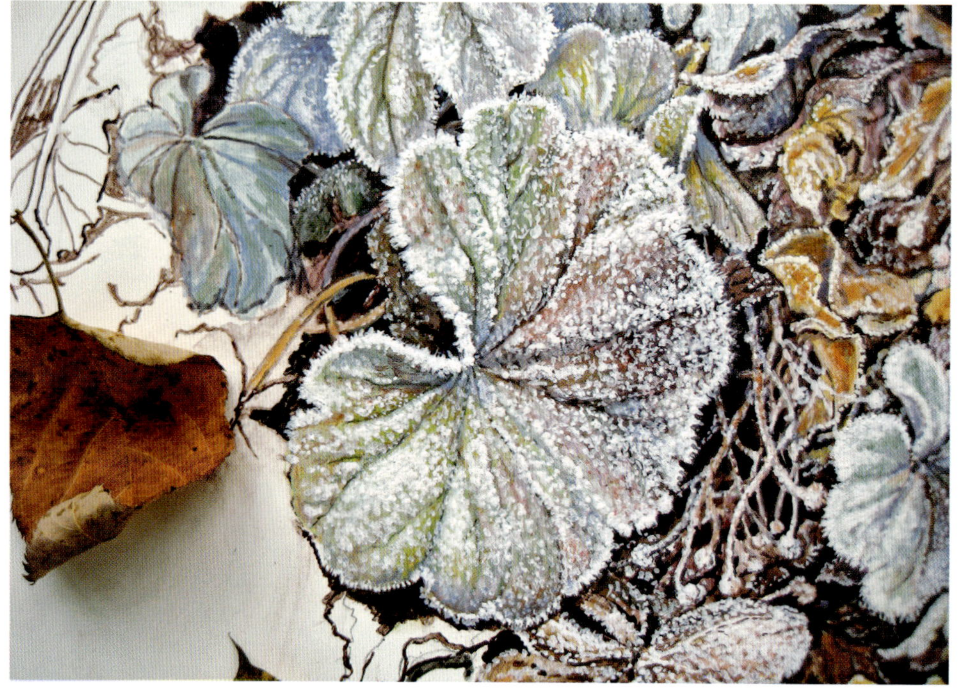

3. More leaves are added and the composition is built up.

4. The finished painting (opposite) – see how well the moth blends with its surroundings.

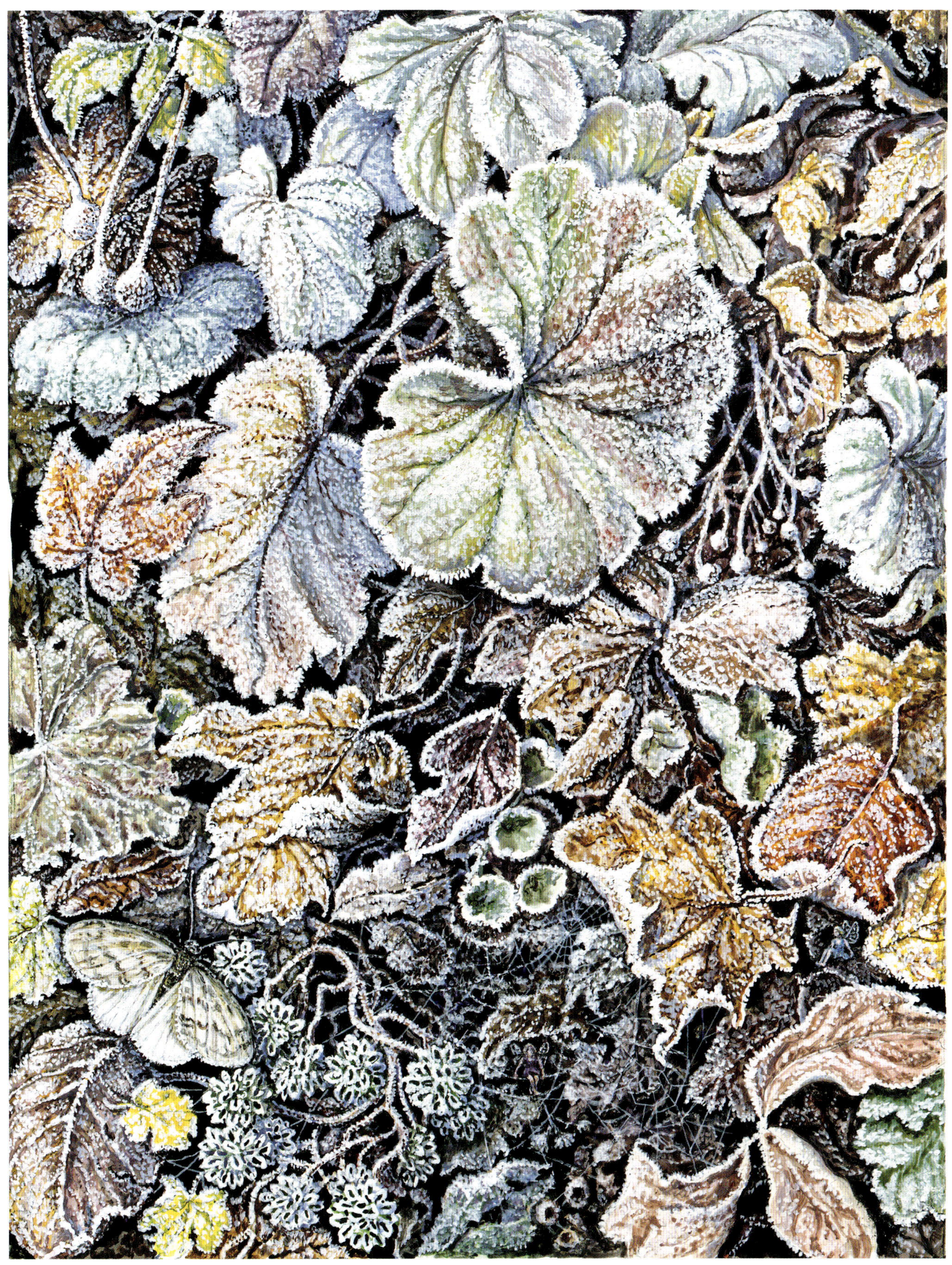

Rosa 'Golden Wings'

MARION PERKINS | Gesso board

Choosing which medium to use when starting a painting is often determined by the subject itself. With *Rosa* 'Golden Wings' I was drawn to the stunning centres of these open roses, reddish-brown changing to a rusty brown as they age. Painting this part of a flower is difficult to achieve in watercolour, especially the yellow anthers on a yellow rose. Unlike watercolour, egg tempera raises the surface of a painting with each application of paint, so a three-dimensional effect is easier to accomplish.

The yellows I used here are Naples Yellow Light, Tartrazine Yellow (the substitute for Indian Yellow when it became apparent that the sole diet of mango leaves resulted in cruelty to Indian cows, whose urine had previously been collected and dried to make the rich yellow pigment) for the anthers and Red Ochre for the stamens, all available from ww.cornelissen.com.

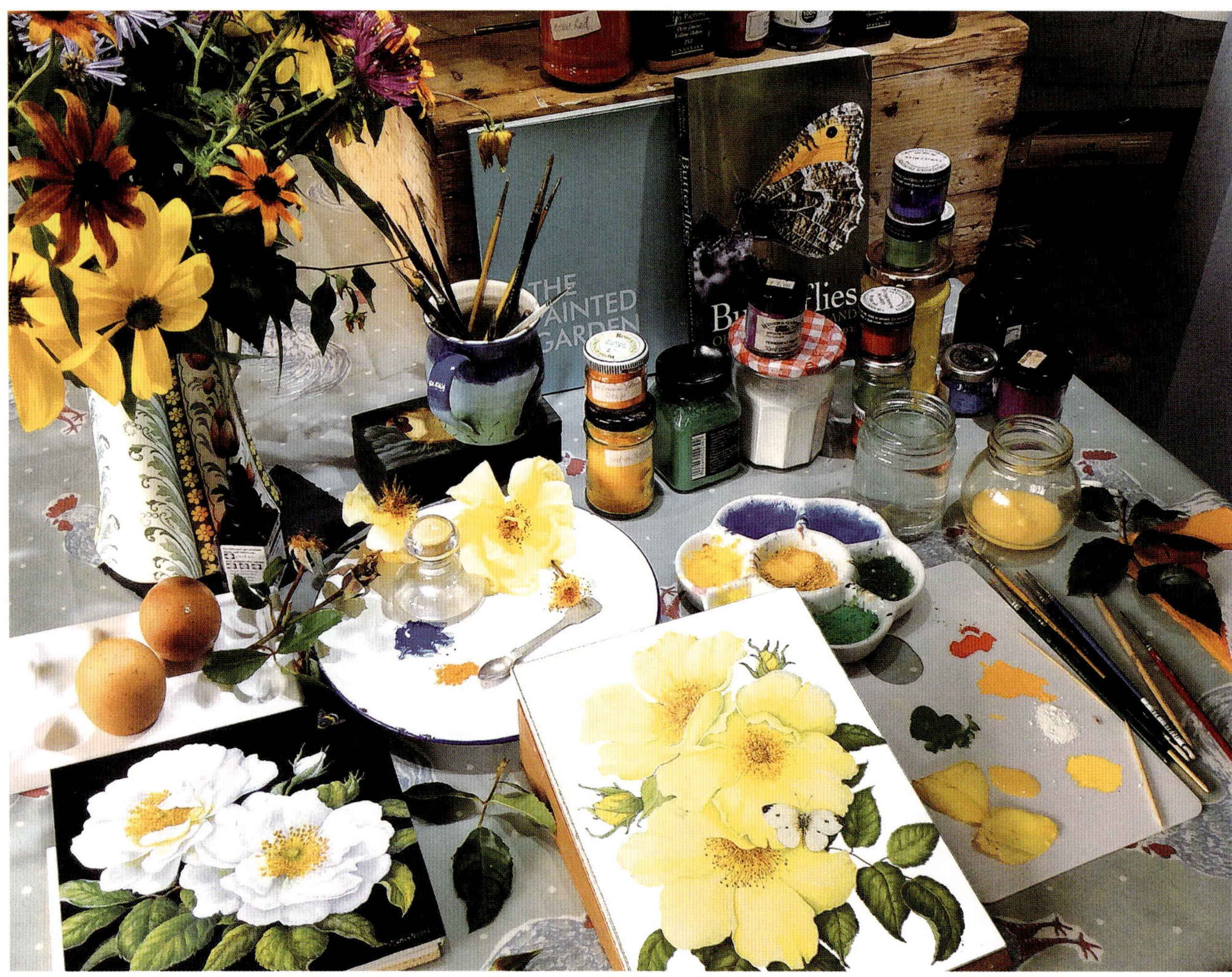

A close-up shot of Marion's desk as she works on *Rosa* 'Golden Wings'. It is important to have everything close at hand and what might seem cluttered to the casual observer is in fact a well-organized layout.

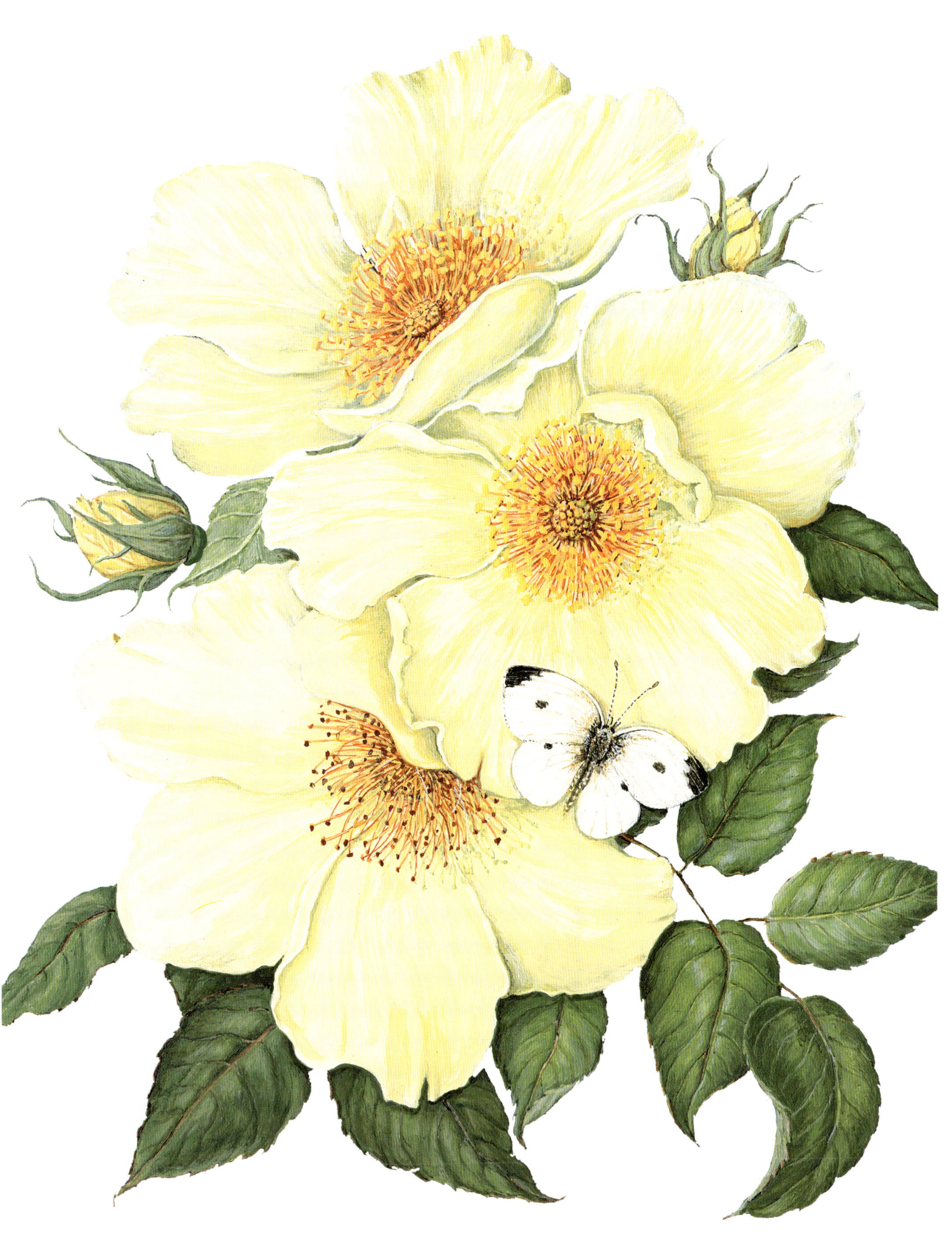

CHAPTER 5

On the Dark Side

In the previous chapter we saw how Marion Perkins achieves the rich backgrounds to her paintings in egg tempera. To the watercolourist this can often seem challenging, so in this chapter you will find suggestions for creating a classic way in which to showcase a beautiful specimen. Of course you can choose to work with designer gouache or a combination of watercolour and white body colour on a coloured board; archive-quality Daler board gives a wide choice of colours which can be chosen to complement the subject matter. The late Sally Keir worked on this support, drawing and painting the whole subject in white paint, then building up the picture with layers of watercolour. The result was always a brilliant, often apparently back-lit painting, full of glowing colour.

Nowadays some artists choose to use a white acrylic base, but I have achieved good results using Winsor & Newton Chinese White. As with egg tempera, you will need to take care not to pick up the underlying white paint as this will create an opaque watercolour and the effect will be lost.

RIGHT *Wisteria floribunda* 'Pink Rain' | Kate Green | Watercolour on paper
This charming painting measures a manageable 33 x 23cm (13 x 9in), which is quite important for the artist working up a dark background for the first time. Kate plotted her composition and drew it using a light mix of botanical grey – French Ultramarine and Light Red. At the same time as she built up the colour of the image she gradually worked up the background using an increasingly strong mix of French Ultramarine and Burnt Sienna. Such a mix of colours enables light to bounce off the background rather than be absorbed, as it would be if one used solid black paint. Kate lifts off paint to achieve a middle ground and holds on to highlights at all costs, very rarely resorting to the use of body colour.

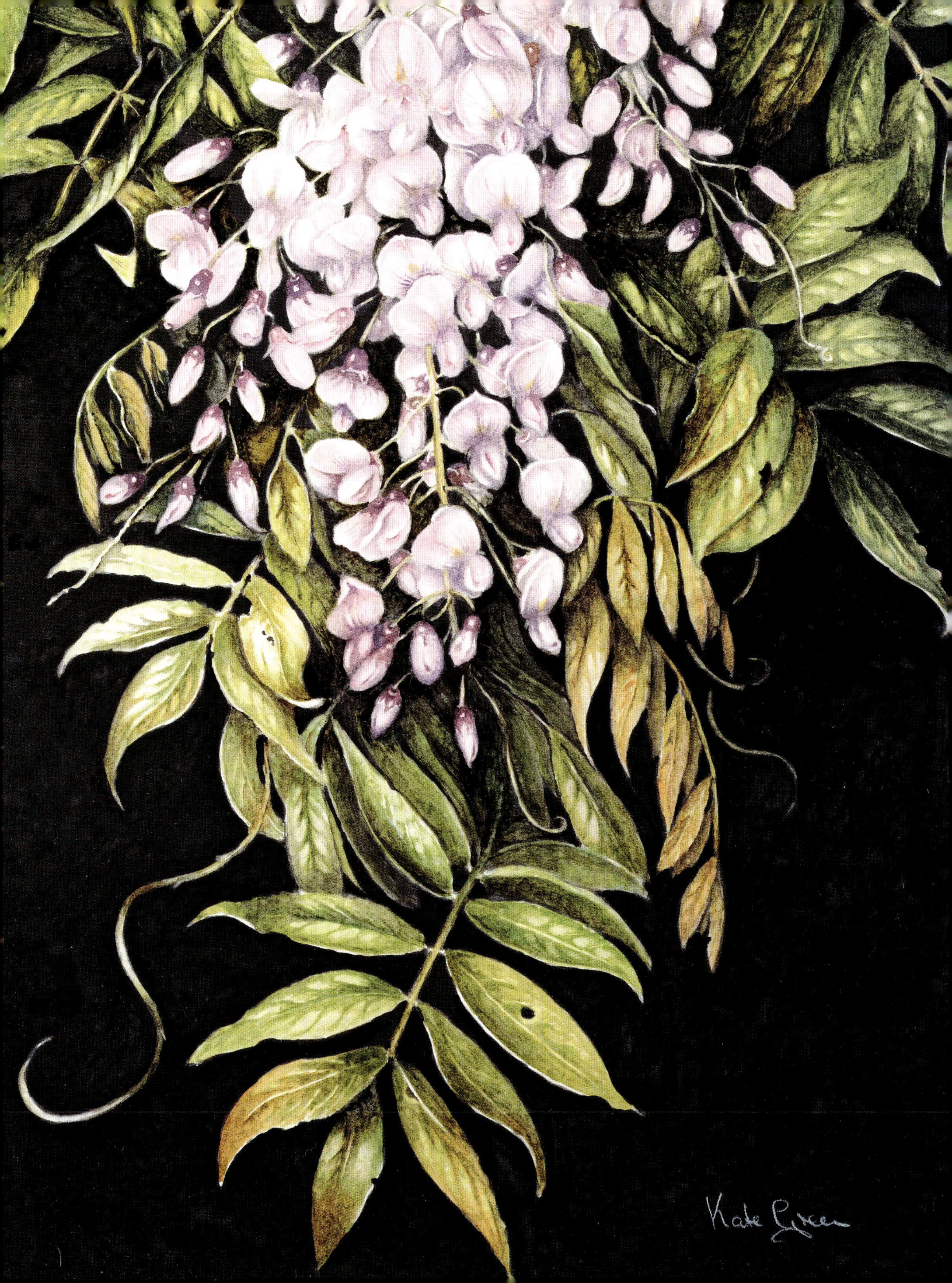

Kate Green

Body colour and designers' gouache
by Margaret Fitzpatrick

Body colour simply means watercolour with an additive to make it opaque. Painting with body colour was in use in Ancient Egypt and the artists of early illuminated manuscripts such as the Lindisfarne Gospels and the Book of Kells added white pigment, usually white lead, to their colours to give them opacity. These manuscripts were produced on natural animal skins, which were pigmented, so the addition of body colour was needed to increase the covering properties of the paint.

In his portrayal of the plants in *Great Piece of Turf* (1503) Albrecht Dürer used watercolour with body colour to great effect, as did many botanical artists including Georg Ehret and the brothers Franz and Ferdinand Bauer in the 18th and 19th centuries. A number of botanical artists today continue to use the traditional method of adding body in the form of white pigment to transparent watercolour for the portrayal of detailed aspects such as veining, fine hairs on leaves and stems and the spines on cacti.

In the 1930s, paint manufacturers produced commercial designers' gouache paint, which is an opaque form of watercolour. Increasing numbers of botanical artists today are using designers' gouache to great effect, for example, Simon Williams, Director of the DLDC. Designers' gouache contains high levels of concentrated pigments specifically created to give a smooth matte finish with great covering quality, which means it can be used over coloured grounds to good effect.

Various grounds are available, but note that surfaces such as mount board, while providing a good range of colour choices, are not designed expressly for artwork.

These surfaces can be absorbent and therefore need sealing before use. This can be done by coating them with a layer of white acrylic ink, acrylic primer or a layer of white gouache paint and leaving it to dry before you start the painting proper. Unlike transparent watercolours, which soak into and stain the surface of the paper or watercolour board, designers' gouache creates a layer of paint that lies on the surface of the support, be it white paper or a prepared coloured support.

The smooth, opaque quality of designers' gouache enables the paint to be blended in a similar way to oil paint and acrylics. Mix it with water to the consistency of thin cream; this both enables the paint to be blended smoothly and also avoids it becoming too thick and prone to cracking. With transparent watercolour one has to work from light to dark, whereas designers' gouache is more versatile and can easily be used from dark to light. When layering the paint, allow each layer to dry before applying the next or the earlier layers will lift – though blending previous layers can be used with care for certain effects. To create tone, use areas of cross-hatching and stippling with a dry brush.

Designers' gouache colours should be put on the palette fresh each day; if they are left overnight they give a chalky finish to the work, particularly in the case of white pigment. The paints are extremely vibrant and lend themselves to illustration work for reproduction, but for fine art work you need to bear in mind that some of the pigments are not lightfast – check the lightfast ratings if you want your work to survive long term.

Cereus (Queen of the Night)

VALERIE BAINES | Watercolour and body colour on paper

Most botanical painters are conversant with the life and times of Margaret Mee, who fulfilled a long-held ambition to paint the night-flowering Cereus in its Amazonian setting shortly before her untimely death. Valerie did not have to go to such lengths as she has one in her conservatory which flowered at midnight and obligingly lasted throughout the following day, giving her time to work on this stunning painting.

She first drew the plant on tracing paper, then back-traced it and rubbed it down with the edge of a coin onto her watercolour paper. She used the tracing reversed to copy the shape of the flowers on to the backing paper of some low-tack film (rather than masking tape), then cut out the shapes and attached them to the picture before painting in the dark background around the leaves, flowers and bud. She left the moon as white paper, then shaded it to make it appear distant. The stars were added later using white gouache.

The all-important background colour is Winsor & Newton Payne's Grey, which Valerie finds just right for the dark yet soft tones appropriate for a night sky. She left the petals chiefly as white paper shaded with a mix of French Ultramarine and Winsor Violet. The final touch was to add white gouache to the flower centres.

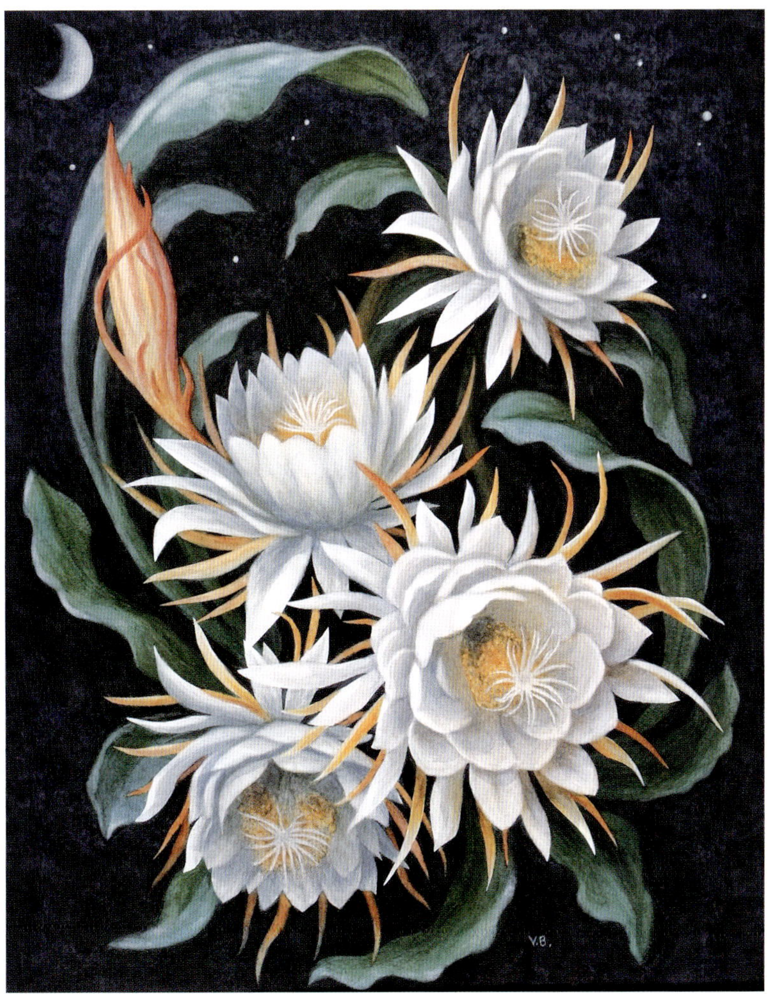

Step-by-Step

SUNLIT ROSE BY MARGARET FITZPATRICK

In this painting, I used black mount board as the ground to support the work. Background colour is obviously a matter of taste, but you only have to look at the work of the 17th-century Dutch flower painters to see how those intensely dark backgrounds they so often employed were contrasted with light on the subject to such dramatic effect.

As gouache is an opaque medium it is possible to paint directly onto coloured mount board, but for two reasons I feel the mount board benefits from some preparation before painting. The mount board is a slightly absorbent surface not designed for painting and of course very dark in colour. Laying a white base coat on the area where my painting will be done seals the surface, enabling the paint to be applied smoothly. In addition, the white undercoat means that the top coats of paint do not have to be applied too thickly in order to maintain their freshness.

STEP 1

The first step was to place my subject in a strong light to create dramatic areas of shadow and highlight. I then made a detailed drawing of the subject. Once I was happy with the drawing, I took a tracing of the outline and transferred it using yellow Tracedown paper, which leaves a clear pale outline on the mount board.

STEP 2

Next I painted a white base coat over the entire image, using white acrylic ink. This both dries quickly and gives a smooth opaque finish. I then traced the details of the rest of the drawing onto this as one would when working on white paper in the usual way.

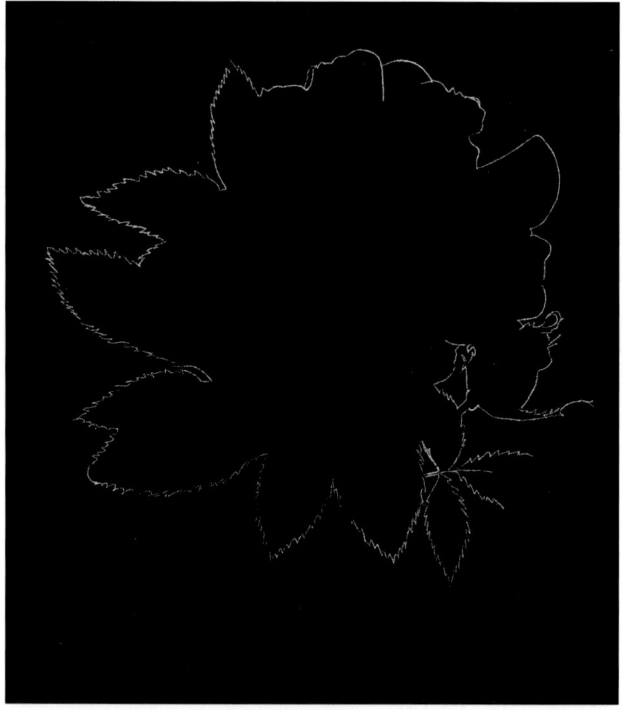

Step 1

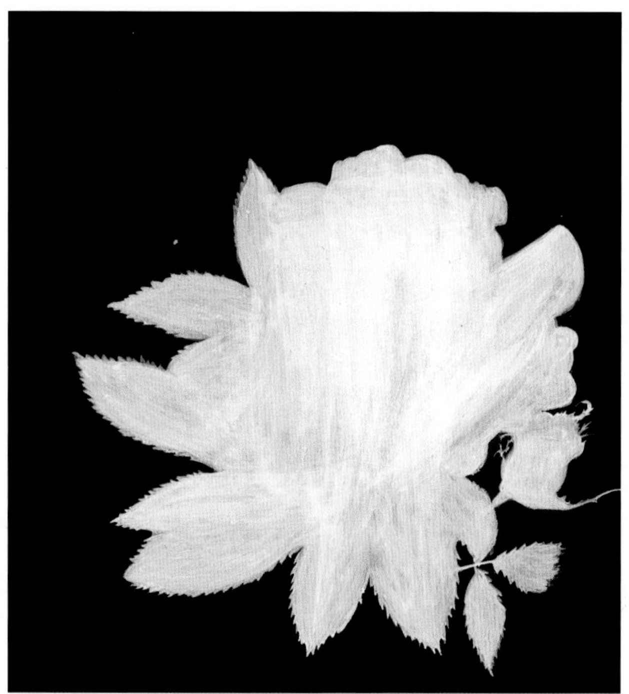

Step 2

STEP 3

As the flower would fade first I started with this, working from the outer petals inwards and completing each petal before moving onto the next. With gouache I like to put in the mid-tones first, building the darker tones and shadows from there. Then I add the lighter tones and finally the pure white highlights at the end. Once the flower was complete I painted the leaves, once again starting with the mid-tones and building the darks and finally the highlights.

At this stage with any painting I like to take time to look at the work and check I am happy with the balance of light and dark. I intensified some of the shadows where I felt they needed it to emphasize the strong sense of light. A touch more white was added to the highlights and finally I sharpened any edges where necessary.

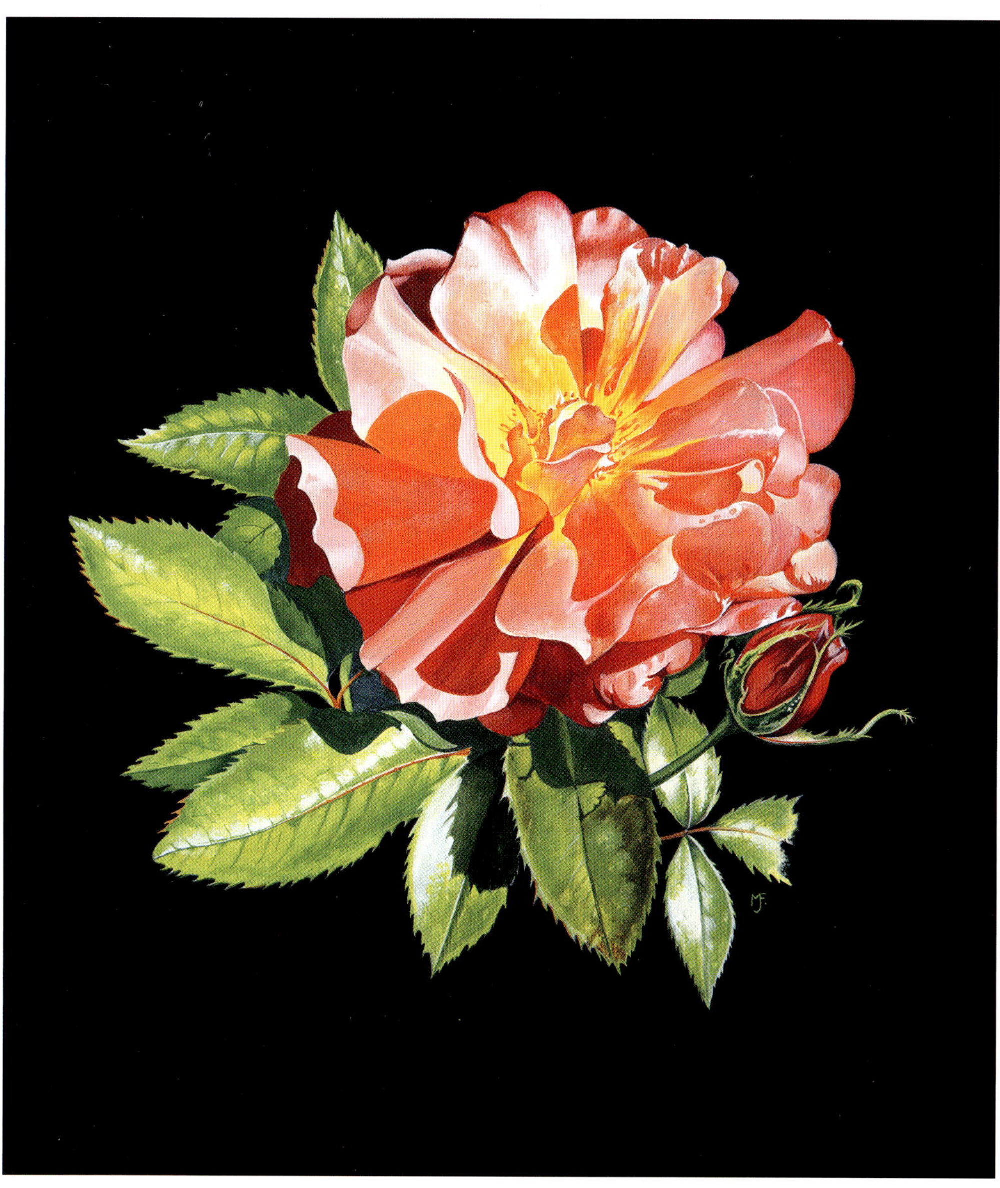

Step 3

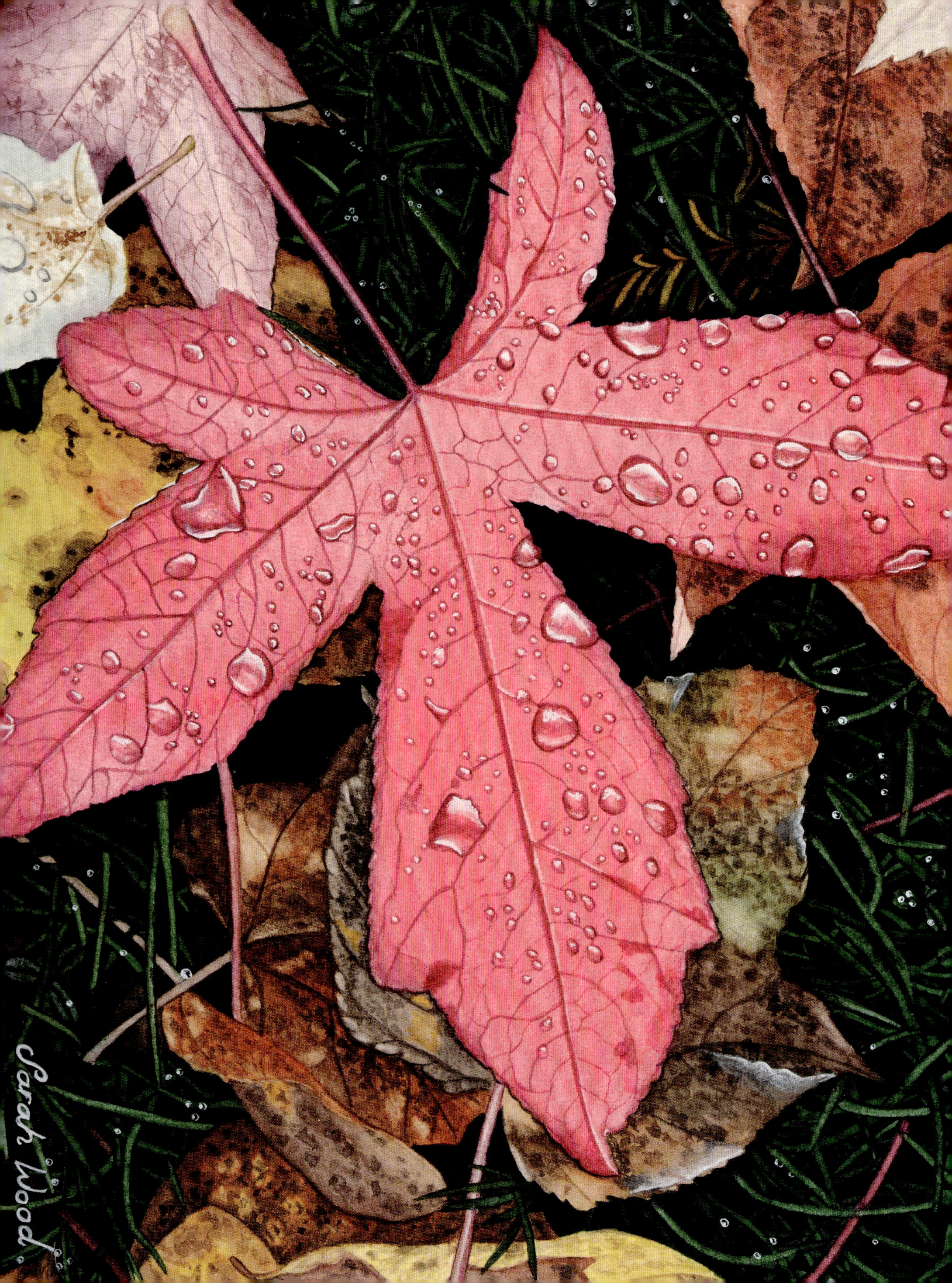
Sarah Wood

Liquidambar styraciflua 'Worplesdon'

SARAH WOOD | Watercolour with gouache on paper

Sarah came to love botanical painting after taking the SBA DLDC and became a full member of the SBA in 2014. She has already received a number of prestigious awards and written a number of articles for well-known art magazines. This 20 x 29cm (8 x 11½in) painting is based on sketches and photos taken at Ness Botanic Gardens on the Wirral.

Sarah drew the composition freehand on her paper of choice, Langton 425gsm (200lb) watercolour paper. She starts the painting process by blocking in areas of colour using light washes, which enables her to see the overall composition, particularly when it is complicated. Here, to make the liquidambar leaf the main feature, she kept the background and grasses dark, using mixed washes of Winsor & Newton Neutral Tint, Terry Harrison Midnight Green and Daler-Rowney Sap Green. The mixed leaves were painted with Cadmium Yellow, Vandyke Brown, Burnt Sienna and Crimson Alizarin, all Winsor & Newton pigments. For the vibrant liquidambar leaf she used Daler-Rowey Quinacridone Magenta and Cobalt Magenta, with Daler-Rowney Permanent Magenta for the darker veining, applied with a No.1 brush.

Sarah created the raindrops by lifting out some of the paint with a damp brush, or tissues for the lighter areas. Observing the direction of the light carefully, she added a mix of Permanent Magenta and Neutral Tint to the shadowed areas of each raindrop, using a No.0 brush. Highlights were picked out with Permanent White Gouache.

Once she feels a painting is finished, Sarah puts it away for a couple of weeks to help her to view it again with a fresh eye, at which time any corrections can be made. This is something all artists should do as there is no better way of truly assessing one's work.

Café Crème Irises

SARAH CASWELL | Acrylic on deep profile canvas

These irises grow against a south-facing wall where Sarah can see them from her studio, and she has painted them several times with various backgrounds, including silver leaf. This almost black background evokes a 17th-century still-life tradition, while silver conjures up images in her mind varying from iconography to a silver *fin de siècle* gown with panne velvet and bugle beads. Such is the imagination of the true artist when planning a composition.

Irises, according to the language of flowers, represent valour, faith and friendship, which one might associate with the virtues of the Three Musketeers and the symbolic fleur-de-lis of France. This design forms the basis of Sarah's composition. One bloom looks bravely into a sunlit future while the other is more gentle, looking out at the viewer, head on one side. They are a kind of family group and also show flowers at different stages of development.

Sarah works with a variety of acrylics, mainly Liquitex Heavy Body Acrylics. Here she used Dioxazine Purple for the background to complement the yellow tones of the flowers, although she often chooses Hooker's Green as in general it suits most colours. She started with the white primed canvas and built up thin layers of this transparent paint, making use of the fact that light will travel through the layers, hit the opaque white and travel back to the eye, giving glow and depth. The finished result may read as black but is actually much richer.

For some commissions Sarah will match the background to the site where it will hang so that the flowers appear to float away from the wall. For this she uses a commercial wall paint with a very low sheen and a chalky finish. For her own collection she favours Farrow & Ball Estate Emulsion. Sarah's commissions include 36 large-scale pieces for the Oriental restaurant on the P&O Cruises superliner *Azura*, launched 2010, and subsequently the only figurative painting on *Britannia*, launched 2014. Measuring 7m (23ft) long, it was hung behind the reception desk and depicts white parrot tulips.

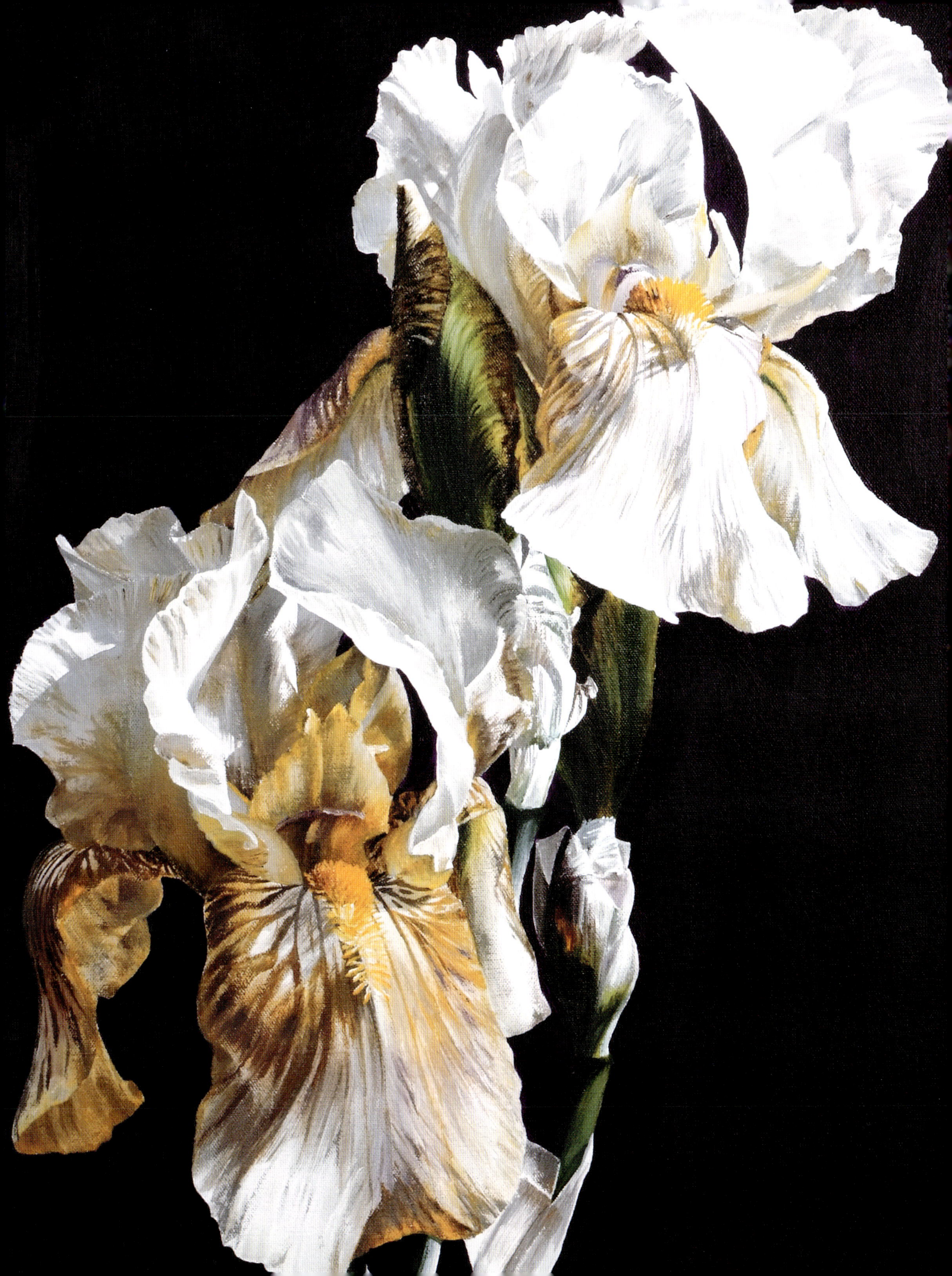

Bramble Leaf

DENISE HEYWOOD | Watercolour and gouache on paper

This 23 x 18cm (9 x 7in) image is a fine example of the glowing intensity of colour that can be achieved when enhanced by a dark background. Denise used a lightbox to transfer her tracing onto Fabriano Artistico Hot Pressed watercolour paper. Her watercolour pigments included Daniel Smith Quinacridone Gold, Hansa Yellow Medium and Green Gold and Winsor & Newton Yellow Ochre, Indanthrene Blue, Perylene Green, Permanent Rose, Perylene Maroon and Perylene Violet. She also used Winsor & Newton designers' gouache in Ivory Black and Permanent White.

Denise worked up the leaf in the usual manner by applying washes of watercolour, wet-on-wet, as required. Her first wash on the background was of Perylene Green, after which she rubbed out all pencil lines. She finished the leaf using a dry brush and a stippling technique for the fine detail.

To paint the background, she dampened the surface and dropped in Indanthrene Blue and Perylene Green to achieve a dark but vibrant colour. She then feathered out a little black gouache from the outside edges of the leaf into the background to define the leaf. A little white gouache was used to pick out the edge of the leaf and it was allowed to dry thoroughly. Denise then painted this over with Hansa Yellow Medium and Green Gold as required. She also painted parts of the leaf that she wanted to emphasize in the same manner, thus adding texture and form.

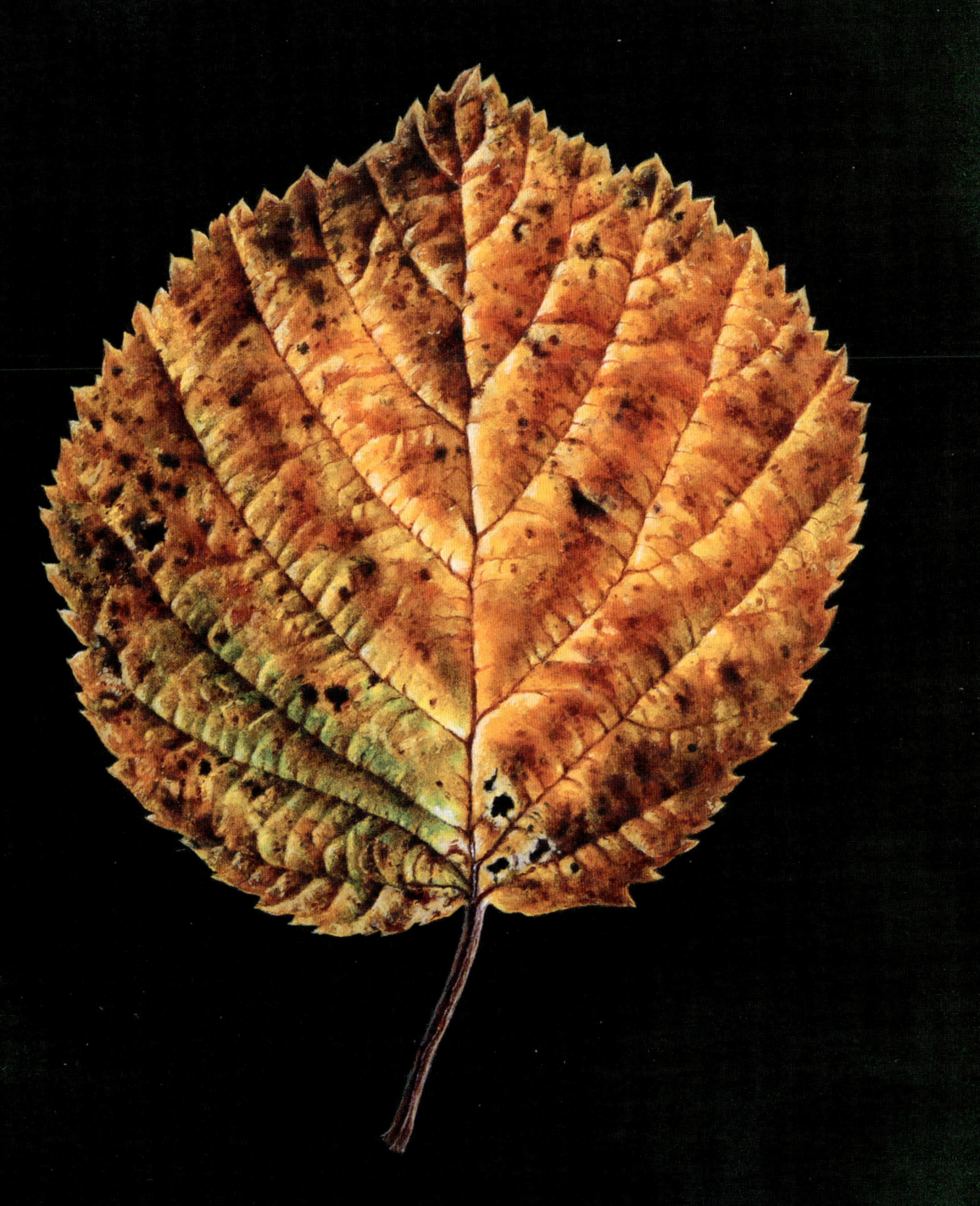

CHAPTER 6

Plant Portrait or Botanical Illustration

In this section I have grouped the often disputed styles of plant portrait and botanical illustration together, as both endeavour to show the subject at its very best, but the latter leans towards a scientific approach and contains more botanical information. Over the years I have come to realize that both have equal value and good work will always find an appreciative admirer. Clearly, if an artist is painting to commission for a strictly botanical magazine or text book they will need to measure and record every stamen and sepal using dividers, dissect as required and refrain from taking any short cuts. On the other hand, they may just want to capture the spirit of the plant, something which can frequently be lost in the quest for botanical accuracy.

These days there is so much emphasis on tracing rather than freehand drawing that students tend to forget it is through that first contact between pencil and paper that the essence of the specimen is captured. I was encouraged to draw from the age of four by a father whose art school training was undertaken before the First World War so please accept that my views will be considered old fashioned – until there is a rethink, of course, since most things come round in circles.

So here you will see prime examples of both types of portrayal, starting with an unusual subject painted and described by Barbara Munro, who gained a Distinction on Course 5 and is now established as a regular exhibitor and artist of considerable merit. Barbara gives a good account of the method employed when the eye is caught by something growing in the wild and then of course one is bound to rely on sketches and photographs.

RIGHT *Clematis* 'Lincoln Star' | Joanna Craig McFeely | Watercolour on paper
Joanna takes pleasure from watching the flower emerging from the bud, noting the subtle colour change as it reaches maturity. She takes the trouble to get to know the plant, studying its growing habit and sketching various parts, particularly the more complicated ones and those that might fade first.

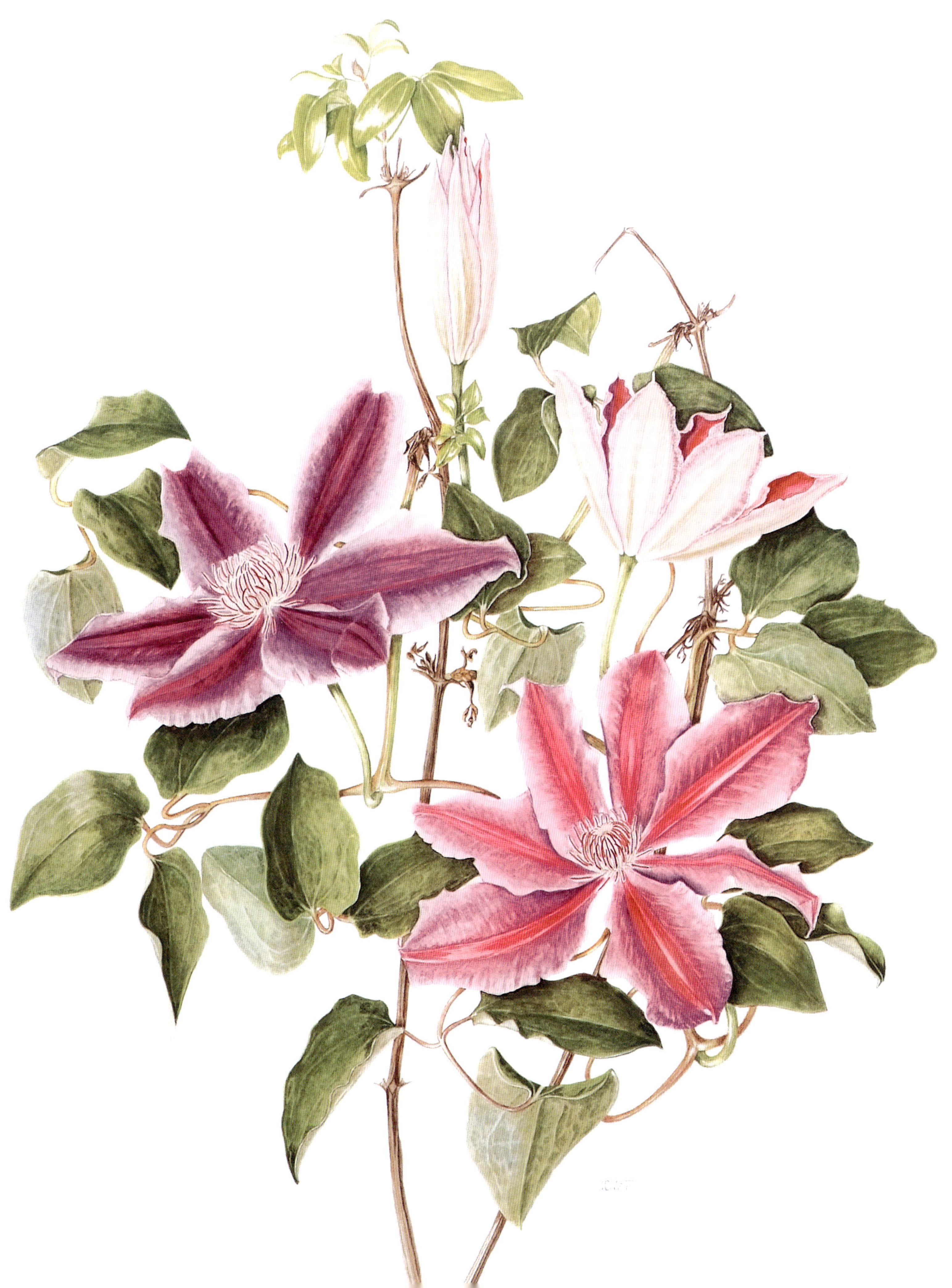

Step-by-Step

HIBISCUS SYRIACUS 'BLUEBIRD' (ROSE OF SHARON) BY BARBARA MUNRO

Barbara was attracted to this small shrub by the prolific violet-blue flowers which appear in late summer; here she describes her working method.

STEP 1

In my painting I wanted to portray all stages from bud to the mature flower. The plant has a long flowering period, so I could take my time with composition and my initial drawings. I drew each element, buds and open flowers, on separate pieces of tracing paper and then combined these in different arrangements until I was satisfied with the composition. I looked for triangular relationships between the elements and a focal point in an appropriate position. The composition was then transferred to paper as a simple, very light, line drawing.

Next I tried out different colours and mixes to cover the range I could see on the plant. This gave me a set of swatches from which I could work throughout the painting. I also took photographs of all the different parts of the plant in case I had to resort to these at a later stage.

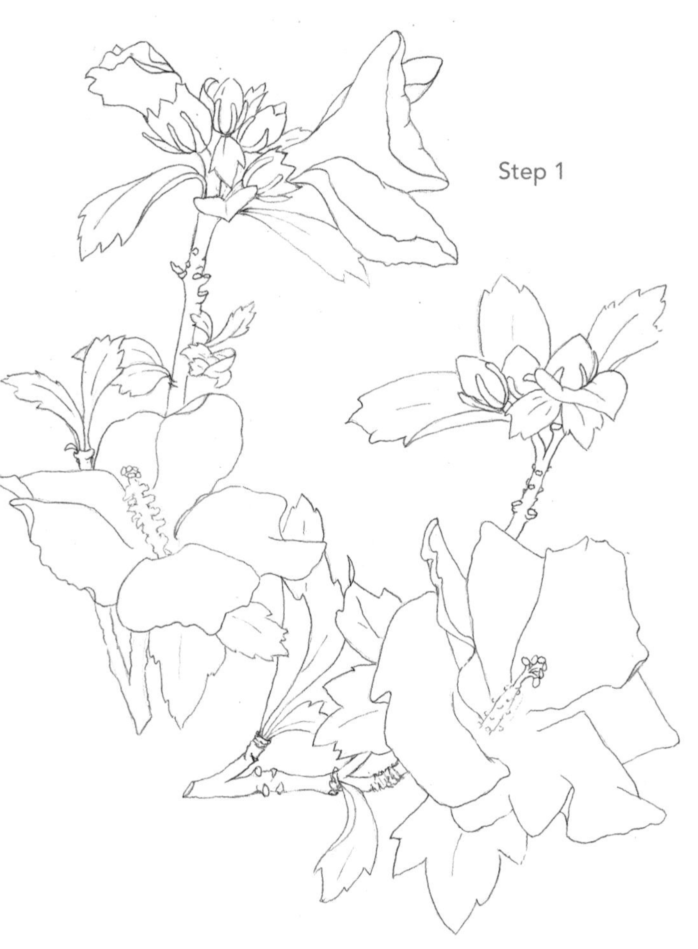

Materials required:

WATERCOLOUR PAINTS:
* Winsor & Newton: Cadmium Lemon, Winsor Violet, French Ultramarine. Daler-Rowney: Naples Yellow, Aureolin. Schmincke: Raw Umber, Brilliant Purple, Cobalt Blue.

GOUACHE:
* Winsor & Newton Zinc White.

BRUSHES:
* Raphael Kolinsky sable sizes 4 and 2 Series 8408.

SURFACE:
* Fabriano Classico 5 Hot Pressed 300gsm (140lb) watercolour paper.

STEP 2

I normally use the same blue in the mix for the leaves as for the flowers, but in this case the result was too bright and a weak mix of Aureolin and French Ultramarine gave a better colour for the leaves. Underpainting in this, leaving areas where the light caught them, allowed me to remove pencil marks without losing the leaf shapes. I used a slightly darker mix to emphasize the shadow areas. A touch of Brilliant Purple added to the mix gave a grey-green shade which was useful for the overlap of petals on the leaves.

In a similar way, I used a dilute mix of Cobalt Blue and Winsor Violet to show where petals overlapped, together with any folds and creases, which helped to develop a three-dimensional appearance. Where hard edges were not wanted I softened shadow colour with a clean damp brush. For the complex structure of styles, stigmas and stamens, I initially marked an outline by using a light wash of Brilliant Purple; the area would need very precise painting at a later stage. This wash was extended onto the petals to show veining. I indicated the anthers with a small amount of Naples Yellow. For the branches I used a dilute wash of Raw Umber which, when dry, allowed all pencil marks to be removed.

As all the buds were beginning to open it was essential to capture them immediately. I used a mix of Cobalt Blue and Winsor Violet in differing proportions to show the veins and undulating nature of the opening petals.

Step 2

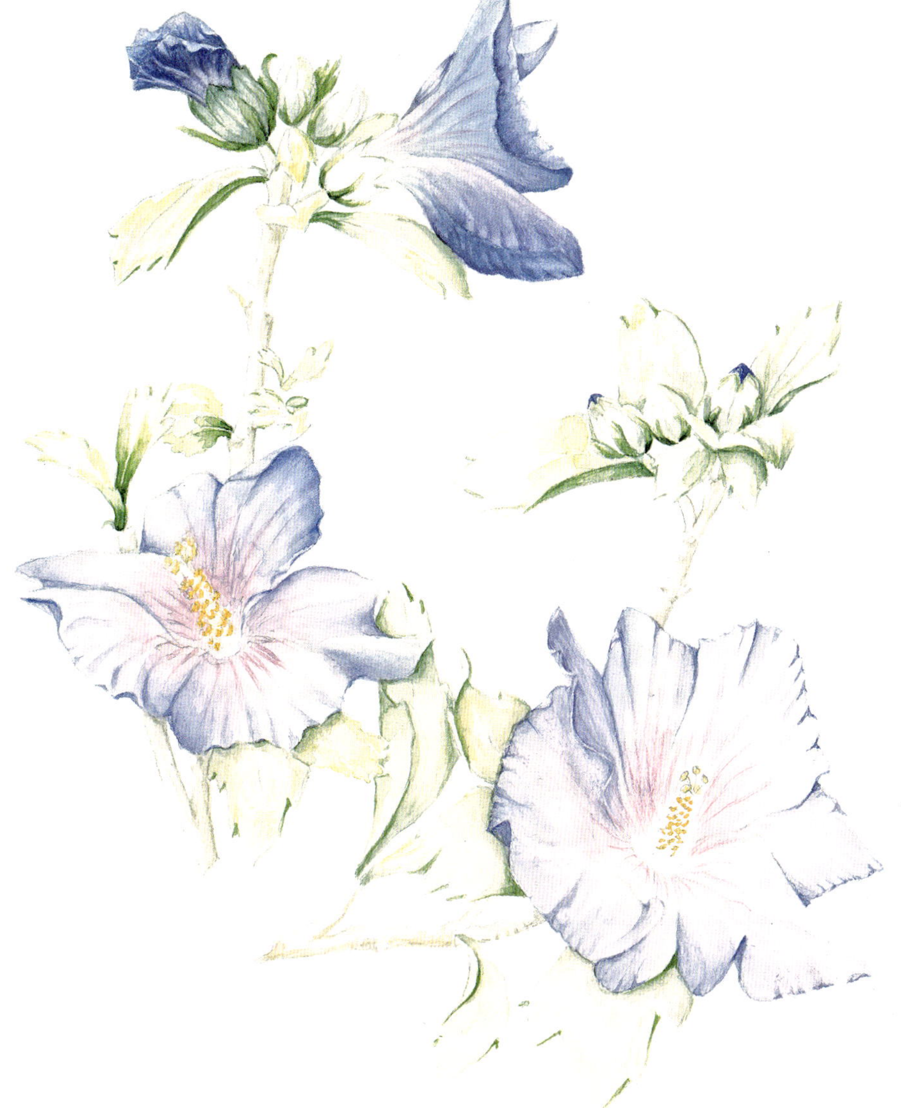

As autumn progressed the flowers began to fall and the leaves were fast changing colour. Usually I would finish painting the flowers first but this time I needed to concentrate on the leaves while I still had fresh material. First I outlined the three main veins, which were washed over with dilute Cadmium Lemon once the rest of the leaves were completed, using a mix of Aureolin and French Ultramarine. I painted overlapping shadow areas with a grey-green mix made by adding a touch of Brilliant Purple as before. As these hibiscus leaves were not shiny, highlights were best achieved by lifting out rather than avoiding those areas altogether. I also checked for connections between buds and leaves as it is essential to ensure that each appears to grow from the correct part of the plant, even if the actual joining point is obscured.

As the flowers mature the colour becomes less blue and more violet. I used a mix of Cobalt Blue and Brilliant Purple in different proportions to indicate the amount of light received – a more violet colour for the lighter areas of the petals and a bluer mix for shadow areas, using French Ultramarine for a darker tone.

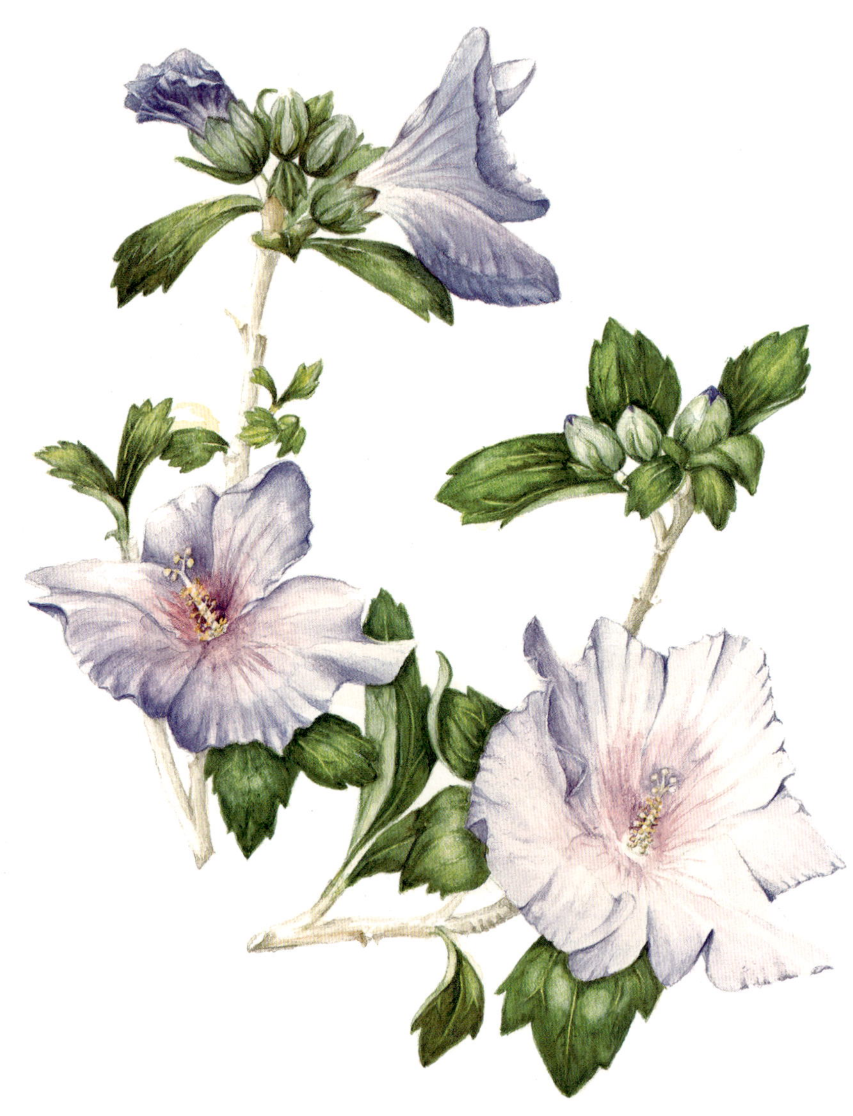

Step 3

STEP 4

The twigs of the hibiscus are ridged and light grey-brown, so a mix of Raw Umber and French Ultramarine gave an appropriate colour. The leaves arise from rather knobbly structures and these together with ridges on the twigs were indicated using lines of a stronger mix. I gradually strengthened the petal colour by repeated washes and softened the edge around the lighter areas with a clean, damp brush. I painted the centres of the flowers using a strong mix of Brilliant Purple with a touch of Winsor Violet, carefully avoiding the styles and stamens. The colour paled towards the centre. Although white paint is not normally used in botanical studies, a small amount is sometimes needed to correct unwanted colour, as the Brilliant Purple is very staining; for this I used Zinc White gouache. The stigmas also needed a highlight of this on the lighter side.

Finally, I checked the work with a hand lens to ensure that all the edges were clean and free from drips of paint or pencil marks. One last check a day or two later is always a good idea as the eye sometimes spots a detail which needs attention before the work can truly be said to be finished.

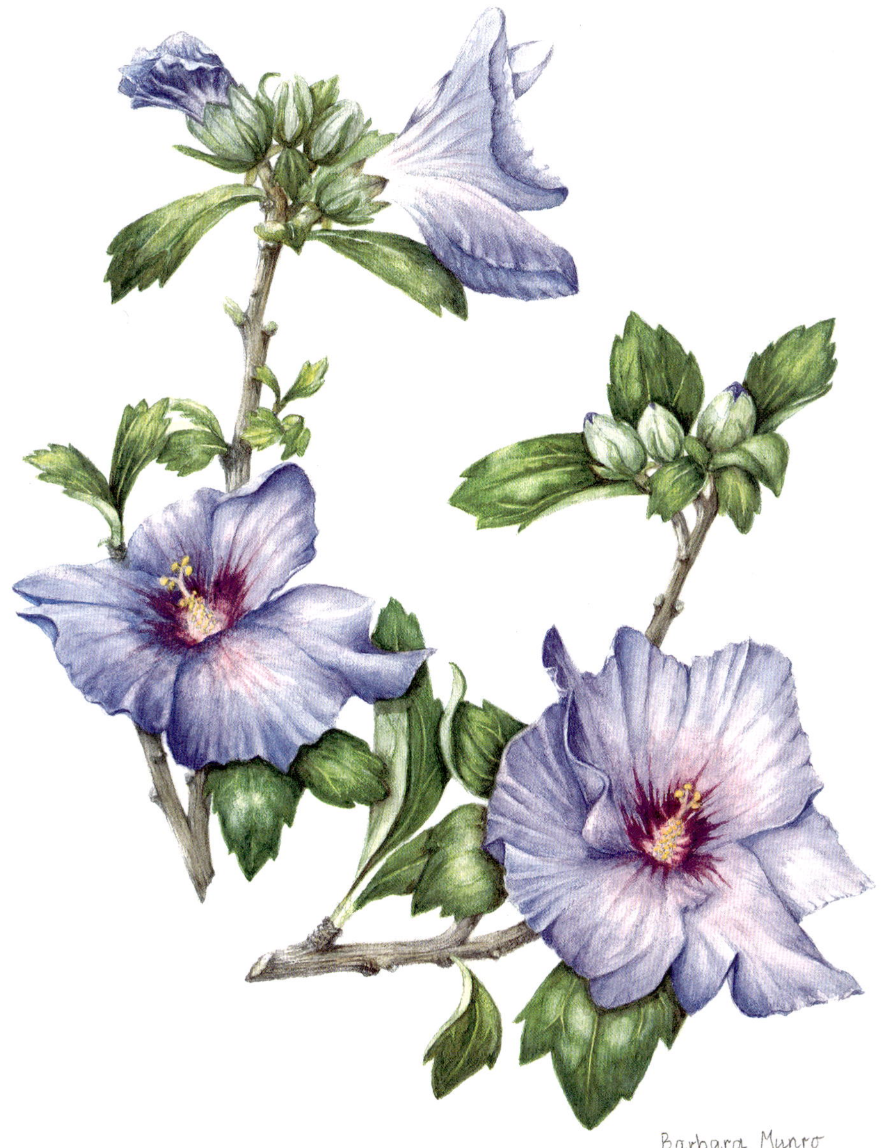

Step 4

Liparia splendens (Mountain Dahlia)

BARBARA MUNRO | Watercolour on paper

During my visit to the Cape region of South Africa I was greatly attracted to this shrub with showy flower heads the size of oranges. Thought to be a type of protea at one time, it actually belongs to the pea family and is pollinated by sunbirds. After making several sketches on site and closely examining the flower head, I realized that it was like a giant red clover in its floral structure. It is a plant that is almost impossible to grow in a garden, so I knew that I had to make a very good photographic record if I were to have any chance of painting it when I got home; there is no chance of finding it in a supermarket bouquet!

As this is such a complex flower I decided to draw my composition on tracing paper first so that erasing would not mar the surface of the Hot Pressed paper. As I wanted to show the nodding posture of the flowering branches, I chose to have them arching in from one side of the paper. I then transferred the composition to Hot Pressed watercolour paper.

For the dark green leaves a mix of Aureolin and Indanthrene Blue gave a good colour match, with a more yellow mix for the stems. Cadmium Yellow Deep and Brilliant Purple, used both individually and layered, gave a range of yellow, orange and pink, which can be seen in the gradation of colours in the individual flowers. After painting the mainly yellow flowers first, I used a more orange mix to help differentiate individual ones. The larger, outer flowers were first washed with Cadmium Yellow but not fully, so that when a wash of Brilliant Purple was applied, yellow, orange and pink towards the tips was the result. After intensifying the colour of the pink tips and checking their outlines, I used a mix of Winsor Violet and Brilliant Purple for shadows.

I underpainted the leaves with Aureolin, as both the leaf edges and the veins were this colour. The larger leaves, which were the darkest, needed a deeper mix of Aureolin and Indanthrene Blue. I applied shadows where leaves overlapped, using a blue mix of these colours plus a touch of Winsor Violet to produce a more grey-green. Finally, I checked all edges thoroughly and sharpened them where required.

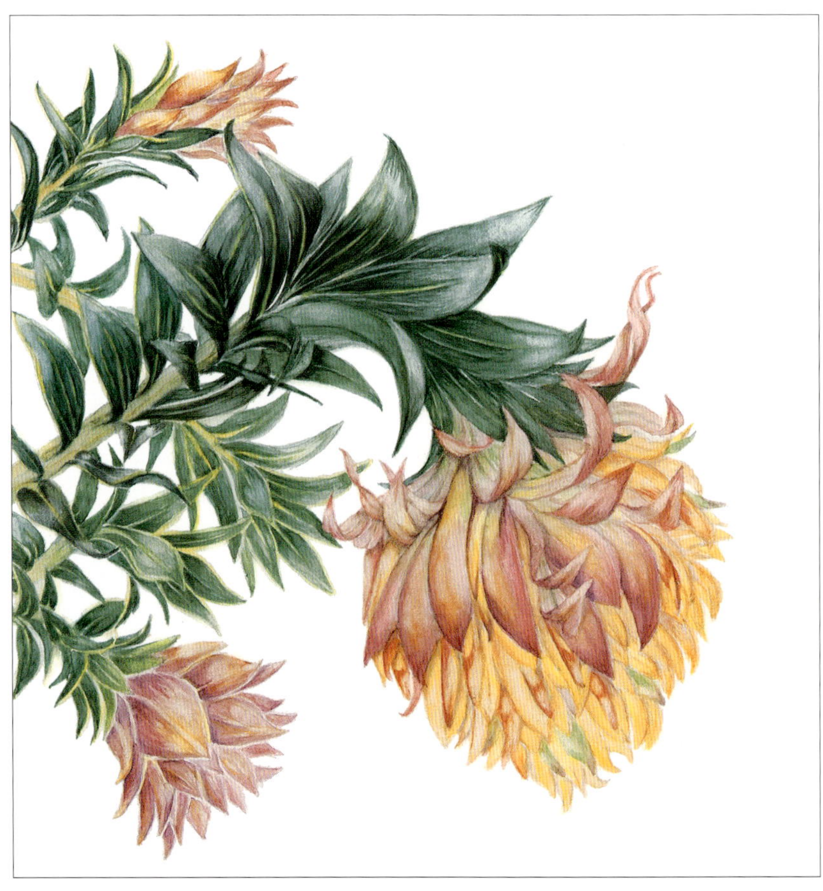

Two Unknown Peonies

MARGARET STEVENS | Watercolour on paper

Although I have never succeeded in growing peonies, they are among my favourite flowers. The buds hold a special fascination for me, particularly those which have the appearance of beautifully marbled end papers in a well-bound book. This little group rising above their parasol of leaves turned out to be the last large painting I could do before chronic arthritis stopped me in my tracks.

Peonies are gentle flowers – working in a silent room you will hear the full-blown flowers fall to the table with a sigh. It pays to work as quickly as you dare with the mature flowers. This painting went to a very good home – that of a fellow artist whose sight has sadly been affected by macular degeneration, though she was able to admire it. There is a moral here for all young and aspiring artists – enjoy every moment of your painting and never let yourself get caught up in all the petty politics which can be a blight on your work and your life. This is as important as knowing which colour to mix!

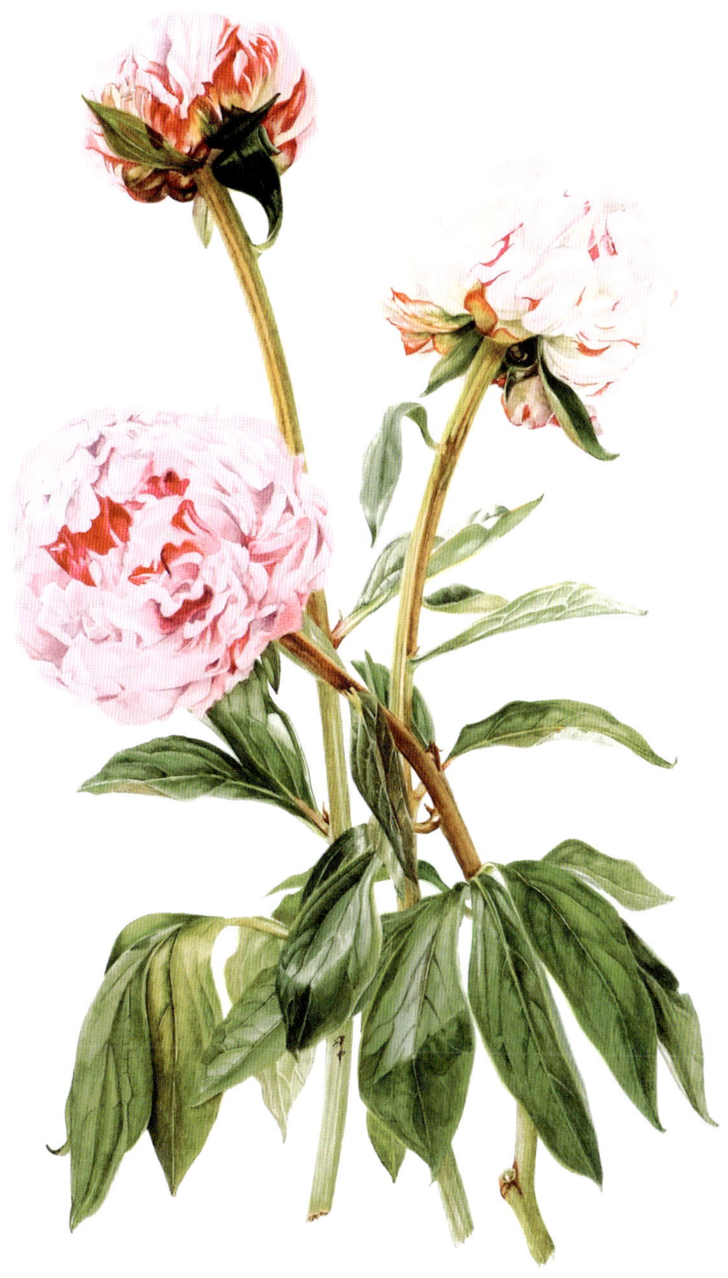

Botanical illustration fit for purpose

I hope this section will help to clarify the matter of when a plant portrait becomes a true botanical illustration. After half a lifetime of consideration I believe it depends on the purpose for which it is created rather than the content. The following contribution by Past President Vickie Marsh is an excellent example and her lecture notes supply the background to a fascinating story.

I have selected a few paintings to illustrate around 12,000 years of change following the melting of the ice sheets 15,000 years ago, when part of what would become Liverpool turned into an area of sparse vegetation later known as Moss Lake, a raised peat bog cut for fuel, then used as a rubbish tip and eventually built upon.

On this site part of the University of Liverpool would be erected and when work was being carried out on the Senate House in the 1950s a core sample was taken. Preserved in the peat were seeds, pollen, leaves and other plant material, and many of the species are still growing in the area today. Through her involvement as a botanical art tutor at Ness Botanical Gardens on the Wirral, Vickie was given the opportunity to record the full list of specimens discovered in the core sample, painting more than 50 of them to form a major exhibition at the university.

Fifteen thousand years ago vegetation was sparse, but among the sedges and grasses one might have found the very familiar *Valeriana officinalis*, whose flowers brighten many a West Country wall or cottage garden today, and the tiny blue flowers of *Succisa pratensis* (devil's bit scabious).

Twelve thousand years ago a warmer climate brought new species, including *Helianthemum* (simple rock roses), and *Armeria maritima* (sea pinks). Open woodland with pine and *Betula* sp. (birch, illustrated) gave some tree cover, and also *Salix caprea* (goat willow), made

an appearance. Over the next thousand years the trees survived a cold period and were joined by a wide mix of familiar plants such as *Filipendula ulmaria* (meadowsweet), *Juniperus communis* (juniper) and *Typha* sp. (bulrush, illustrated).

There was a rapid warming of the climate 10,000 years ago and more trees were established, including *Sorbus aucuparia* (rowan), and *Prunus spinosa* (blackthorn). The lake blossomed with *Nymphea alba* (white waterlilies, illustrated). A thousand years later the woodland became more dense and *Quercus* sp. (oak, illustrated) appeared for the first time. In the lake a floating raft of sphagnum moss appeared, the start of the raised bog which supported *Osmunda regalis* (royal fern, illustrated on page 2). The scent of *Lonicera periclymenum* (honeysuckle) would have wafted on the breeze, another first in our botanical history.

Seven thousand years ago the English Channel breached, allowing the tides to flow around these islands and change the climate to the cooler and wetter one familiar today. *Eriophorum* sp. (cotton grass) appeared on the bog (illustrated).

As a result of peat cutting and use as a rubbish tip, followed by a building site, it is not possible to be exact in the upper layers, so the near millennia cannot be documented in the same way. However I hope this section might encourage anyone with an interest in serious botanical illustration to look for a project. On a DLDC, students are required to use one assignment to work in the field and record plants found on a particular site. This is an excellent starting point and often awakens an interest outside the confines of the garden wall, as well as improving observation. It could well provide a foundation for a more serious study at some later date.

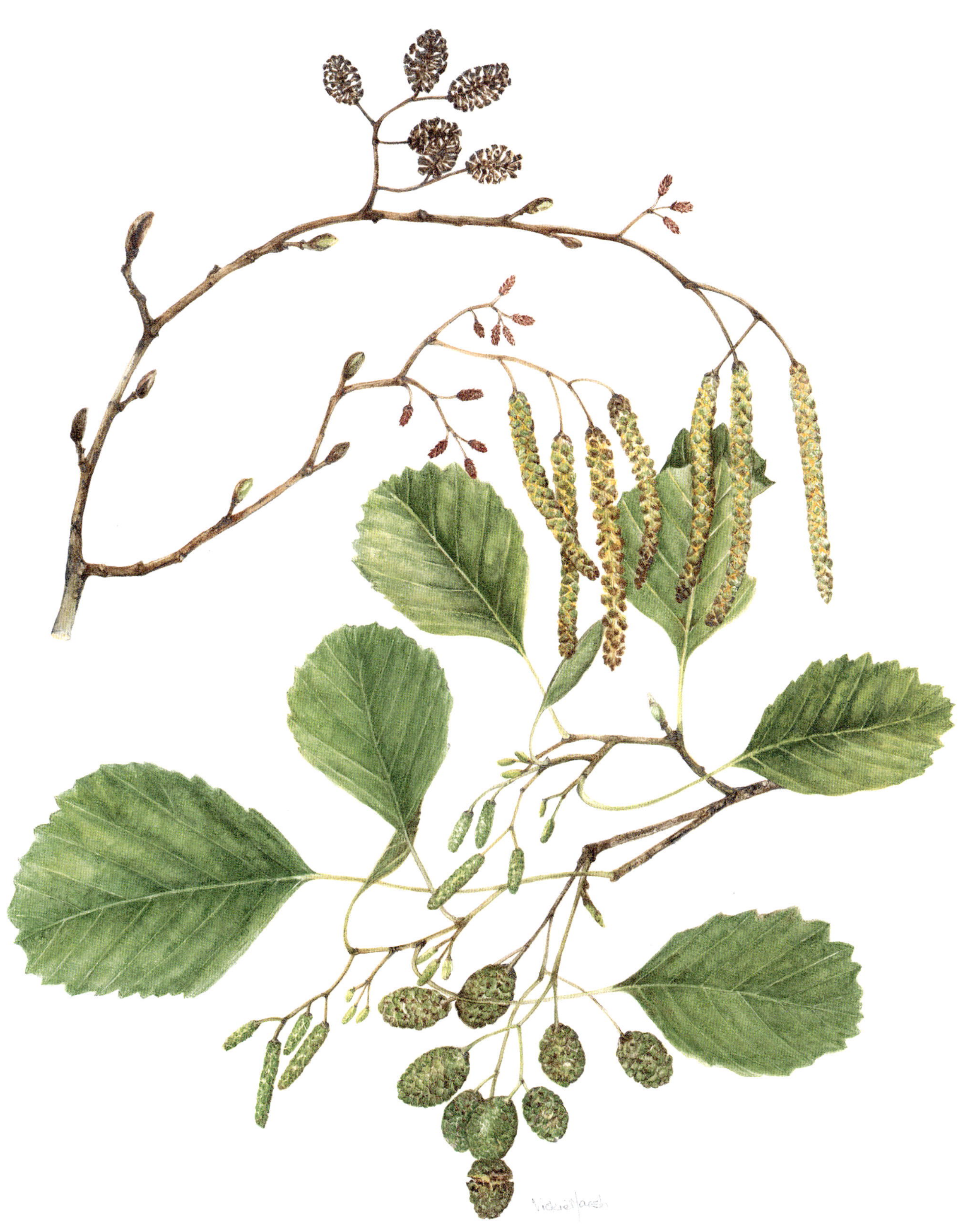

Betula sp. (Birch) from 12,000 years ago | Vickie
Marsh | Watercolour on Fabriano Classico 5 Hot
Pressed paper

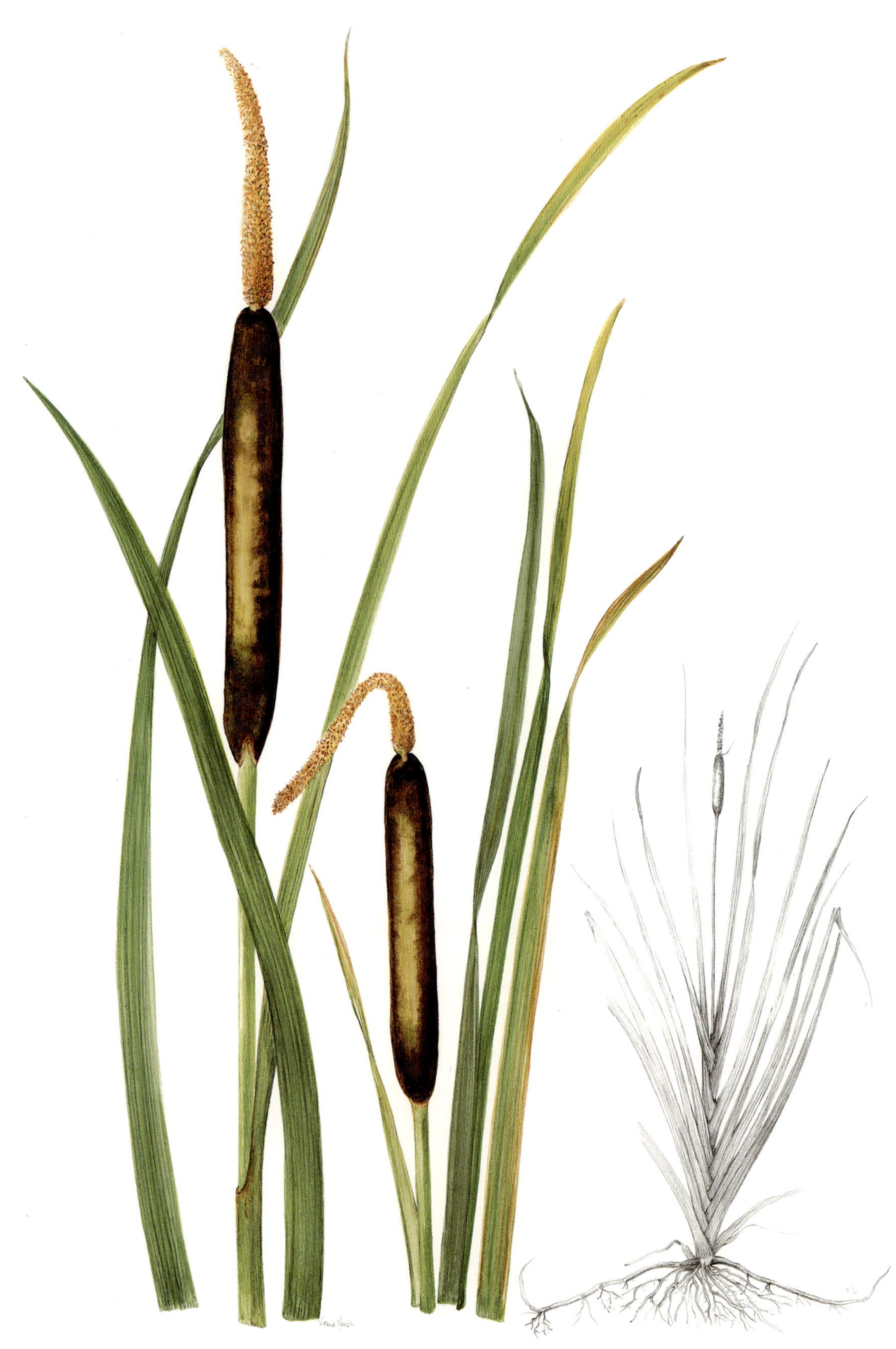

Typha sp. (Bulrush) from 11,000–12,000 years ago |
Vickie Marsh | Watercolour on Fabriano Classico 5
Hot Pressed paper

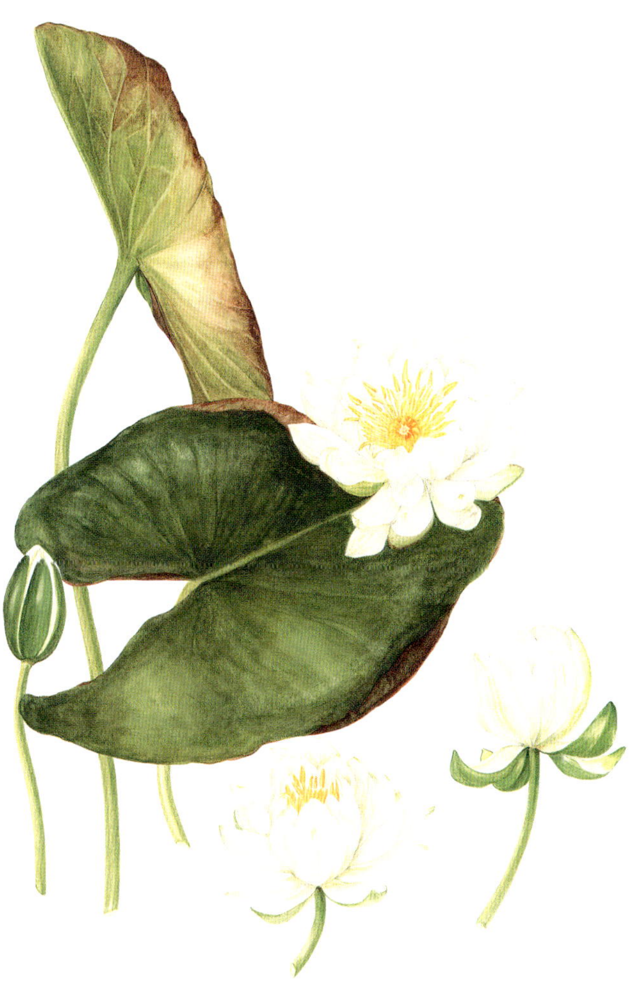

Nymphea alba (White Waterlily) from 10,000 years ago | Vickie Marsh | Watercolour on Fabriano Classico 5 Hot Pressed paper

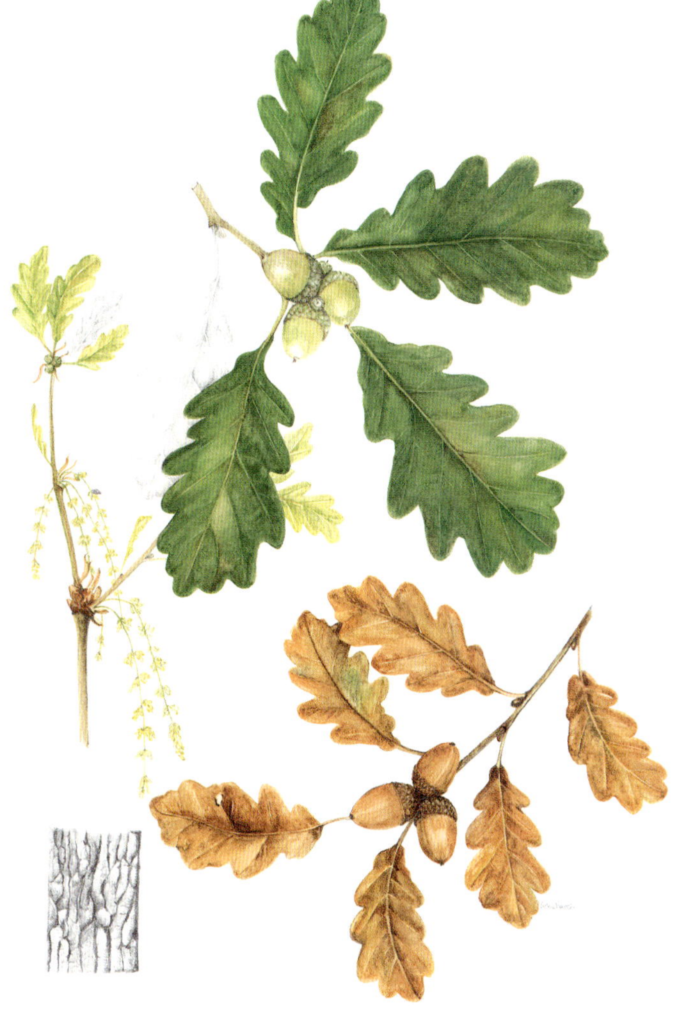

Quercus sp. (Oak) | Vickie Marsh | Watercolour on Fabriano Classico 5 Hot Pressed paper

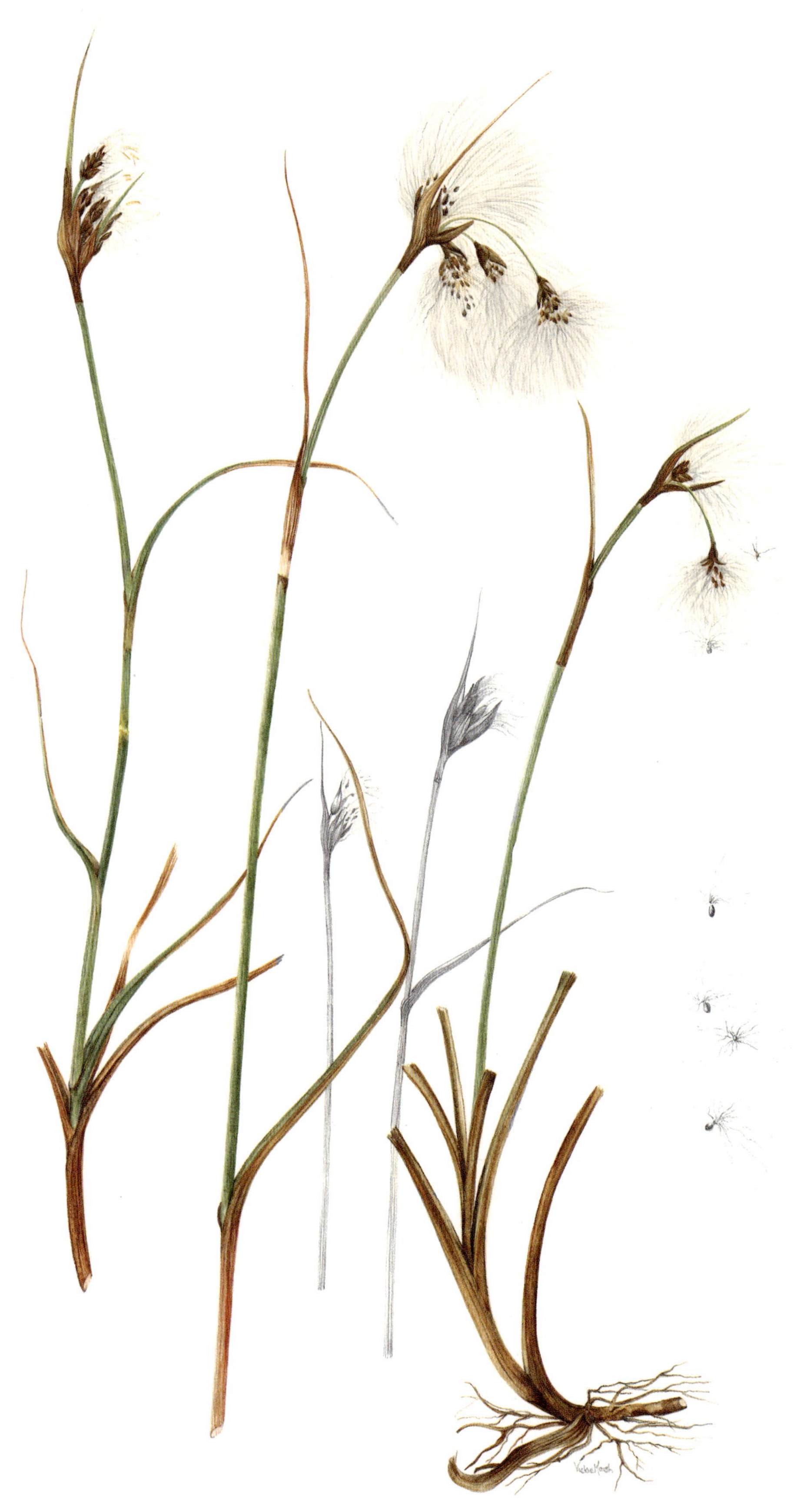

Eriphorum sp. (Cotton Grass) from 7,000 years ago | Vickie Marsh |
Watercolour on Fabriano Classico 5 Hot Pressed paper

A Library Page of Leaves

JIYOUNG KIM | Watercolour on paper

The way in which leaves are painted will make or break a painting, no matter how well the flowers are represented. For that reason we devote a three-month assignment period to their study with the library page a final requirement. This is a good example of a highly competent piece of work showing an assortment of shapes and colours. They may not hold the same attraction as gaily coloured flowers but of course they are essential, not only botanically, but as a foil to floral abundance.

The student needs to prepare a chart of mixed greens which will be useful for matching colours in the future.

Venation also needs careful study – for example, note the way both midrib and side veins narrow towards the tip or edge of the leaf and the side veins curl round to meet their neighbour, never going direct to the leaf edge. They are there as channels to carry food throughout the leaf, not tip it off the edge!

Jiyoung, a DLDC student from South Korea, finds the flamingo willow particularly attractive in spring when the green, pink and white leaves blow in the wind and she compares these to the most beautiful flowers.

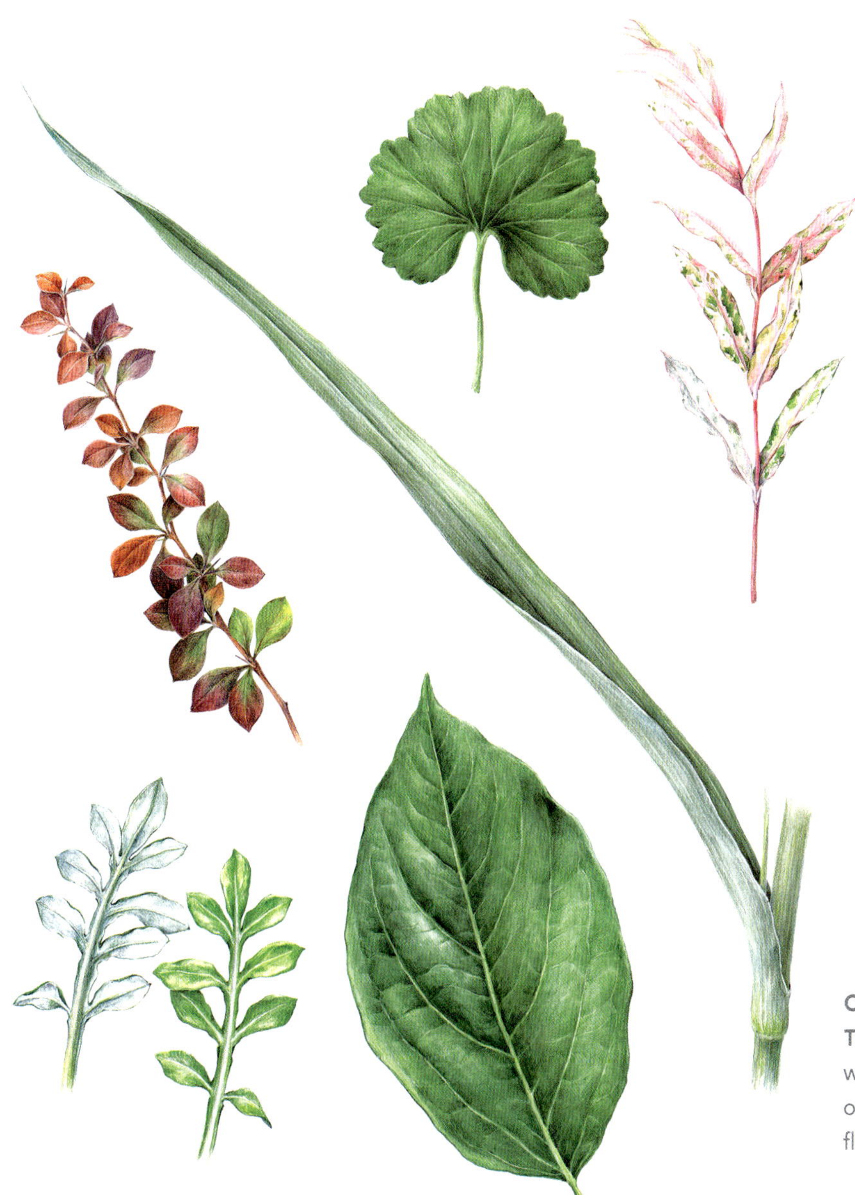

CLOCKWISE FROM THE TOP: *Pelargonium*, flamingo willow, reflexed spiderwort, oriental persimmon, treasure flower, poiret barberry.

Bratonia Shelob 'Tolkien'

SUNANDA WIDEL | Watercolour on paper

Although the name of this orchid was inspired by the giant spider Shelob in *The Lord of the Rings*, this cross between *Bratonia Olmec* and *Brassia Edvah Loo* is beautiful and not at all frightening. It certainly attracted Sunanda when she first found it for sale at a nursery in Singapore. She fell in love with everything about it, from the plant form to its star-like blooms and naturally swaying leaves, which she attempted to show in her composition. The colour combination of spotted, deep rose lip and burgundy-brown and pale yellow long spiked sepals and petals made it enjoyable to paint. The resulting botanical study/plant portrait is one of grace and elegance.

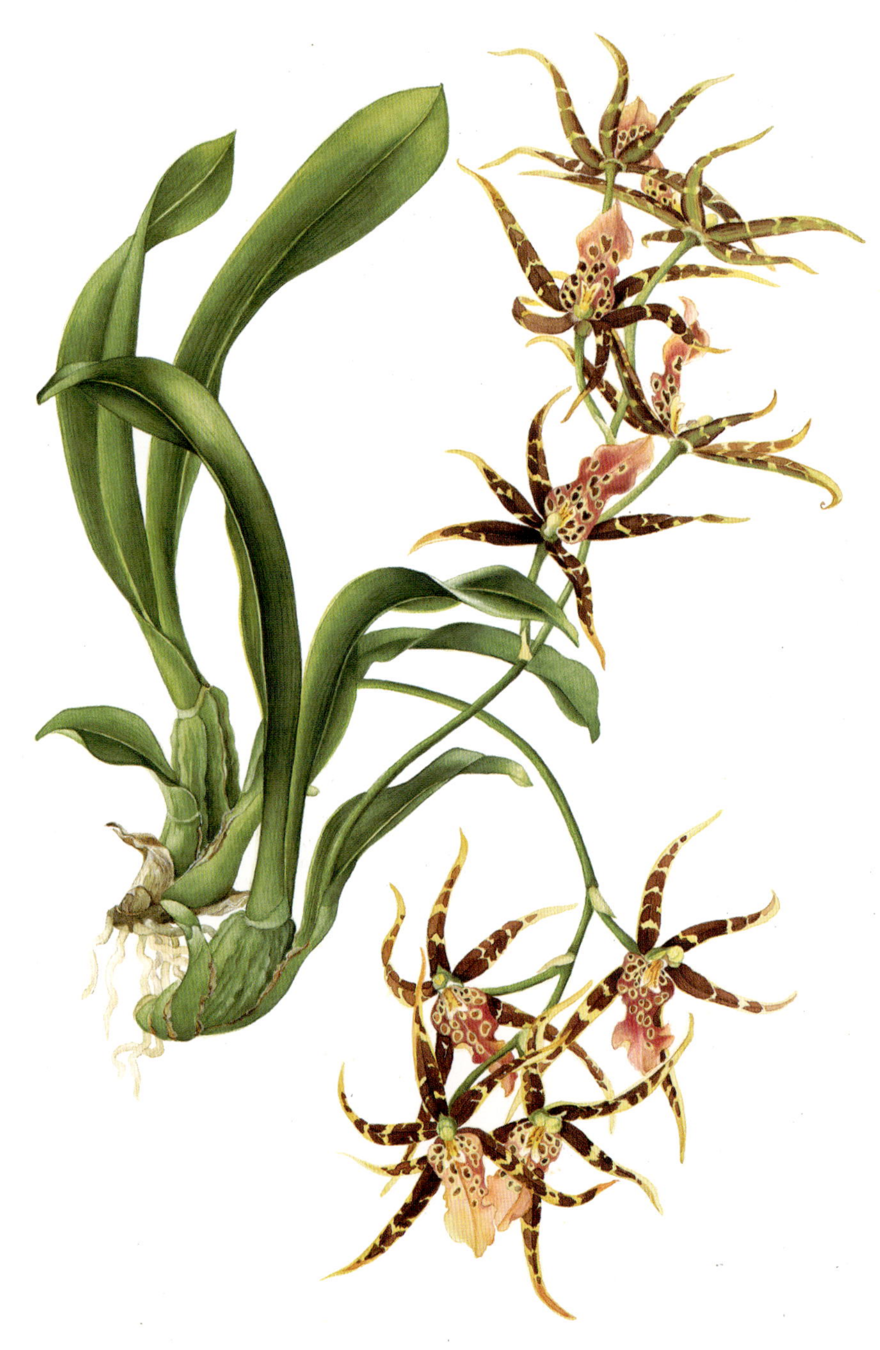

Cattleya intermedia var. *coerulea* x *flamea* x *Cattleya walkeriana* 'Daphne Wenzel'

ERICA HARGESHEIMER | Watercolour on paper

Canadian artist Erica Hargesheimer submitted this as part of her Diploma Portfolio. A few darker tones would have made it a little more three-dimensional, but the drawing is excellent. Students are constricted on the paper size they are allowed to use because of packaging and postal difficulties – ideally she would have had more room to display her very competent dissections.

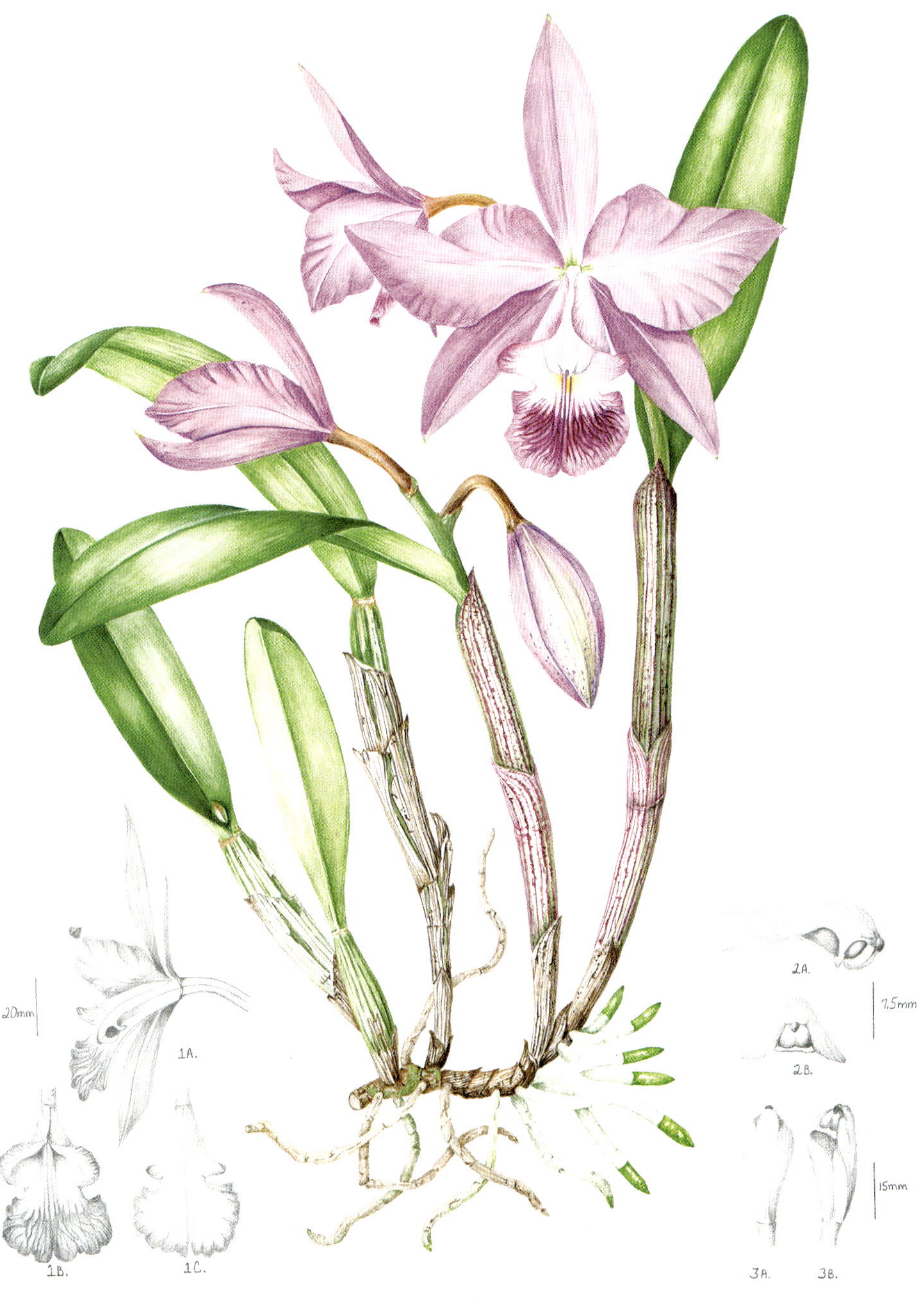

Silver *Banksia*

ALISTER MATHEWS | Watercolour on paper

This plant is probably one of the most challenging subjects a botanical artist can choose, so it is not for the faint-hearted. It is long-lasting, enabling Alister to give time to the complex but primitive flowers, which consist solely of sexual parts clustered tightly on the cone. These produce pollen and nectar to enable fertilization by bees and birds. Alister painted each of the flowers separately as a negative image, painting around each filament individually – a very laborious job. The five studies are arranged diagonally across the page and show the progress from full flower through deterioration to spent cone. Three seeds can be seen at the bottom left, like little brown lips, showing that in spite of their number not every flower produces a seed. The leathery leaves last a long time and, thankfully, can be left until most of the intricate work is well under way.

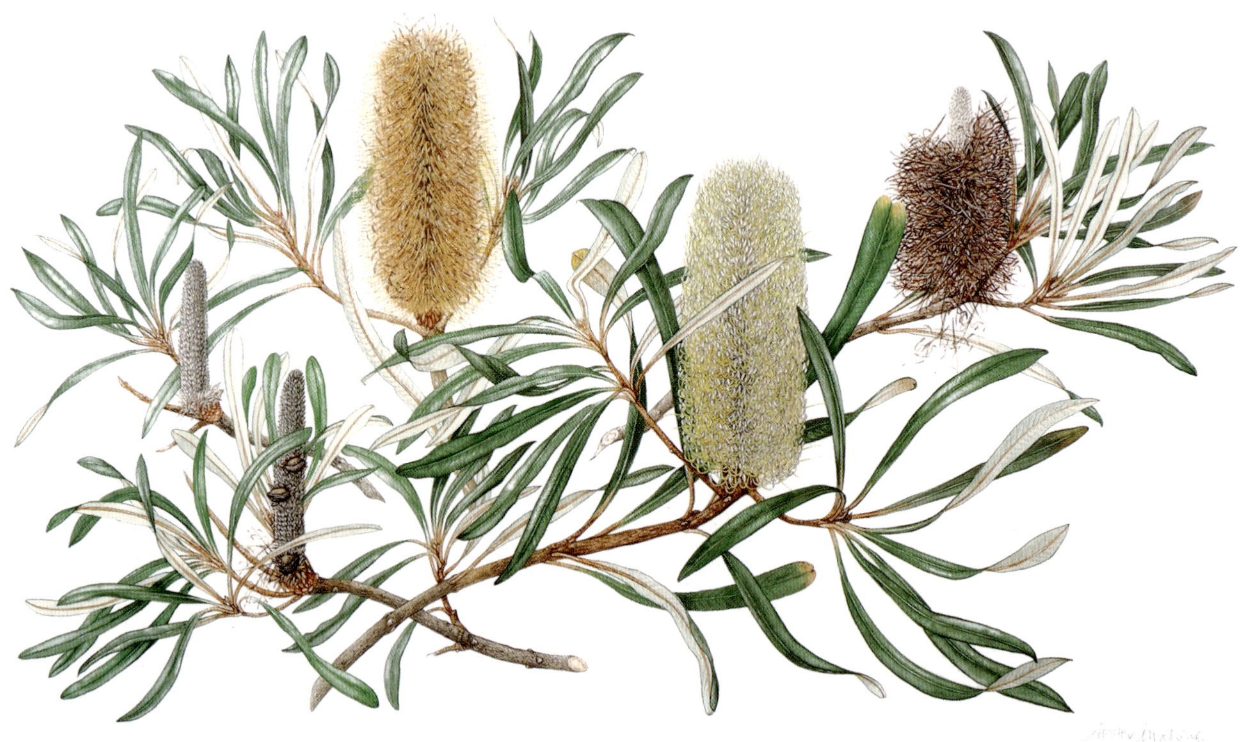

Hippeastrum

KAREN GAVIN | Watercolour on paper

This study of an unidentified hippeastrum was submitted by Karen as the botanical illustration for part of her Diploma Portfolio on completion of DLDC 11 and gained her the full 25 marks awarded for this section. The assessors praised the clean lines, excellent colour and above all the tonal variation, which gave depth to the flower and its parts. The dissections were well arranged and beautifully painted. Tonal variation is the one area that many students struggle with, both in monochrome and colour, yet without it the work will be flat and lifeless. This piece is an excellent example of what the judges look for in this section.

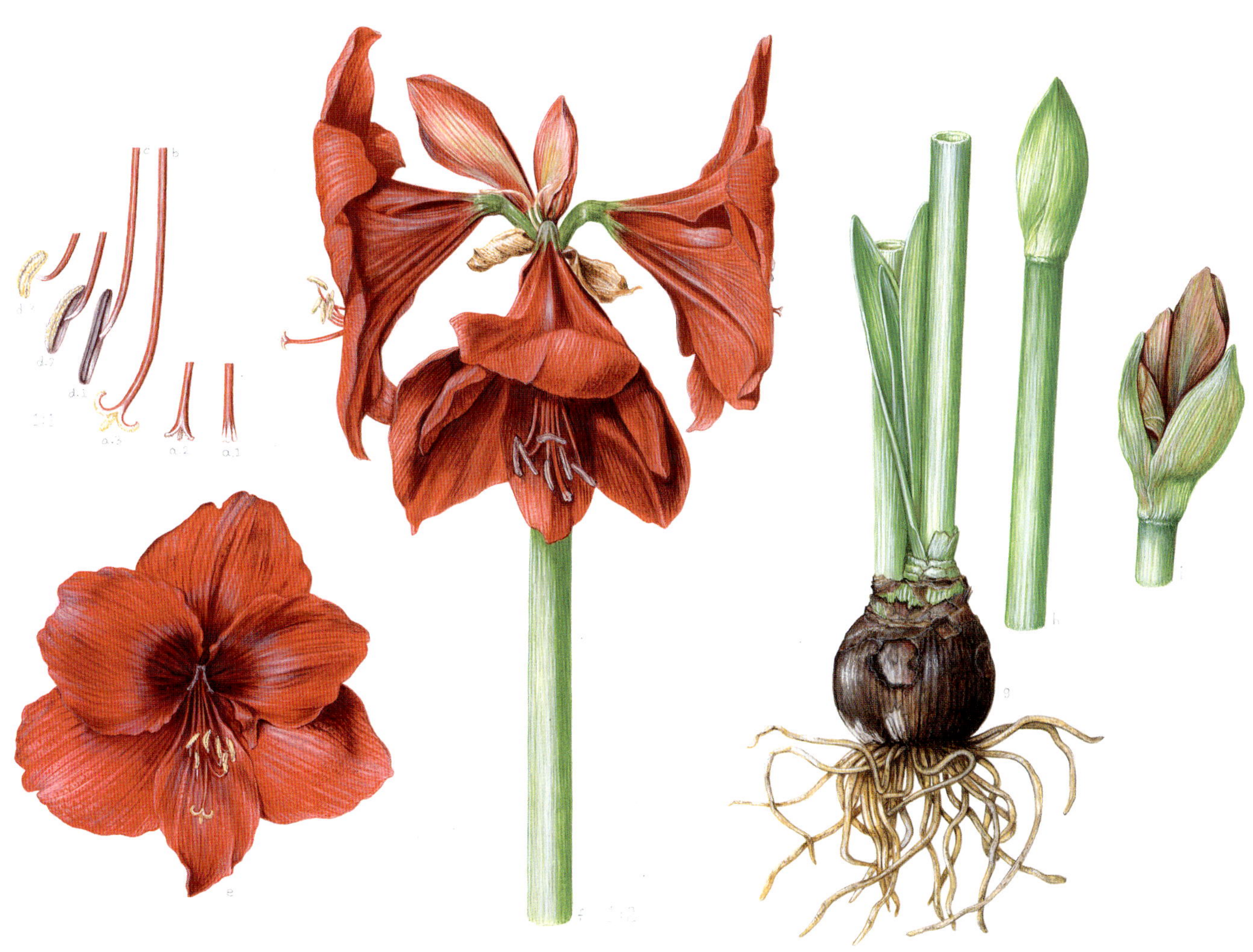

CHAPTER 7

The Mixed Bunch

This is an area of botanical painting that seems to cause many of our students to approach their assignment with a degree of trepidation. Placing one specimen plant on the page does not require a great deal of design or compositional skills, but grouping a mix of different flowers with a variety of foliage and perhaps berries too, is another matter.

As this is the most difficult assignment on the DLDC timetable it is the final one, with nearly two years of preparation preceding it. It also features in the Diploma Portfolio alongside Botanical Illustration and Fruit or Vegetables.

In an ideal world the artist would have a ready supply of flowers and could paint at will, but often, when working commercially, one has to fulfil commissions out of season, which creates a fresh set of problems. Here we see examples of both situations and the step-by-step from Past President Sandra Wall Armitage is an excellent example of the latter.

Immediately before the final assignment the students are required to tackle one on working from photographs, and for this they need to think ahead and collect their own photographic reference material. Even when you are just painting for pleasure, back-up photographs are always a good idea as the subject usually dies before the painting is finished. It is wise to record leaves, leaf joints, stems and so forth as well as the pretty flower! Do not take photographs at midday when the sun is high – choose early morning or late afternoon when light and colour will be more accurate. Take note of the angle of shadows and light source and stick with it throughout your painting; nothing looks more manufactured than a painting where the light is coming from several different directions. While you have a living specimen, also take the opportunity to work out and record a colour mix. This will ensure you have accurate shades regardless of the colour in your photographs, which is likely to vary.

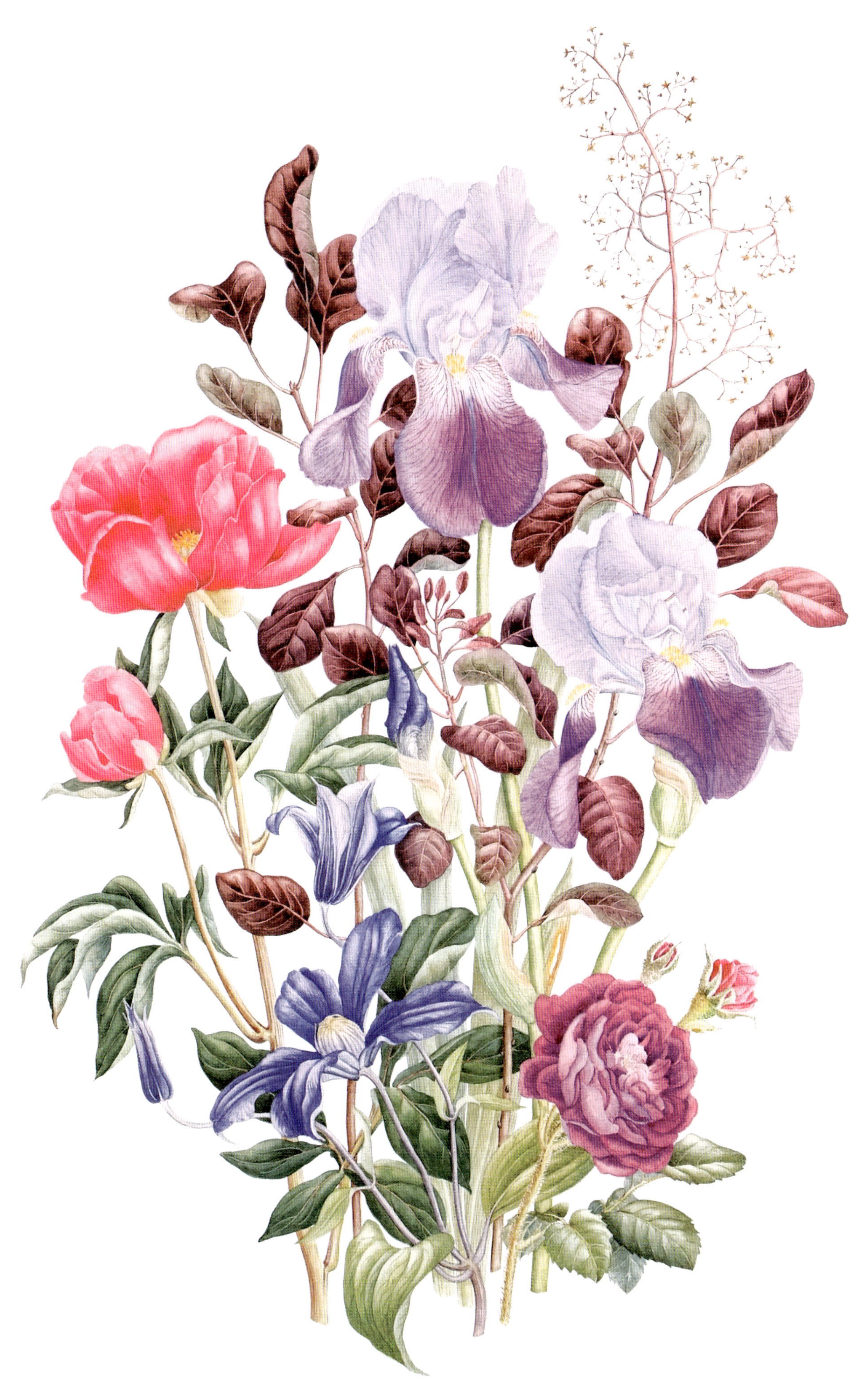

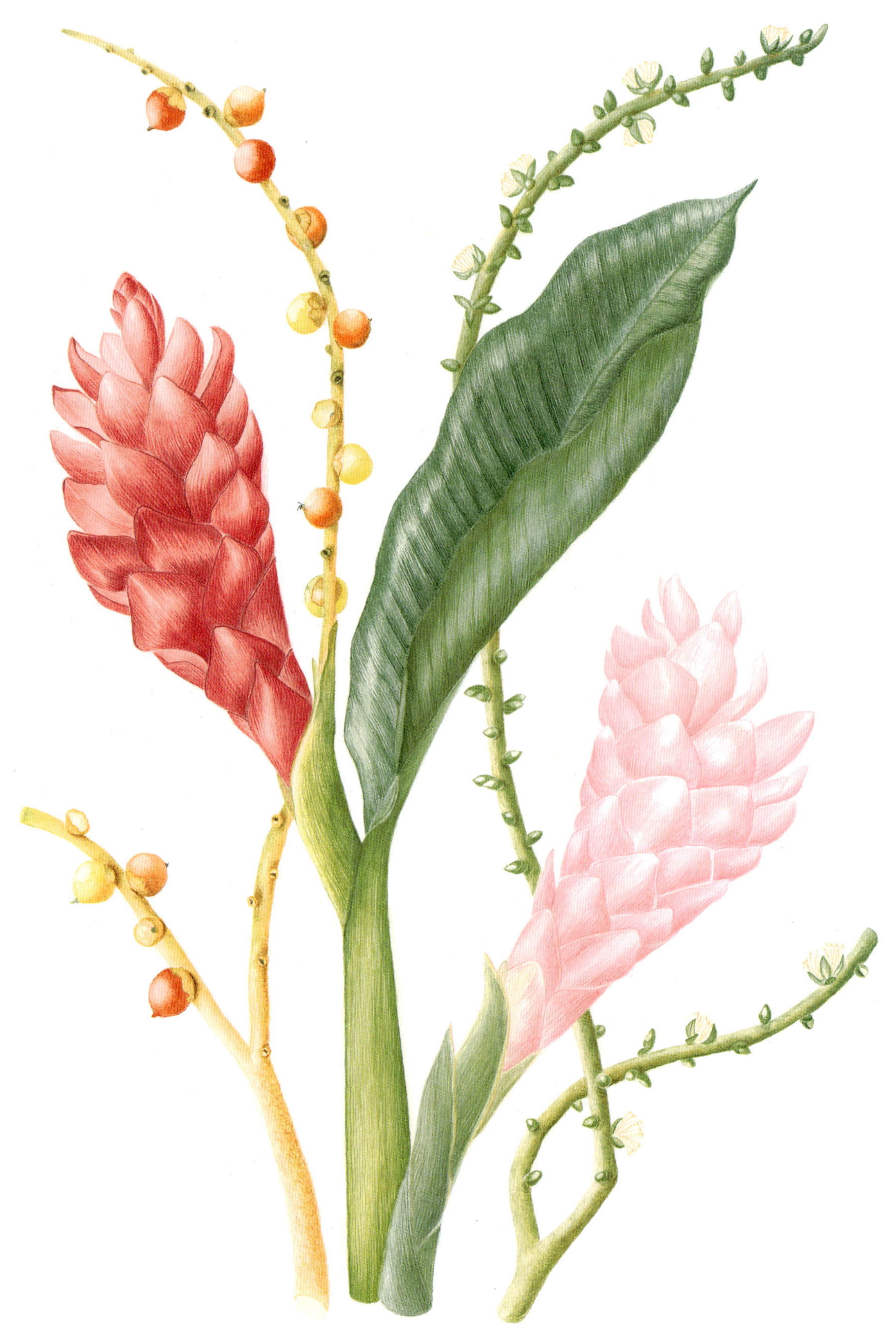

Previous page: Summer Extravaganza

JENNY JOWETT | Watercolour on paper

Jenny is a keen gardener who regularly opens her garden under the National Gardens Scheme, so it is not surprising that she has painted some magnificent mixed flower studies over the years. Working with a limited palette, Jenny chooses flowers which both blend and complement each other. What might appear an artless arrangement in fact shows great skill at selecting just the right specimen, the removal of which would undermine the whole composition. In this case the bronze foliage complements the purple falls of the iris. Let your mind's eye remove this and see how an all-green scenario would lessen the impact of this strong and beautiful painting.

Mixed Study – *Alpinia purpurata* (Red Ginger) and *Ptychosperma macarthurii* (MacArthur Palm)

CHOON-YING TAN | Watercolour on paper

From Singapore came this exquisitely painted example of two exotic species where the colour had been applied with a very delicate touch. Perhaps a little more depth of tone on the pale pink ginger might be of benefit, but here in these northern climes we tend to forget how the light affects our perception of colour so I make no real criticism. The leaf in itself is a thing of great beauty and is among the best I have seen in nearly 40 years of teaching adults the art of botanical painting. The brushwork is faultless and Choon-Ying has set herself a very high benchmark.

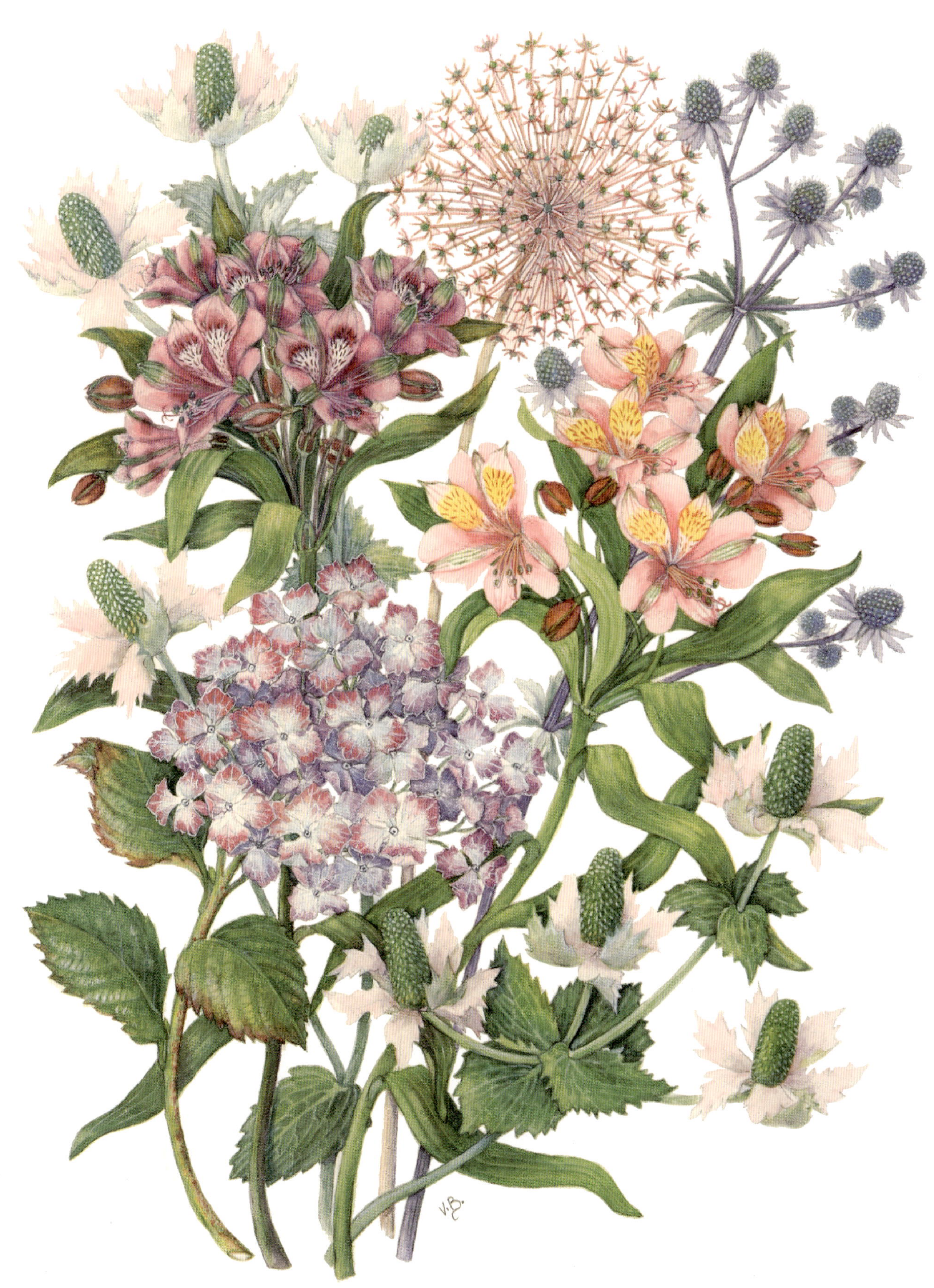

From the Summer Garden

VIVIEN BURGESS | Watercolour on paper

A long-standing SBA member, Vivien never fails to delight with seemingly artlessly arranged flowers that complement each other in both colour and form.

Here she describes how the *Alstroemeria* first caught her eye and she wisely photographed them in order to have a record when they faded. The hydrangea would be longer-lasting so, seeing that the colours were harmonious, she picked both flowers and set about planning her composition on cartridge paper, tweaking stems and leaves to suit.

Using 300gsm (140lb) Hot Pressed paper and an old mount as a guide to the likely finished size, Vivien drew within its borders with a light touch. You can see that those three flowers made the solid triangle at the centre of the painting. Next she looked for something to make a contrast both in colour and shape and for this two species of *Echinacea* were ideal. Again she drew them on cartridge paper but this time she traced them too as this enabled her to move the tracings around the already drawn plants to select their best position. She then drew

them in, passing the stems in front or behind as necessary. Note how each stem follows through, so that none appear to be emerging from another flower or leaf, which is a common fault in this type of composition.

There is a fashion in floristry for the hand-tied bunch, which simply means the stems are brought together at an angle in the hand rather than straight down and you can see elements of that in this composition, and this helps to create a natural bouquet. Finally Vivien added the allium seedhead, which was an excellent choice as it filled the gap without adding unwanted weight at the top of the picture.

With the drawing complete, Vivien began the painting, paying attention to detail throughout. The echinacea were particularly time-consuming and Vivien made sure each centre was accurately painted and shaded. The junctions of stems and leaves were also carefully rendered as were veins and leaf edges. As a final step, she deepened colours towards the back, leaving them lighter at the front, which gives depth to the painting. When it was framed the finished painting measured 60 x 48cm (23½ x 19in).

Zantedeschia rehmannii, *Zantedeschia* 'Purple Moon', *Alstroemeria* 'Solent Crest', *Chrysanthemum* 'Tom Pearce' and *Viola tricolor*

RACHEL HUGHES | Watercolour on paper

Rachel presented this for her final assignment in a recent course and there is much to commend it but also a few valuable lessons to learn. The mix of gold and purple is classic but the little violas, although a useful filler at the bottom of the page, are really out of place.

It is always worth asking yourself if the flowers grow together – not all are natural bedfellows – or if they would look good in an arrangement. Also take care how you portray the angle of the flower heads. Here Rachel happened to have the same chrysanthemums in a vase and noticed that as they matured the stems were not quite strong enough at the neck to support the bloom. This led to some odd angles, such as you can see here, which could easily be misinterpreted as an error of line drawing. Either adjust the angle of the flowers to correct them or alter your drawing so that the stems line up with the centre of the flowers.

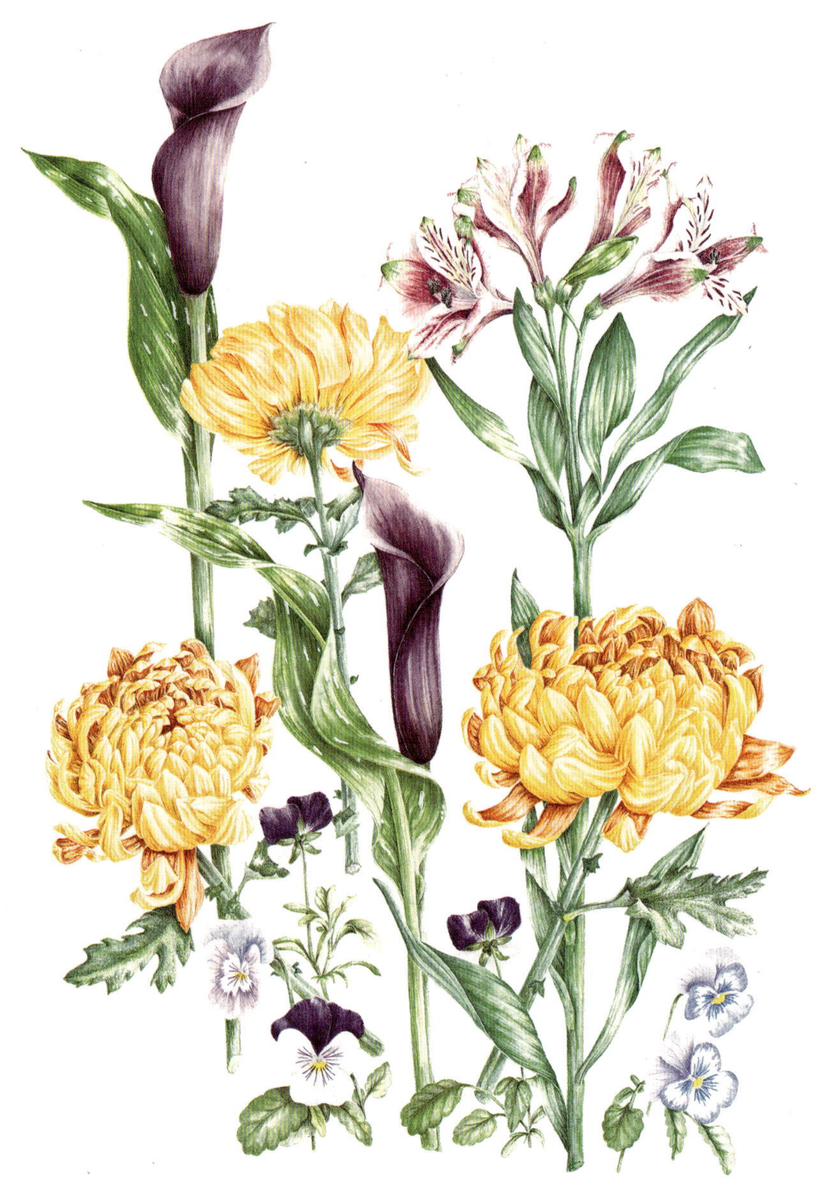

Rosa 'Fragrant Delight', *Alstroemeria* and *Freesia*

MARIA MOLDAVSKY | Watercolour on paper

Maria shows a confident technique which enables her to choose and blend pigments smoothly, achieving tonal variation without losing the purity and richness of colour of the blooms. There is a warm glow at the heart of the rose and some extremely fine painting around the stamens of the alstroemeria. Perhaps a little less highlight on some of the rose leaves would be preferable – if there is too much they can appear metallic – but the alstroemeria foliage is beautifully painted with graceful movement.

It is wise to avoid a gap in the centre of a composition and there is a suggestion of this where the rose leaves curve towards the freesias. This might have been solved by more rose leaves emanating from lower down the stem or perhaps another stem of freesias suggesting a 'back' to the arrangement. I would suggest a few drawings on tracing paper which could be moved around to see how they look before adding with confidence. These are just pointers as it is an exceptionally pleasing piece of work.

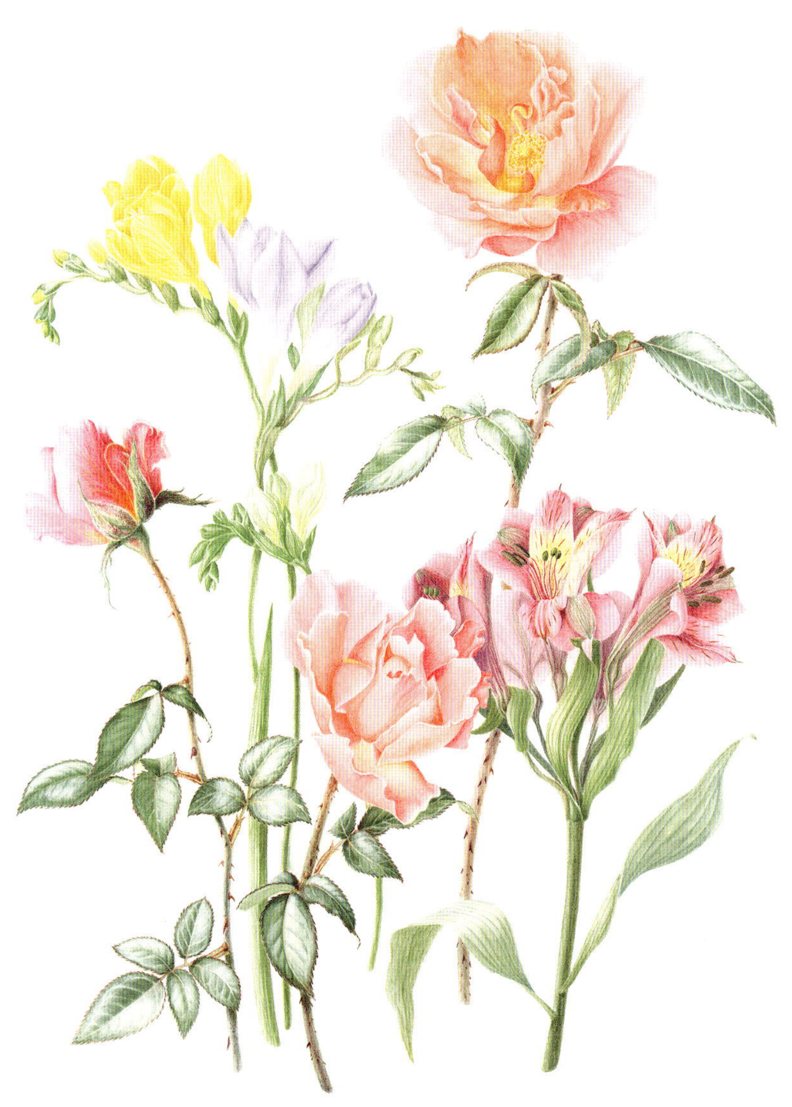

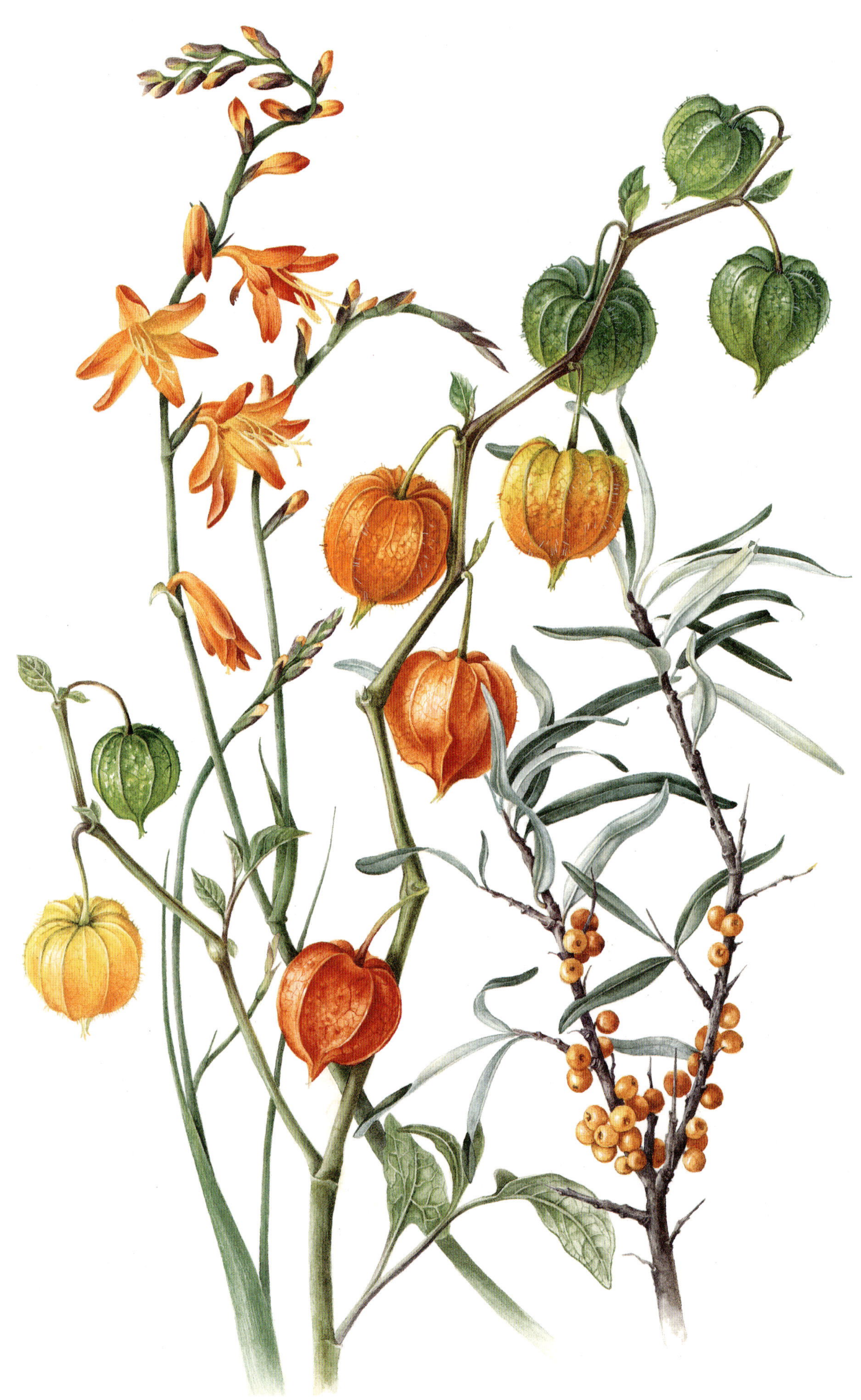

Mixed Study – *Physalis alkekengi* (Chinese Lanterns), *Hippophae* (Sea Buckthorn), *Crocosmia* aurea (Falling Stars)

MARINA PROTSENKO | Watercolour on paper

Throughout her progress on the DLDC, Marina has shown herself to be a highly accomplished artist. She is not afraid of strong, bold colours, but note also the way she has captured the papery texture of the lanterns which shows up the delicate tracery of veins.

Orange, like yellow, is not the easiest colour to handle and shading can easily become dirty or muddy. Here the colours retain their glow yet recession has been indicated among the buckthorn berries, with the darker ones pushing back as the light falls on those in the foreground. The movement of the buckthorn leaves introduces a lightness of line to an otherwise rather linear composition. Note also the way the fine filaments of the crocosmia flowers stand out as they emerge from the tubes. This all indicates keen observation on the part of the artist as well as praiseworthy technique.

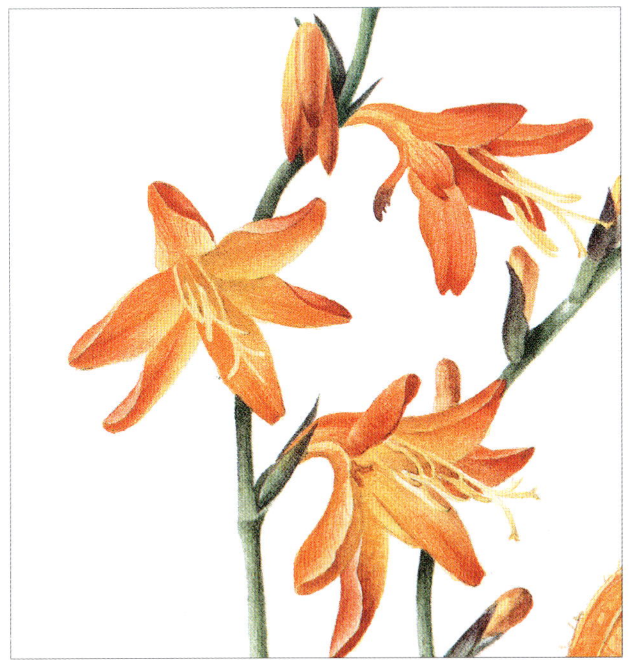

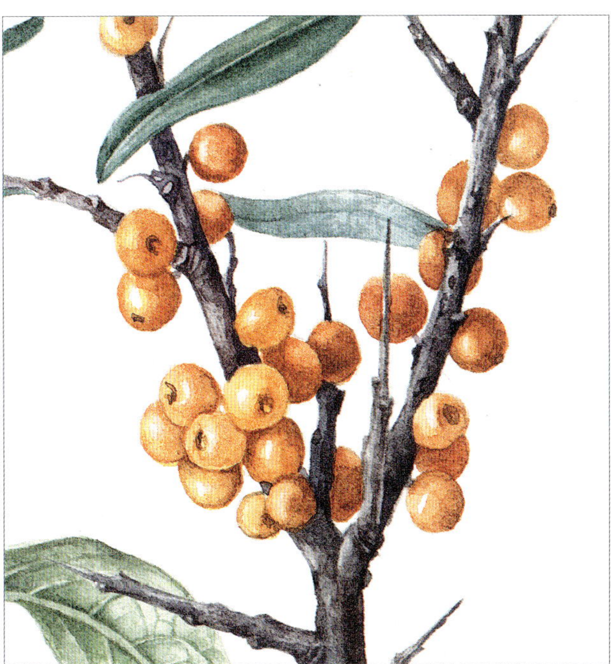

Step-by-Step

It is one thing working up a composition using living plants when there is an abundance of reference material to choose from, with a modicum of back-up photographs; it is quite another to be asked to produce a composition from scratch with no living reference, just photographs and sketches, because the work is required out of season. This is frequently the case with commissioned work and requires a level of experience to fill in the information that a two-dimensional photograph by itself cannot provide. In addition, if possible, you need informative sketches as well as a strong working knowledge of your subjects. Having a full awareness of the habit and structure of your plants makes them grow convincingly on the blank page; it also enables the artist to make adjustments to stems and overlay plants in a convincing and realistic way.

In this composition I selected two familiar plants, cosmos and Michaelmas daisy *aster* x *frikartii* 'Monch'. I have a working knowledge of both these subjects and the colour range is harmonious. However, as both plants are inclined to be quite leggy, a third and larger flower head was required to give more weight to the composition. After rejecting several options I selected stokesia as its soft colour related well to the Michaelmas daisy but provided more volume. After preparatory planning with thumbnail sketches I moved on to larger, loose drawings and colour-washed compositions to anticipate how the colour and scale might work. Finally I began work on the painting proper.

STEP 1

I normally work directly on to the paper when using living plants that are growing *in situ*, grouping, selecting or omitting as I develop the work. In this particular case I used tracing paper, having mostly sketches and photographs and little visual aid to refer to. Working with tracings to plot a composition allows one to shift shapes around and erase poorly placed components until the basic composition is achieved. In this way there is still a degree of flexibility to rearrange or add as the work develops.

Once I was fairly satisfied with the arrangement I could transfer the image to the final support in stages. Cosmos usually grow in profusion so initially I distributed the flower heads liberally across the page. The aim was to give a spread of colour and shape through the group. I selected pink and magenta for contrast and portrayed the flower heads from different angles. At this stage I don't put in the stems and this allows me to make adjustments as I build up the composition, with no need to erase a wrongly positioned stem and risk roughening the paper. I painted the flowers almost to completion to provide detail and depth of colour and tone – I do this at every stage when adding more parts to the composition in order to gain the right tonal balance.

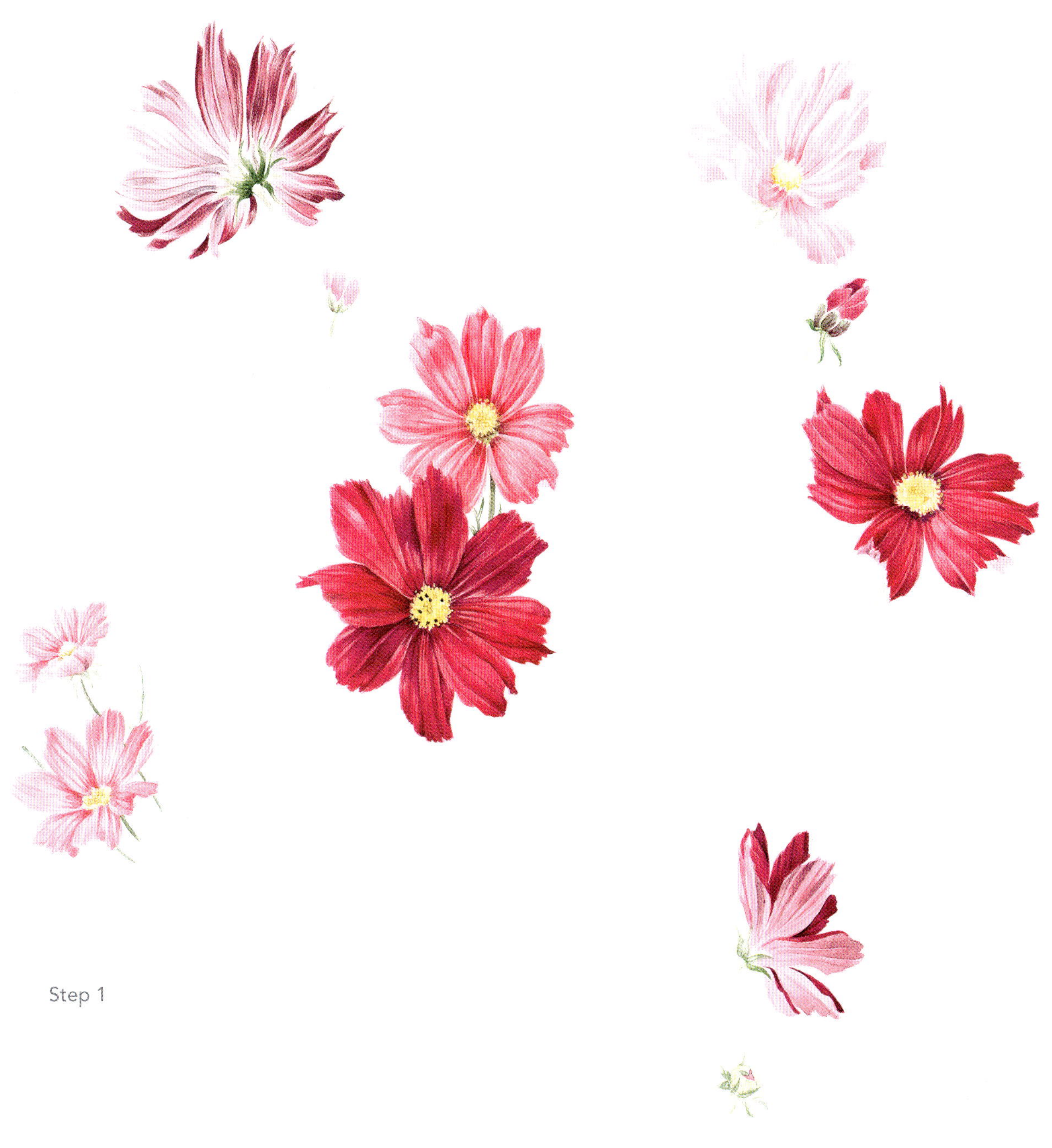

Step 1

STEP 2

Many artists deliberate with drawings on separate layers of tracing paper until they know exactly where everything is placed. I prefer to be more flexible to avoid the work becoming too static and to allow the group to evolve as it grows in nature. Tracings are useful for creating a skeleton plan of the layout, but until the colour is set down it is hard to gauge whether the placing works, or if there needs to be more adjustments. I added the stokesia heads next as this plant and its foliage takes up more space and provides balance to the cosmos. I limited the number of stokesia so as not to overcrowd the group.

At this stage I felt it necessary to add another two cosmos, because there were no pink flowers in the lower quarter and I needed to break the vertical line that I had inadvertently created by the placing of the two central flowers. By dropping in a pink cosmos immediately behind the stokesia on the right this problem was corrected and created more perspective to the composition. I also started to add foliage and stems and you will see I have discontinued these in places to allow for the positioning of the Michaelmas daisies and crossing stems later. All the time it is essential to check the colour balance and to check that there is good movement to the composition.

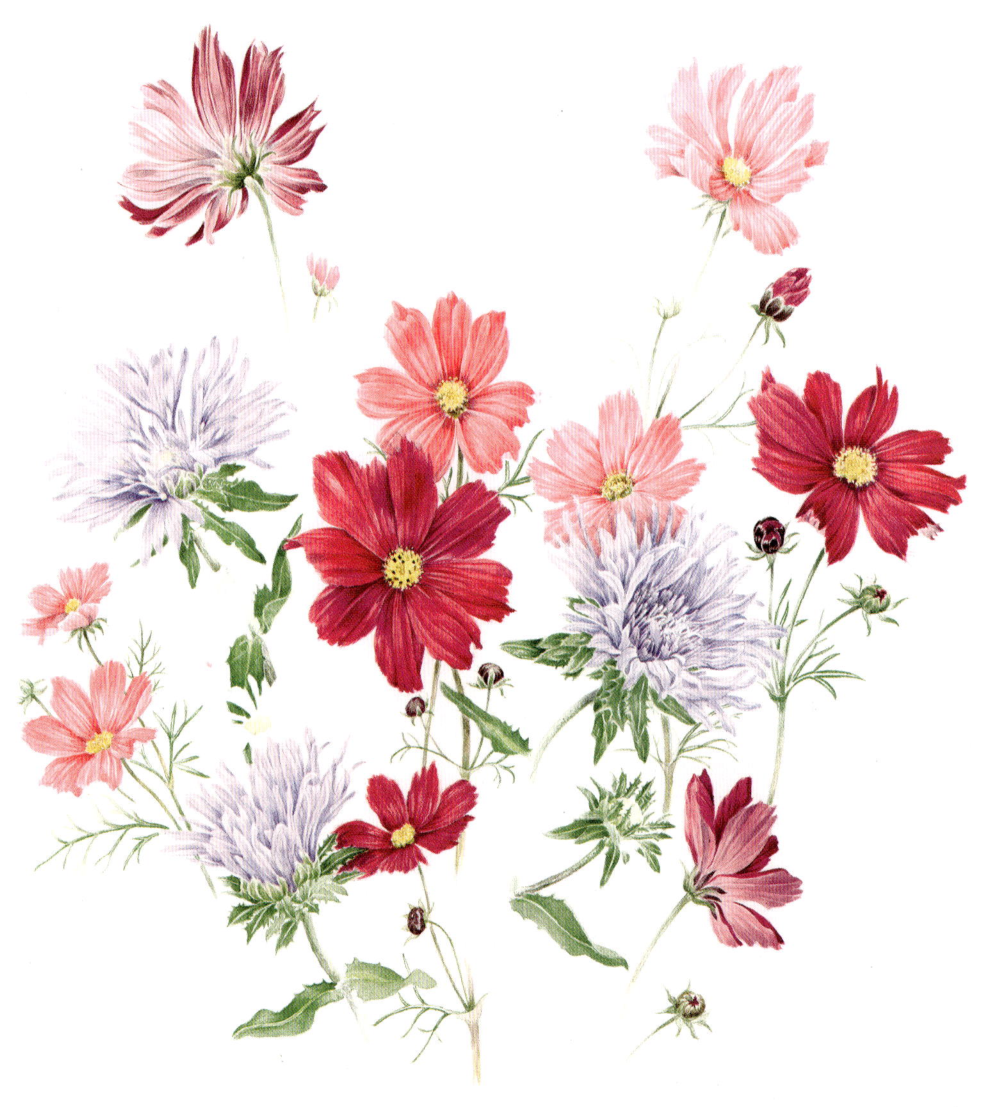

Step 2

STEP 3

At this stage the working out and placing becomes more complex and is inclined to slow down. I began to add the Michaelmas daisies so that the composition started to look more like a section of a perennial border with accents of bold colour and gentle drifts of soft lavender colour to create movement. I also began to add additional foliage throughout and pulled some of the stems further down toward the lower portion of the paper, while still reserving areas where I might need to add further plant form.

The introduction of the smaller, more ethereal heads of the Michaelmas daisies works through the whole composition and the flower heads are positioned at varying levels in the background or foreground areas. I also felt it necessary to include another magenta flower nestling behind the left-hand stokesia flower.

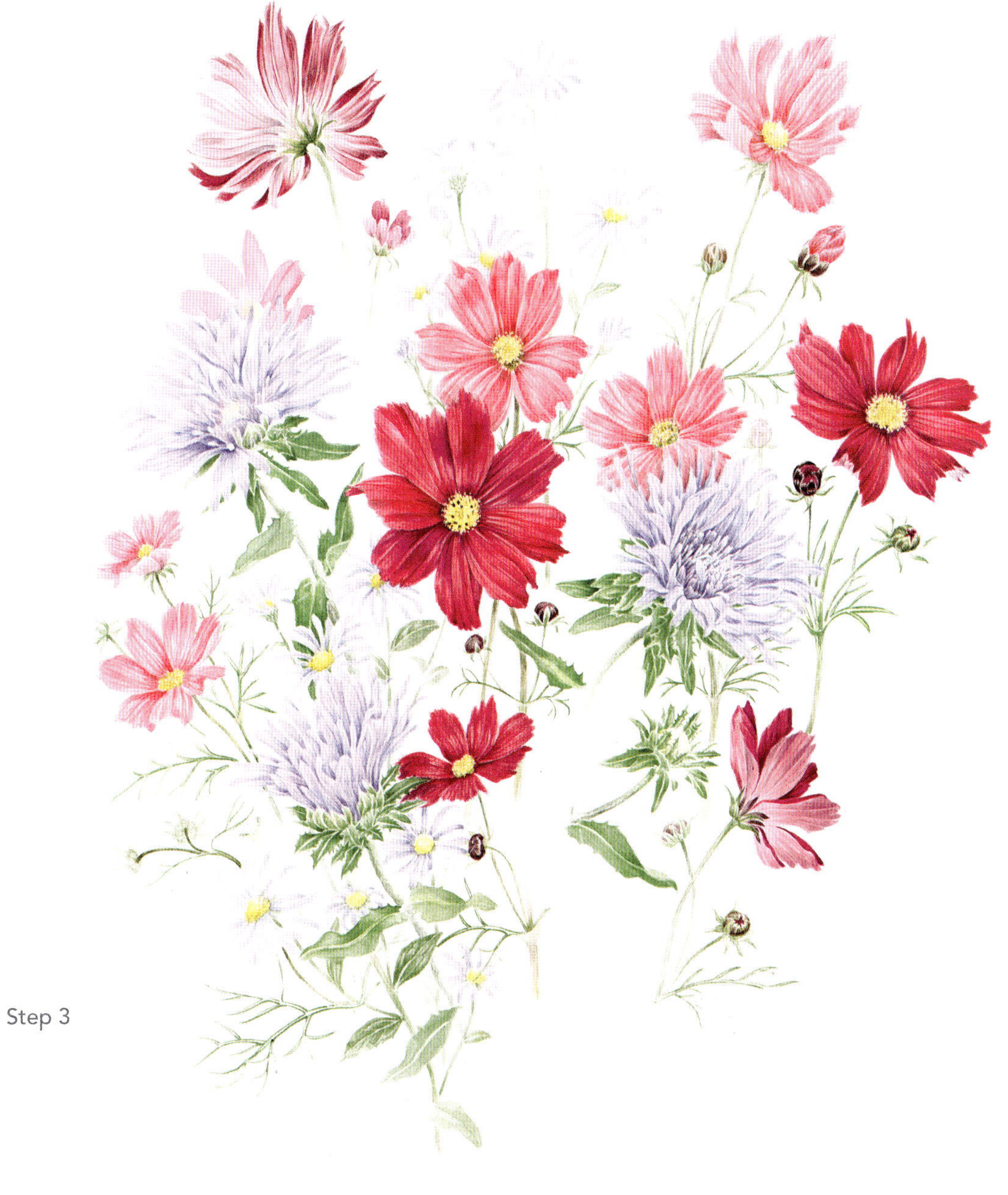

Step 3

Another semi-open cosmos on the right side completed the distribution of darker pink through the composition. I added a bud and strengthened the tones of several of the stalks and leaves. I also added extra Michaelmas daisies, filling in some of the voids and in some areas superimposing them to create more depth of field. I also decided that it was necessary to add further stokesia buds in the foreground and extend their stalks, while at the same time noting where I might add additional daisies.

This was the final stage of the picture and for this I again employed the use of tracing paper. There was so much information on the page now that I needed to be sure that any adjustments or stems would follow through and relate to the relevant flower. In a garden flowers and stems can disappear into the dense foliage around them, but working on a white background means there is no hiding place so it was worthwhile taking time to see how they intertwined with one another and that stems

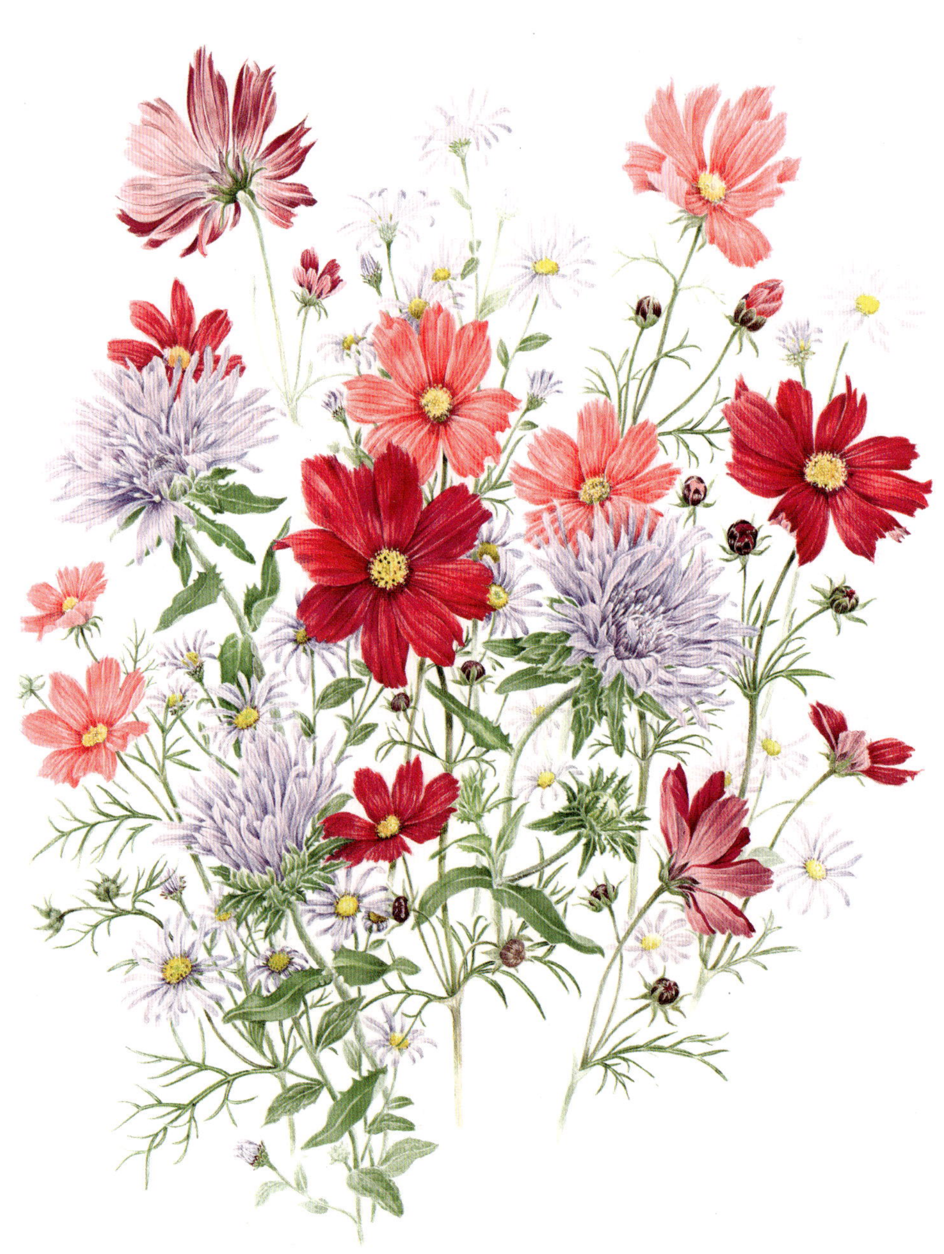

Step 4

came to a natural conclusion. The tracing paper allowed me to isolate areas where I could add flowers, stems or foliage that were needed, like fitting the final pieces of a jigsaw. All the foliage needed strengthening and detail added where relevant. I added shadow to some of the background Michaelmas daisies and those placed one behind another. Next I looked carefully at all the stems and worked out where I felt the natural ending to each would occur, to avoid them all ending on the same level.

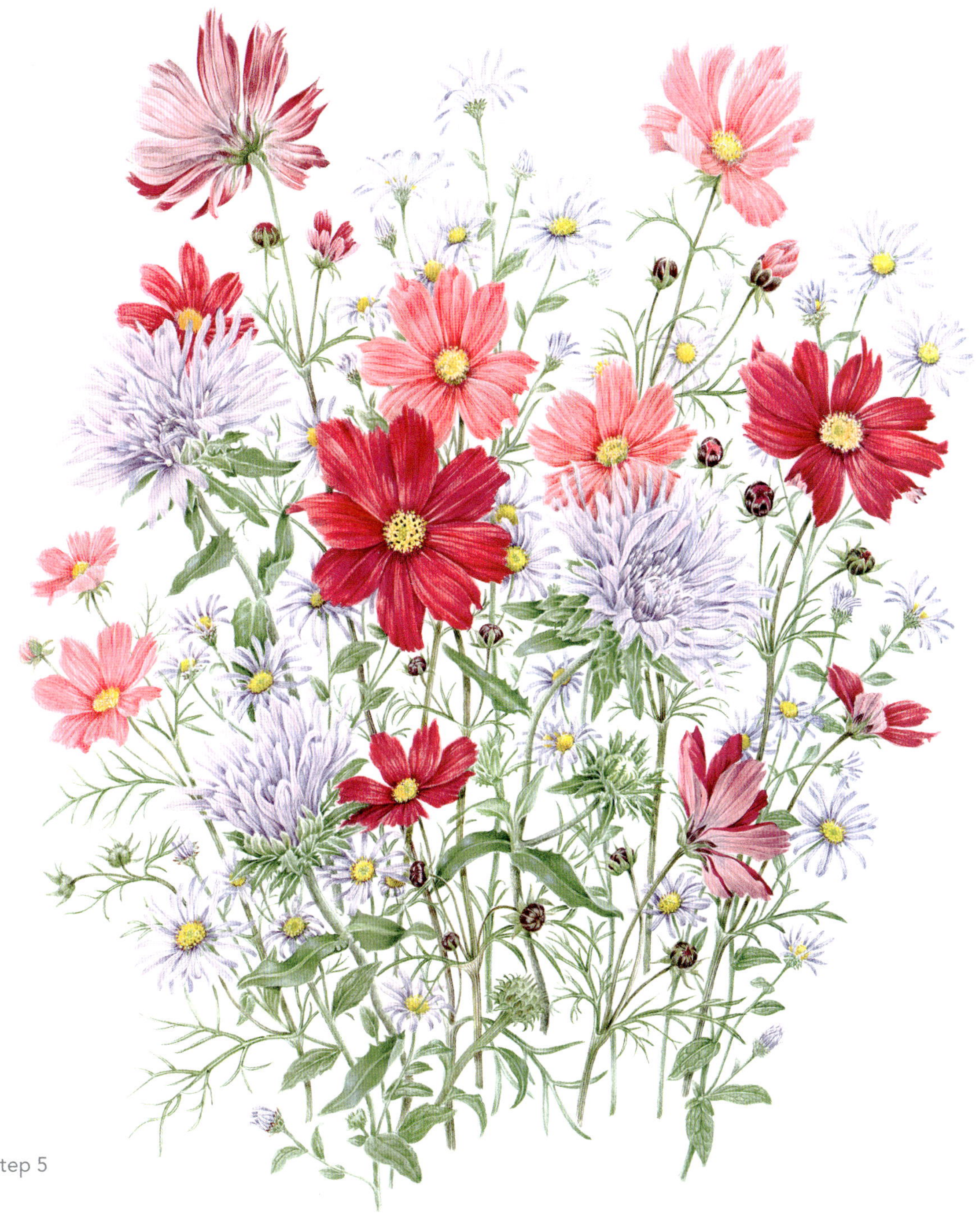

Step 5

CHAPTER 8

Fruit and Vegetables

My grandfather died before I was born, but as a child I remember seeing a postcard he had received sometime around the turn of the 19th and 20th centuries from Suttons the seed suppliers. At that time he was a gardener at the Royal Agricultural College, Cirencester, now a university. I was enthralled by the picture of beautiful velvety pansies, rich purple and yellow, such as I had never seen in real life. Long before the days of easily achieved colour photography, it is hard to imagine just how eye-catching such an image would have been and only an artist would have been able to capture it. So not only flowers but fruit and vegetables depended on such talent.

Sadly those days have gone as modern technology replaces human endeavour and rarely are commissions forthcoming. Fortunately that does not stop the dedicated artist from seeing the beauty apparent in often the most commonplace thing and they will seek inspiration in the greenhouse or on the market stall. Apart from colour there is the added attraction of a wide range of textures to represent and sometimes the resulting painting can be a breathtaking surprise. I hope the examples here and in the Gallery section (see page 142) will encourage more people to look beyond the obvious flower borders and make for the allotment or vegetable patch.

RIGHT *Cucumis sativus* (Cucumber) | Diane Marshall | Watercolour on paper
This painting formed part of Diane's Diploma Portfolio when she took Course 11 and showed great skill in representing the texture of the cucumber peel. Of particular interest to me was the way that, although she clearly shows this part of the vine in isolation, the lack of studio-style light (that is, religiously from the top left), suggests it is hanging in the greenhouse where it is subject to shading from other vines. This is an area of realism that is so often ignored by judges and its absence tends to lead to sterile work where the spirit of the plant and its habitat are lost.

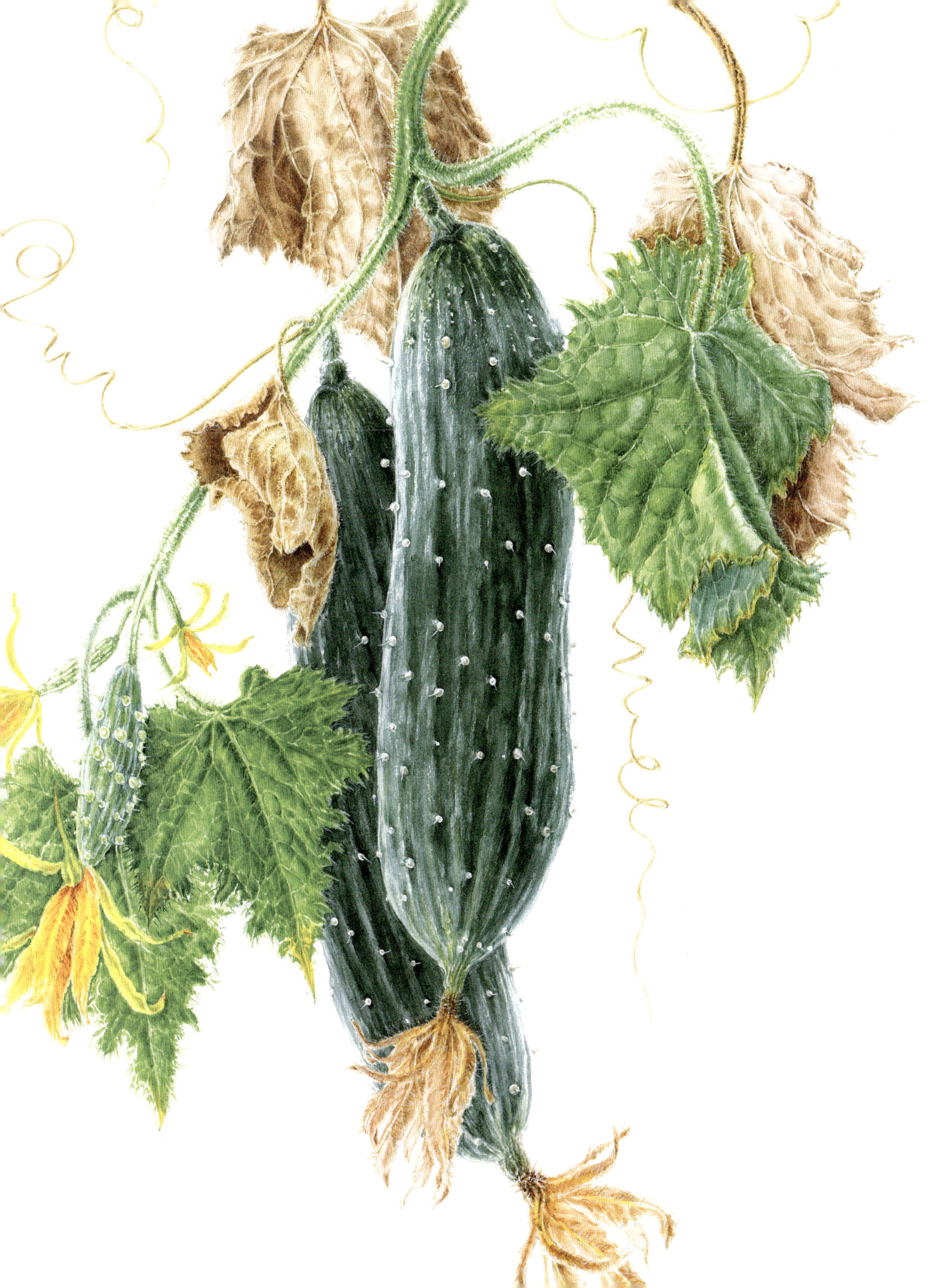

Two Red Onions

DIANNE FRANK | Coloured pencil on paper

These onions are eye-wateringly good, with beautifully blended highlights and
perfectly textured papery skin. Note also the way the roots are displayed showing
depth so that they do not hang like a fringe from the bottom of the bulb – a
common fault that totally destroys the illusion of a three-dimensional image.

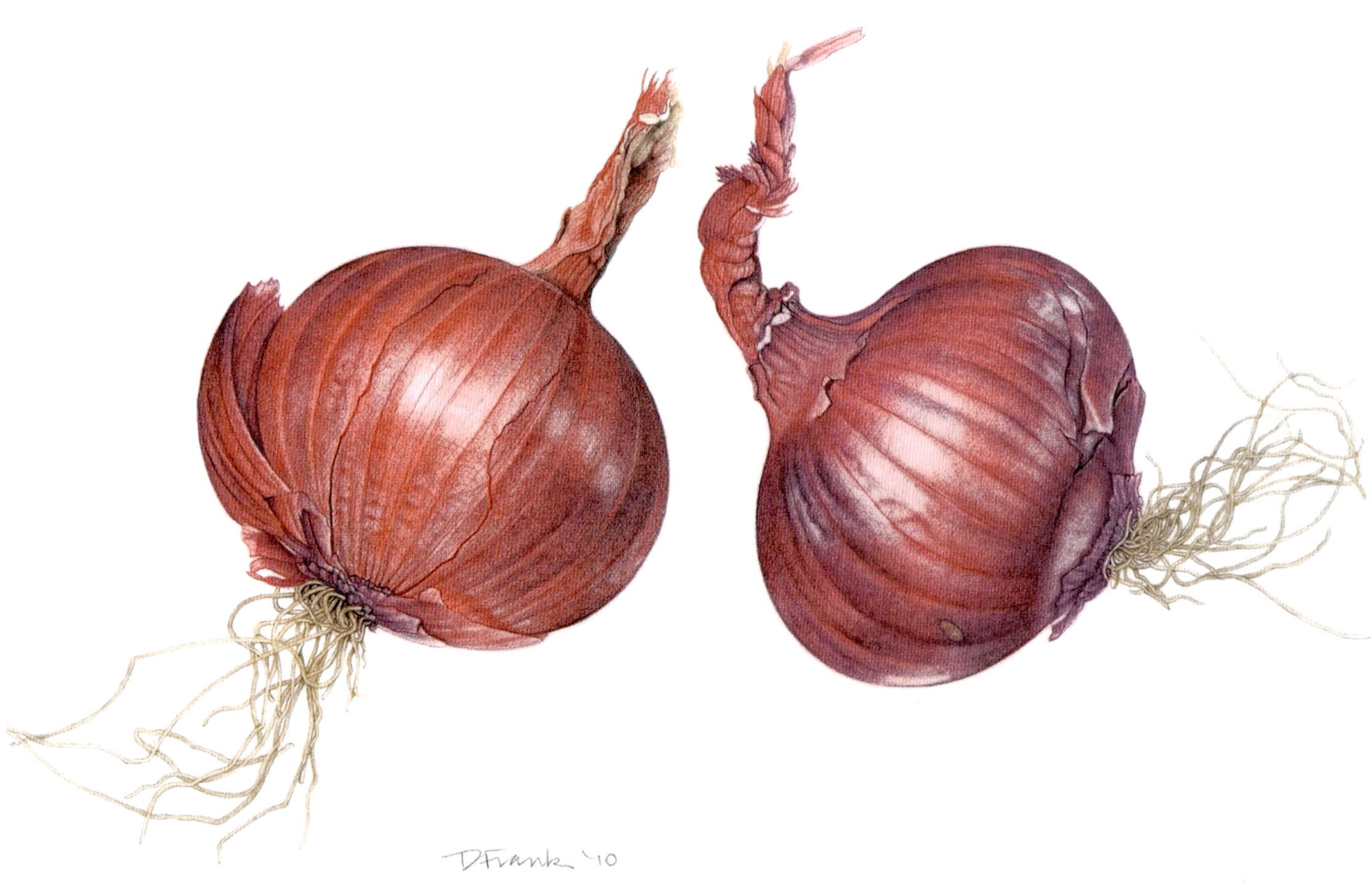

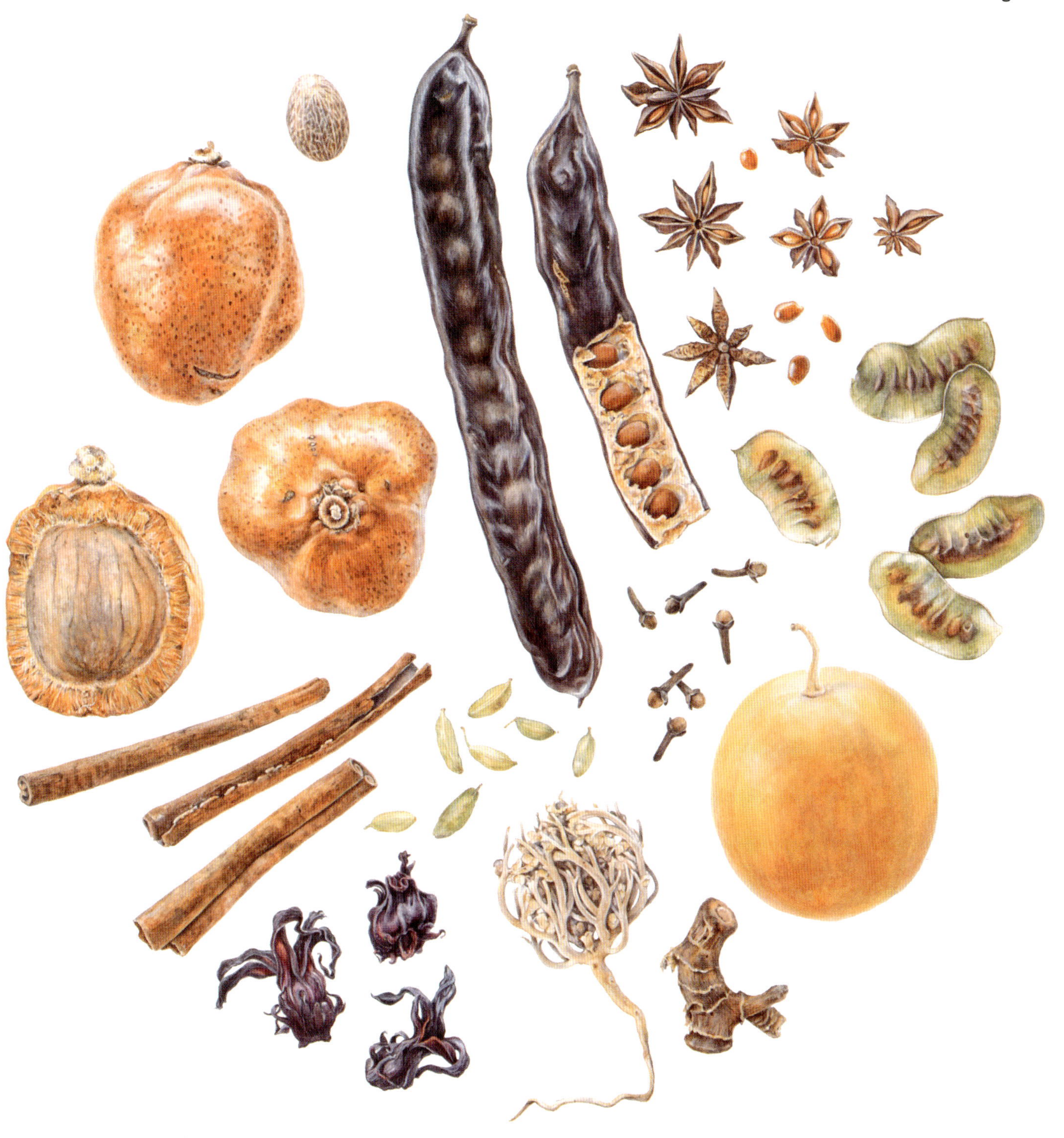

Seeds and Spices

SHEVAUN DOHERTY | Watercolour on paper

The colour and perfume of spice-sellers' stalls were
familiar to Shevaun when she lived in Cairo and she
could not resist painting this wheel, including cardamom
and cloves, anise and cinnamon, to name but a few.

Squash

KAY REES-DAVIES | Watercolour on paper

Rather ugly vegetables also have an appeal (although to be exact, squash are actually fruit). This seriously disfigured squash caught Kay's eye and she tackled it in a way that would not necessarily be the most obvious as one might be inclined to start with a yellow wash over all. In fact she first drew in the green stripes with a brush using a very pale green, and on to the stripes she drew each 'wart'. It was important to show the tone on these so they were painted in a darker green. She then painted the whole length of each stripe making sure the highlights on each 'wart' were retained.

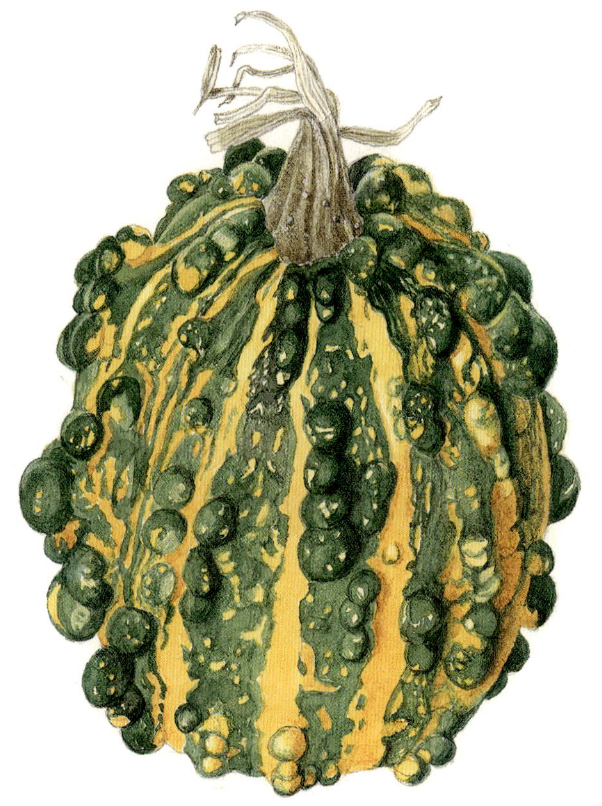

When the green areas were completed she added the yellow together with any visible markings. To complete the warts she blended the dark green into the pale areas. Finally, she emphasized all the tonal values, strengthening any which needed it and making sure each 'wart' cast a shadow. Markings on the actual stripes were put in at the very end.

It is important to realize that every artist develops their own way of working and with experience built up over many years comes a knowledge of what can or can't be done. I would never recommend a beginner to attempt such a complicated specimen as it is likely to lead to disappointment. Too often I have seen students tackle something that is beyond their present capabilities and this can be off-putting, so the advice is, be patient and let the passage of time and practice work their magic on your skills.

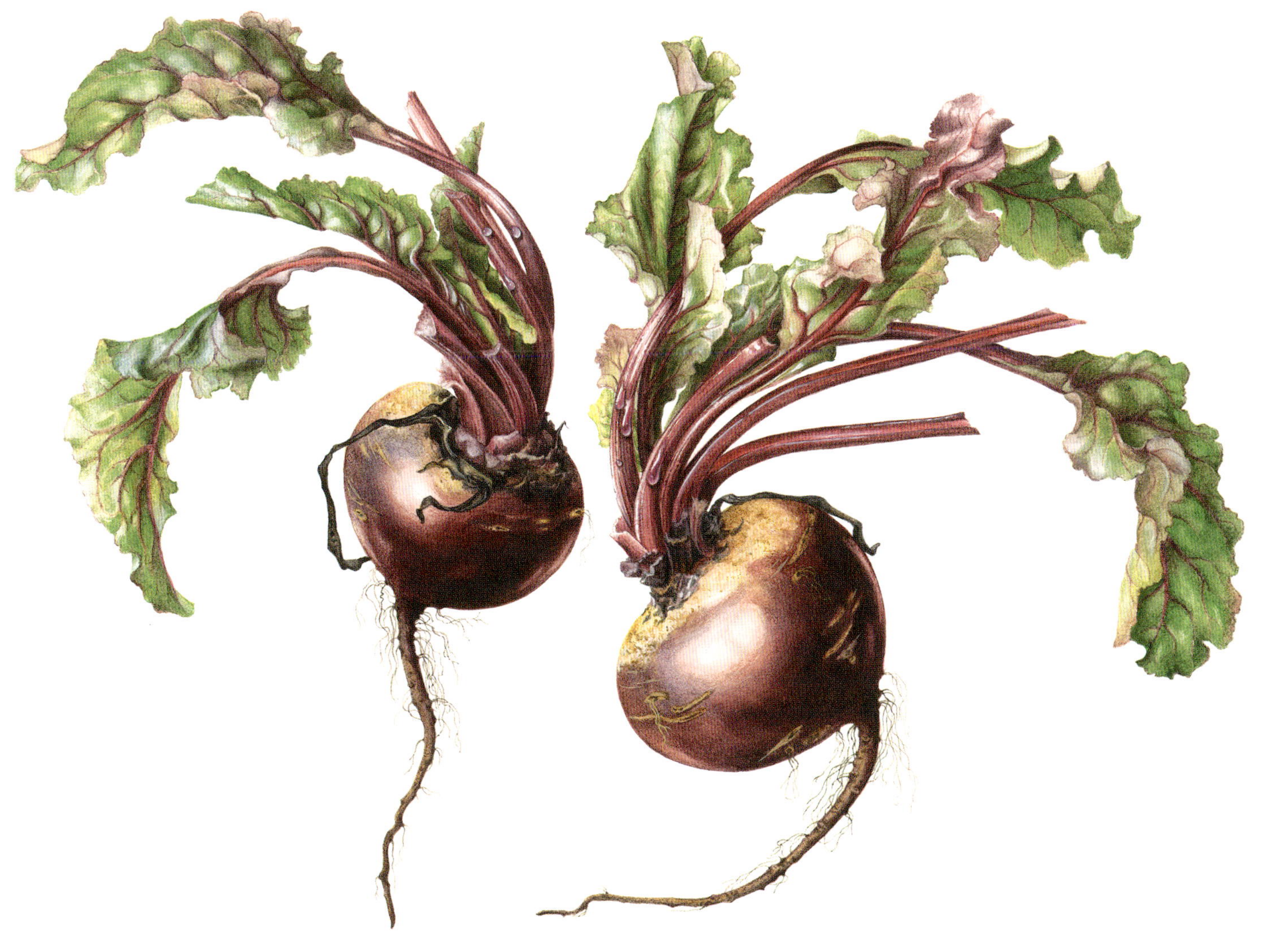

Beetroot

SUNANDA WIDEL | Watercolour on paper

I would never have expected to be deeply moved by
two beetroot, but I actually feel privileged to have seen
the original in this case. A conversation piece, a balletic
movement on stage, a flirtation – the composition allows for
many interpretations. Above all, the painting technique is
exquisite; from the texture on the globes, to the hairs on the
roots and the leaf venation, it is faultless.

William Pears

DIANNE FRANK | Coloured pencil on paper

Also from Dianne, a former DLDC student, we have this stunning representation of the humble pear. The stomata (cells of the skin), the slight bruising which so easily occurs, the ruddy glow of ripeness all are shown to perfection. For me the outstanding element is the cut section showing what happens if you do not drop the cut fruit in lemon and water immediately! The discoloration is photographically shown and the only thing missing is the taste.

Runner Bean Seeds

SALLY JANE PERRIN | Watercolour on paper

Sally has always shown an outstanding knack for choosing things that are often overlooked, and over the years we have marvelled at the intricacy of a feather, or a curled leaf set in a small painting of found objects. Here she has focused on bean seeds just ripe for planting, the crisp pod holding the promise of many highly nutritional meals. The pendant-style composition adds another layer of attraction and the gentle cast shadows create a truly three-dimensional work.

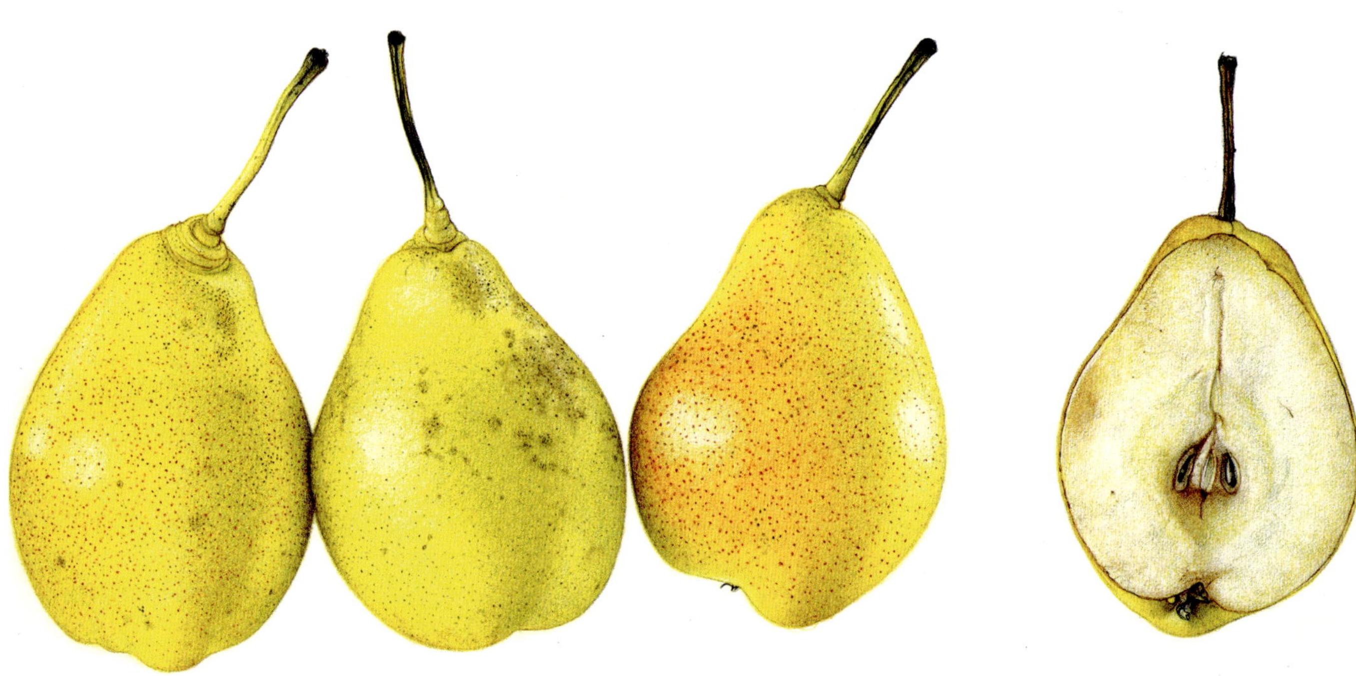

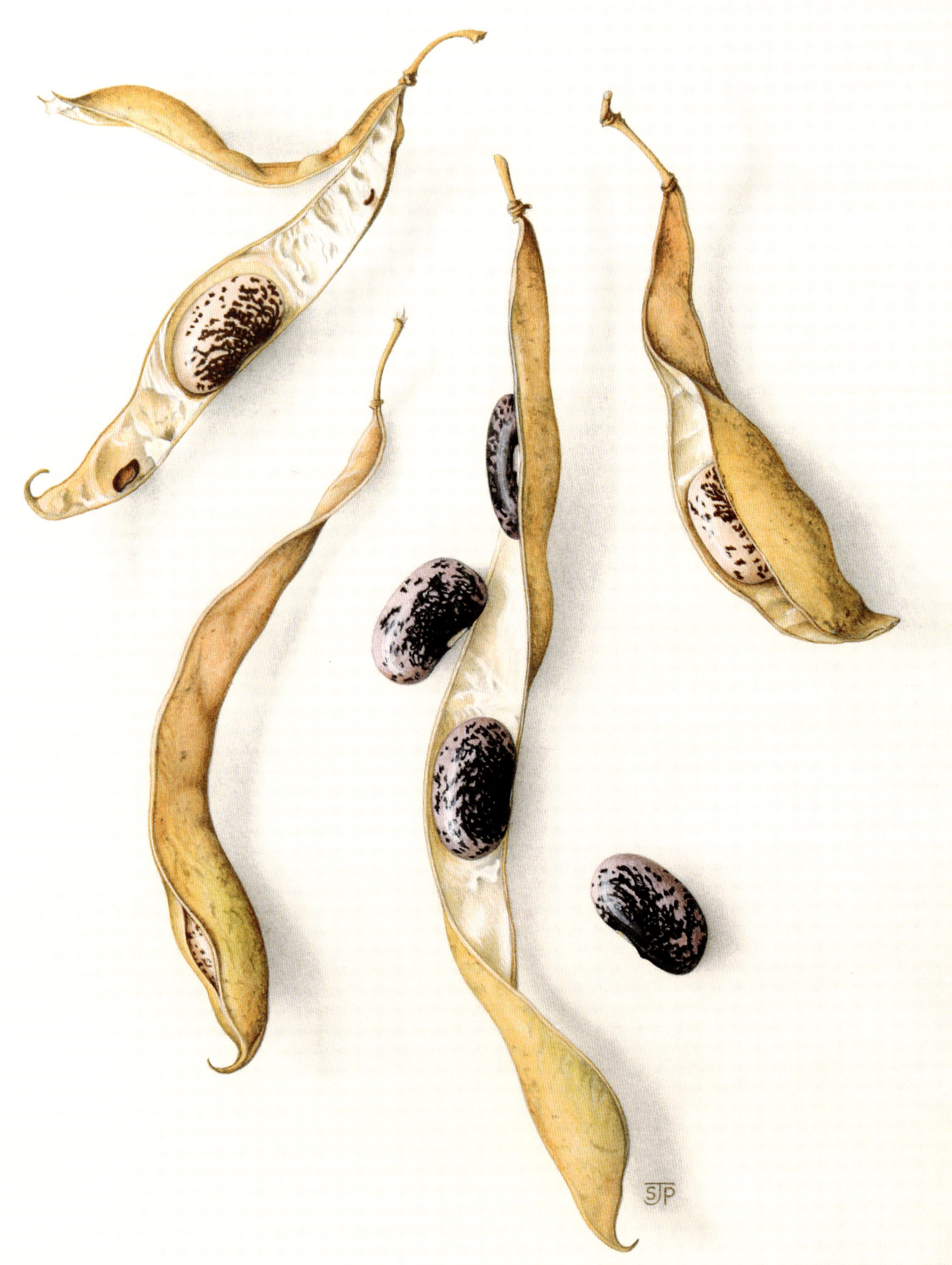

CHAPTER 9

The Great Outdoors

From its foundation the SBA was intended to be a broad church, bringing in members whose work would add interest to each exhibition, provided it showcased talent, skill, dedication and an accurate portrayal of the wonderful plant kingdom. This of course includes habitat and the most obvious area is the garden. Sadly, these days there are few garden painters of note, such as Helen Allingham, whose evocative pictures of Kent cottages and gardens conjure up unrealistic ideas of an earthly paradise, but nevertheless give a good idea of the flowers and vegetables available to the common man. From cabbages to lilies and sweet william, all are recognizable even when painted on a small scale. However, one of today's most respected garden painters is Margaret Eggleston, and the step-by-step of her work on page 120 shows you how to tackle a complex scene.

Working from shadows to full colour in the manner of a Renaissance painter is made possible with watercolour by the use of masking fluid. Photographs can be adapted to improve composition, something Helen Allingham would have surely welcomed as she had to rely on props in her studio – so why not sort through photographs taken on a garden visit and try your hand at something different? It would be an engrossing and cheerful thing to do on a dull winter's day and interest in botanical art does not need to be deadly serious all the time. In fact, I worry when students start to become too anxious about their work, full of self-doubt and angst. Nothing will inhibit development more, so my message here is to relax, never take yourself too seriously and above all enjoy your painting!

RIGHT Flowers from the Gulf of Finland | Marina Protsenko | Watercolour and graphite on paper
St Petersburg artist Marina Protsenko has set brilliant, glowing colours against a gentle sketch of this northern shore. She has handled the paint beautifully, capturing both detail and texture, particularly the leathery leaves and silky petals of the rose. Notice how each leaf has been given its own individuality with the play of light contributing to its form, so that what could have been just a green mass now demands attention.

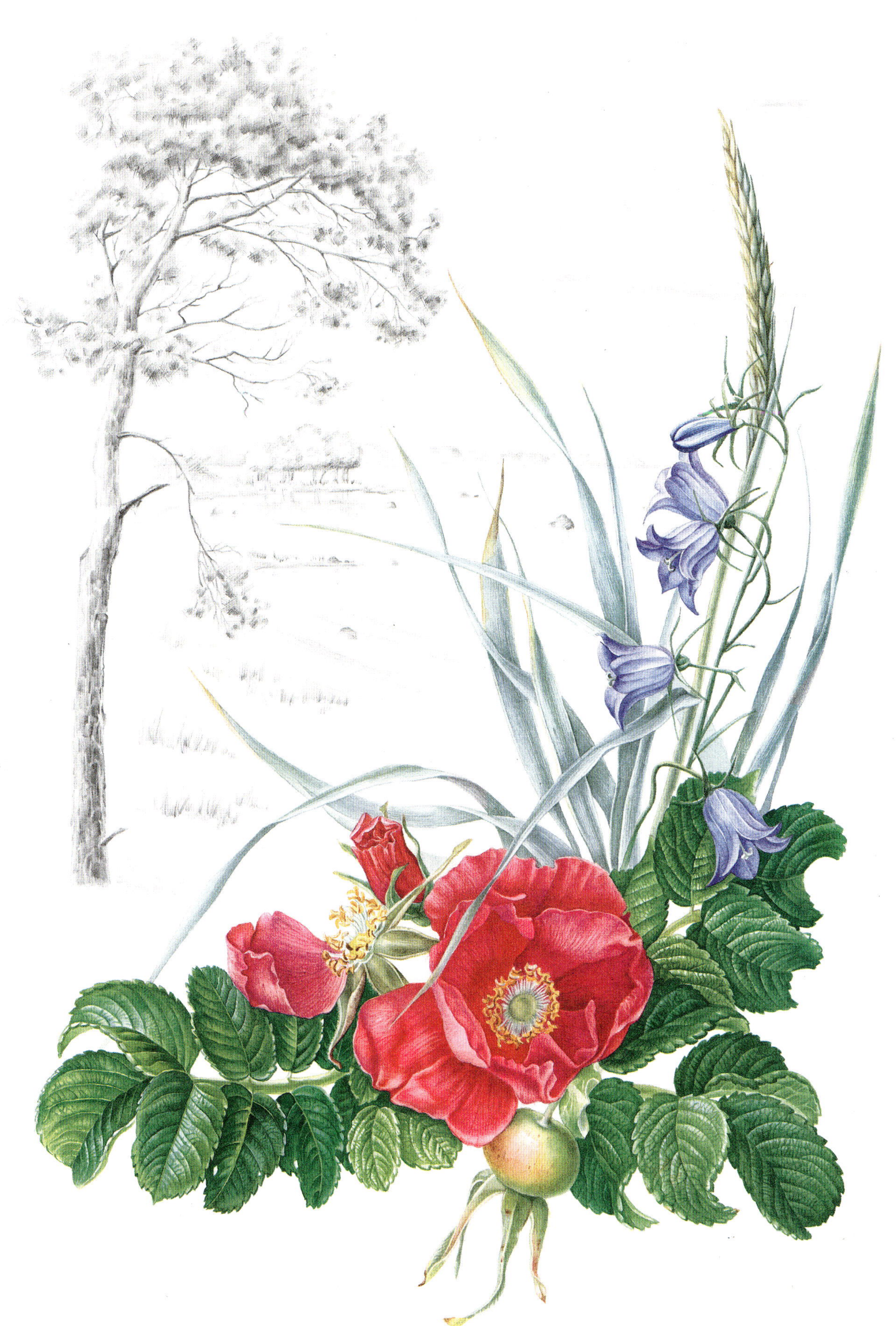

Step-by-Step

STEP 1

Based on her original photograph, Margaret drew a simple but accurate outline, with the plant pots in the foreground contrasting with the curve of the lawn beyond to create a pleasing composition. She applied masking fluid to the highlighted areas using either a pen or brush.

STEP 2

She then prepared diluted washes of Raw Sienna, Cobalt Blue and French Ultramarine before wetting the whole paper surface with clear water and applying Raw Sienna to the sky just above the tree line, French Ultramarine at the very top and Cobalt Blue in between, adding a little clear water (not too wet) in places to give a cloud effect. Next she prepared two dilute washes of Burnt Sienna mixed with Lemon Yellow, adding a small amount of Payne's Grey to one to make a darker wash that she applied to the trees and shadows. It was important that this wash was not wetter than the water already on the paper.

Materials required:

PAINTS:

* Winsor & Newton Artists' watercolours in Raw Sienna, Cobalt Blue, French Ultramarine, Burnt Sienna, Lemon Yellow, Payne's Grey, Quinacridone Gold, Permanent Rose, Carmine, Cadmium Red, Cadmium Red Deep. Designers' Gouache in Permanent White.

BRUSHES:

* Rosemary & Co size 0 mop, series 109. Kolinsky sable squirrel mop 10/0 series 1, pointed round pure squirrel size 2, series 42. Derwent small comb brush and Derwent small flat brush. SAA blue masking fluid, a ruling pen and a masking fluid brush.

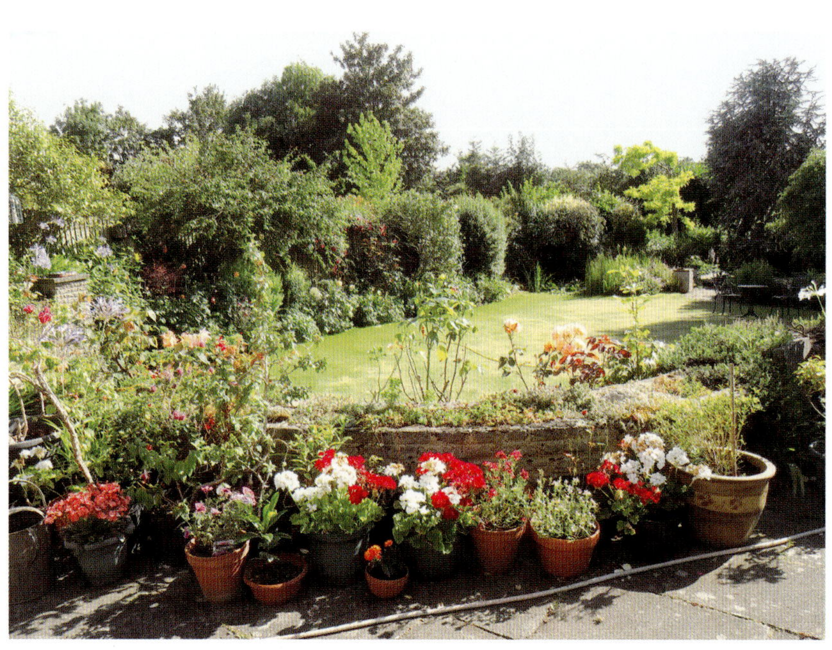

Step 1

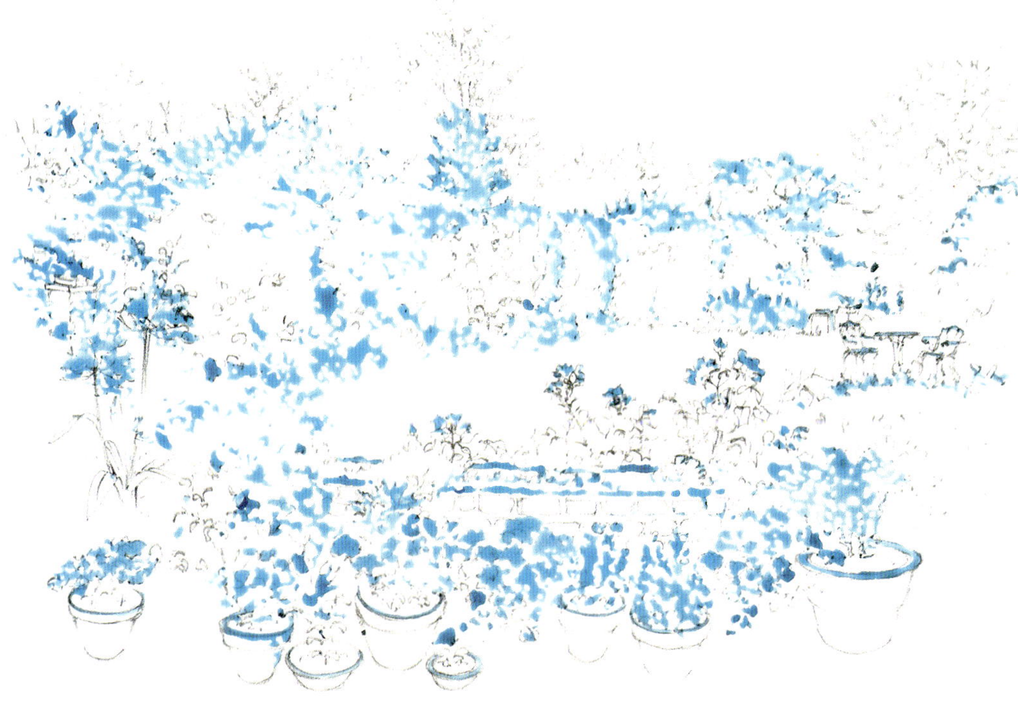

Step 2

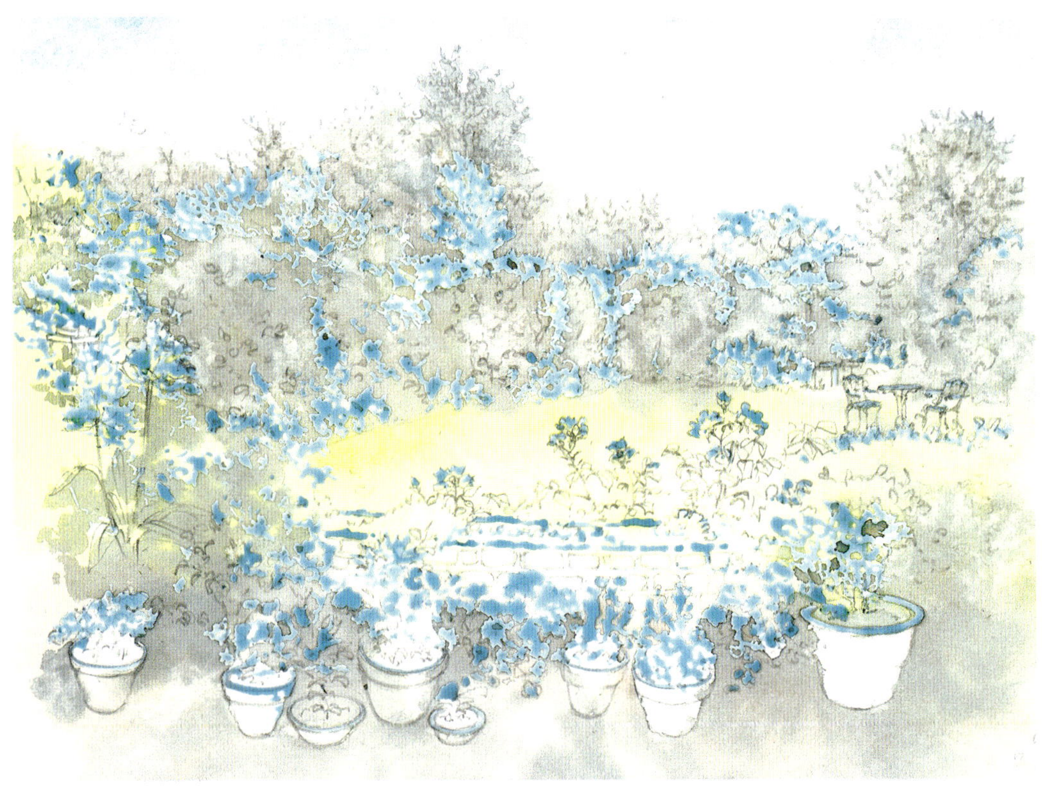

Margaret then mixed a stronger wash of Burnt Sienna and
Payne's Grey and added this to the shadows around the
plant pots, making it weaker towards the front. She painted
a dilute wash of Burnt Sienna on the wall, blending it into
the shadows before leaving it to dry naturally.

Step 3

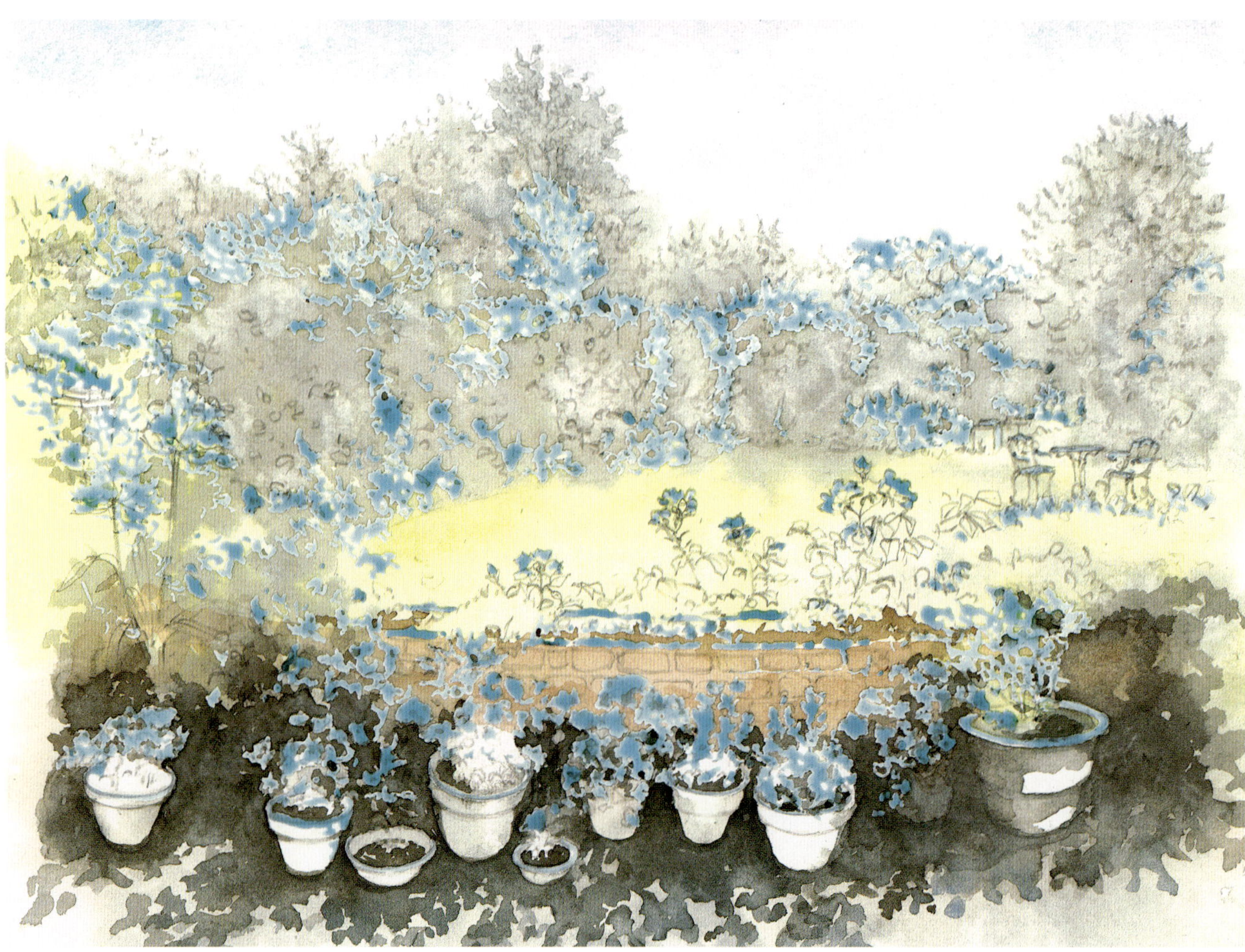

STEP 4

Using a small round brush, or a comb brush on its side, Margaret painted the trees at the back using a semi-dry mix of Burnt Sienna and Payne's Grey, making them gradually weaker, paler and more blue as they receded. She added Quinacridone Gold or more Burnt Sienna to the same wash for the nearer plants and leaves, making them stronger, darker and more yellow in the foreground. She carefully washed away some shadow from the pot on the extreme right, blotting it dry with a tissue, the better to reveal its shape.

Step 4

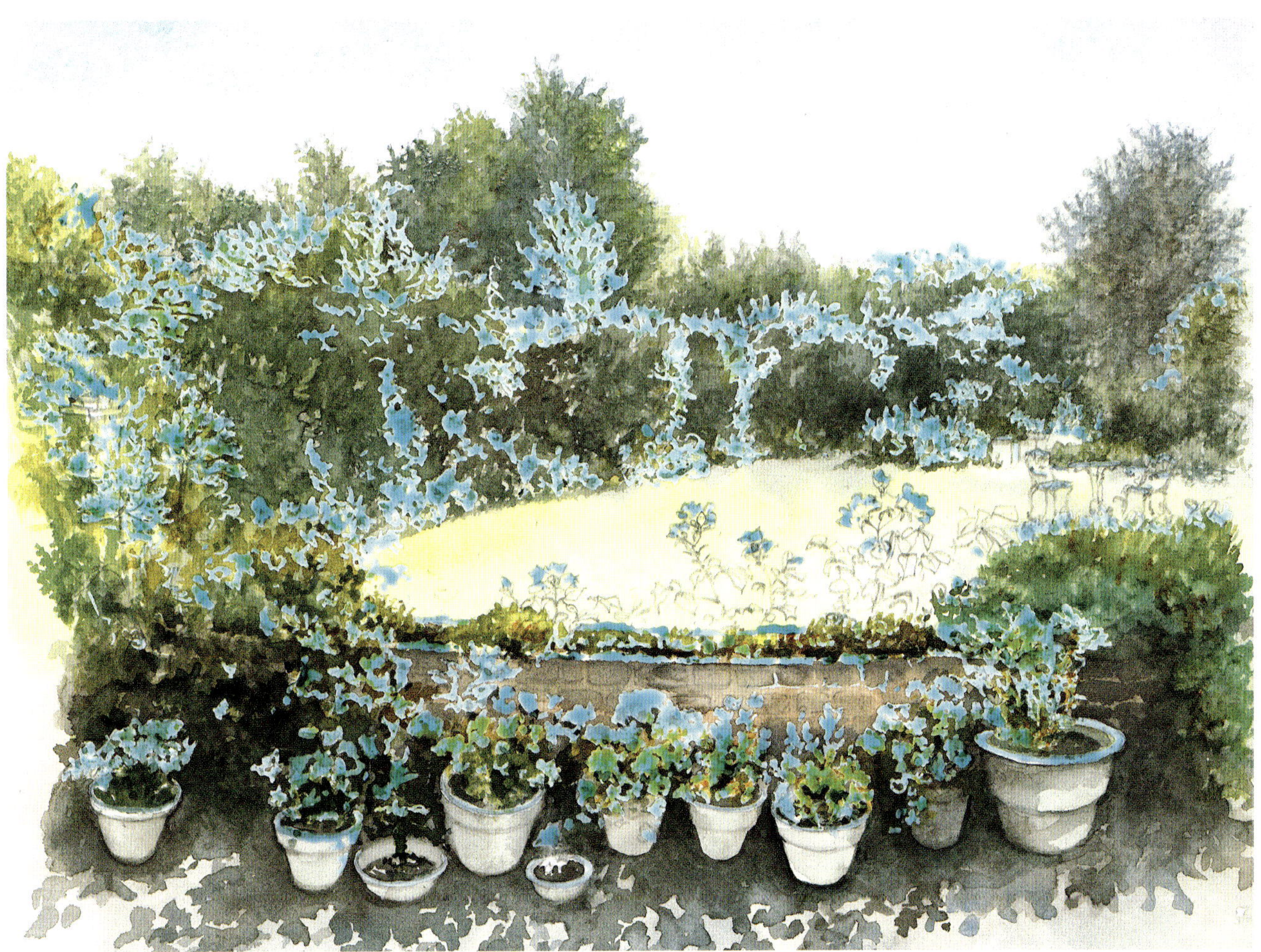

Next, Margaret removed the masking fluid and, using the same flat brush, painted the lighter leaves on the trees and bushes with Lemon Yellow and Quinacridone Gold, blending them, while still wet, with Cobalt Blue into the shadowed sides. She painted over part of the right-hand side of the lawn with this shadow colour. The next stage was to bring the painting alive with added colour. For the roses she used Permanent Rose or Carmine with small touches of weak Lemon Yellow while still wet. For the rose leaves she mixed Quinacridone Gold with a little Payne's Grey and Cadmium Red Deep. The zonal and regal pelargoniums in the pots were painted with a stronger mix of Permanent Rose, Cadmium Red or Carmine, leaving a thin edge of dry white paper on the right of each flower. For the petals in shadow she used a little Cobalt or Cadmium Red Deep.

The tall agapanthus on the left required various mixes of Cobalt, French Ultramarine and a little Permanent Rose, and for the surrounding foliage Margaret made a mix of Lemon Yellow, Cobalt, Quinacridone Gold and Burnt Sienna. Some of the pots were painted with weak Burnt Sienna and a little Payne's Grey for the shadows while still wet. A mix of French Ultramarine with a little Burnt Sienna was ideal for the blue-toned pots, strengthened for shaded areas. Margaret left the rims pale as they caught the light. She could have finished the picture at this point if she had desired a looser, more impressionistic effect, but that was not her intention.

Step 5

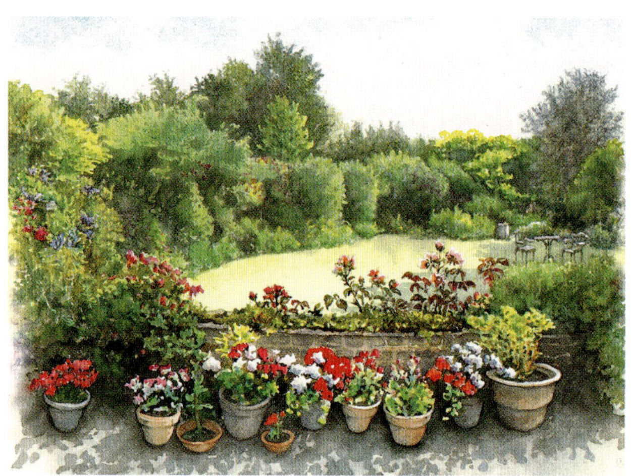

Step 6

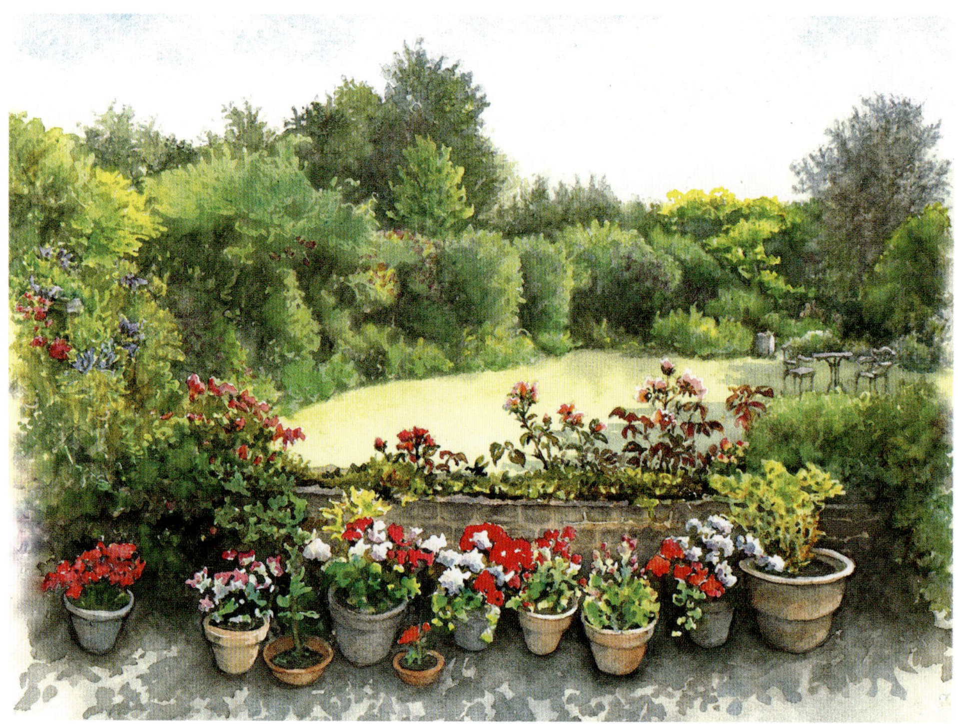

STEP 6

Finally, Margaret extended the foliage on either side of the painting with the same colours to widen the composition. She used a flat brush and a tissue to remove some of the shadow colour on the left, which enabled her to add another blue pot of pale blue flowers that lightened that corner. She mixed Permanent White gouache with water to the consistency of double cream, making it thickly opaque, applied it to the highlights on the roses and the flowers in pots and allowed it to dry. She was then able to paint over the gouache with dilute watercolour in accordance with the colour of each flower, blending it into the original darker tone and leaving a small white edge on the right. This made each flower appear almost three-dimensional in the sunshine.

Step 7

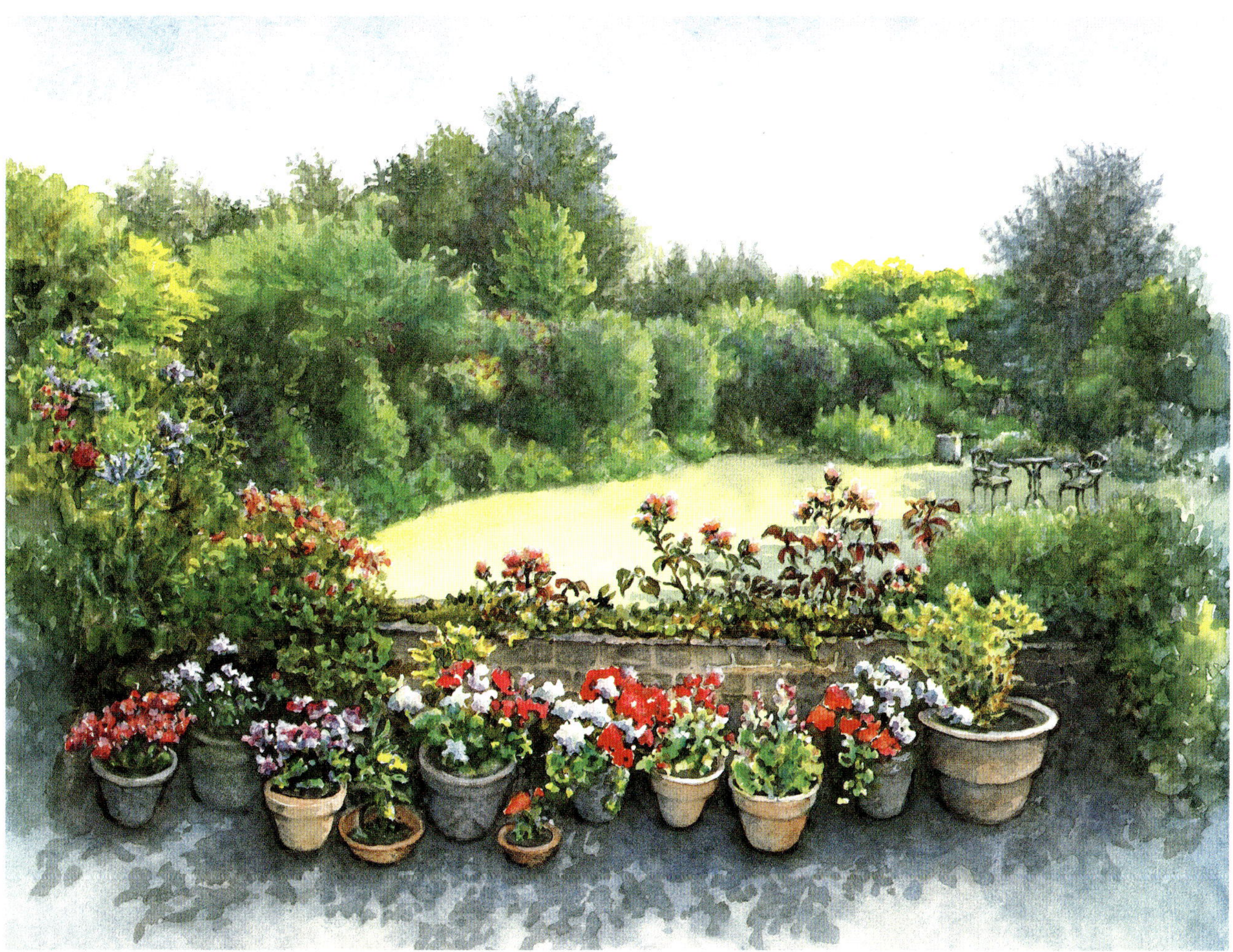

Exbury Gardens, Hampshire

MARION PERKINS | Egg tempera on paper

Famed for their magnificent displays of rhododendrons and azaleas, these gardens also showcase other spectacular plants such as this *Gunnera manicata*, which gave Marion the focal point for her composition. Here she describes how she approached this very challenging subject.
'I visited these beautiful gardens in early summer when they were just bursting into life. There was a slight mist beyond the trees and the high sun reflected on the damp, glaucous leaves of the *Gunnera manicata*, rendering them silvery-white at their tips. I sat down and started to draw with a B pencil in my sketchpad to plan the composition and to give precedence to the gunnera and vegetation at my feet. I also took some photos to capture the light, the colours and the close details, which I knew I would need for reference when painting the intricate foreground.

'Back in my studio, I transferred the sketch to Sennelier Hot Pressed watercolour paper. Once I was happy with the plan I started painting the sky and hazy background trees with a size 3 brush and worked forward using soft subtle colours; Cobalt Blue, Lemon Yellow, Rose Madder, and Potters Pink. I used Cerulean Blue with Cobalt for the gunnera and glazed a light Lemon Yellow on the leaves where the sun shone through them. Changing to smaller brushes, I worked my way through the foreground foliage, constantly assessing the tonal values as the sunlight illuminated the surfaces. My aim was to recapture the moments spent absorbing the beauty of the garden and marvelling at the abundance of nature at my feet. It was impossible to hurry the task but botanical painting does call for patience, careful consideration and a real love and fascination for the chosen subject.'

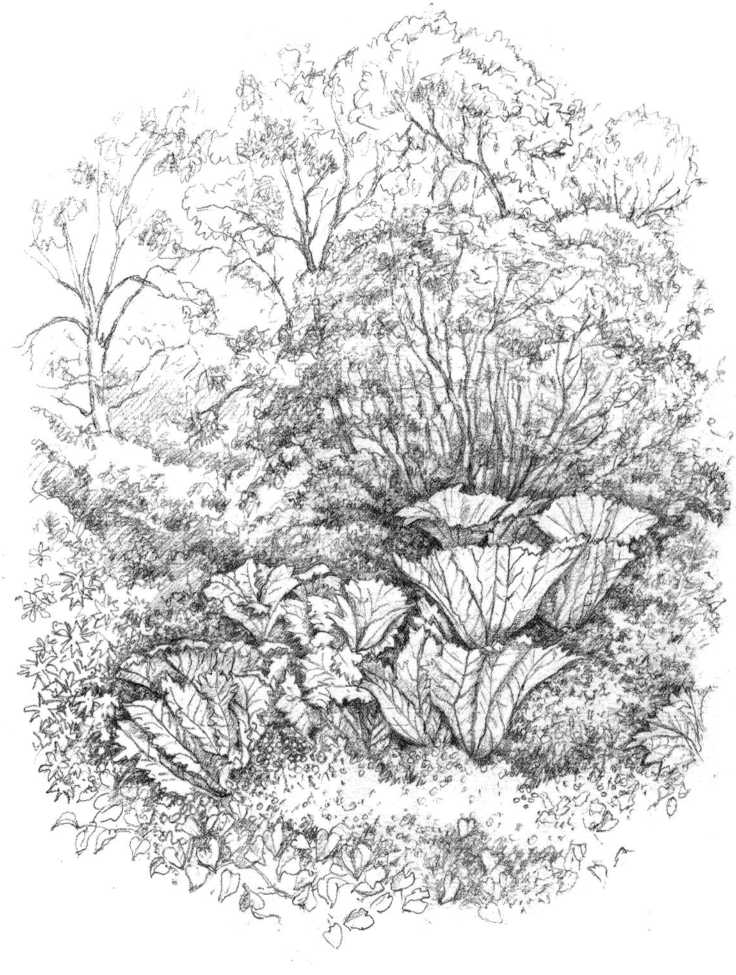

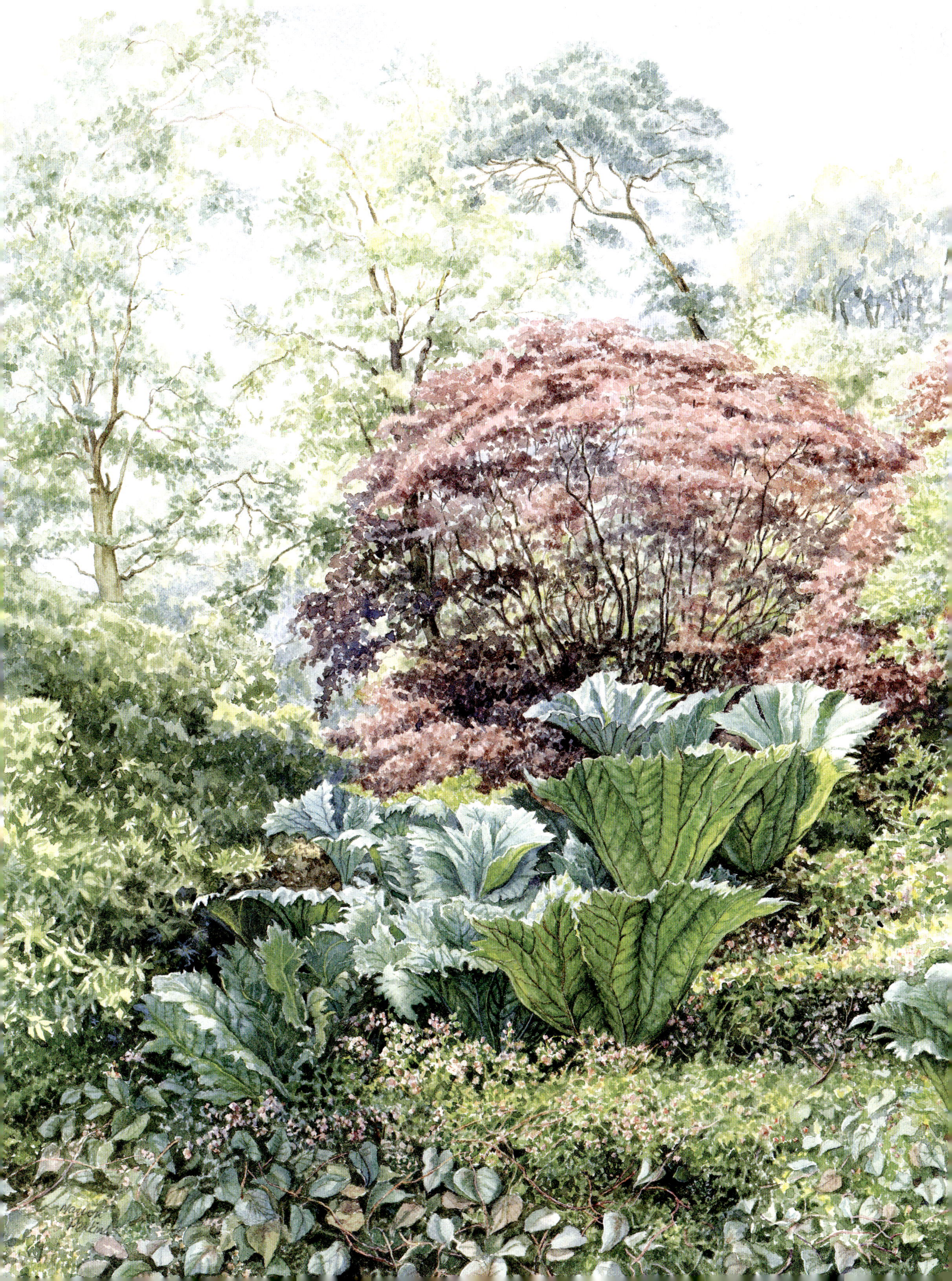

Giant Bamboo, Vergelegen Estate, South Africa

DOROTHY PAVEY | Watercolour on paper

Dorothy took a career change from teaching in 1994 and became a full-time painter. Five years later she became a member of the SBA because, in her own words, 'It maintains and encourages exacting standards in classical botanical work but also values other approaches while maintaining correct botanical content, so my interest in painting plants in their context of garden or natural habitat seems to fit comfortably with their aims.' Dorothy lives in the Cotswolds, but her travels take her further afield and provide inspiration for paintings such as this 46 x 35cm (18 x 14in) depiction of the giant bamboo. Using Winsor & Newton Artists' watercolours in Prussian Blue, Burnt Sienna, Yellow Ochre, Permanent Sap, Cadmium Lemon and Permanent Alizarin Crimson, she was able to capture the effect of sunlight falling across and filtering through this large stand of bamboo. She says, 'The light, or lack of it, causes the stems to merge into, or emerge from, the gloom of the thicket. As well as the light the differing age of the stems creates a variety of subtle colours. Sunlight falling on the earth adds contrast and grounds the scene. It also picks out a few sprays of bamboo leaves against the stems to add interesting detail and gives an indication of the scale of the whole.'

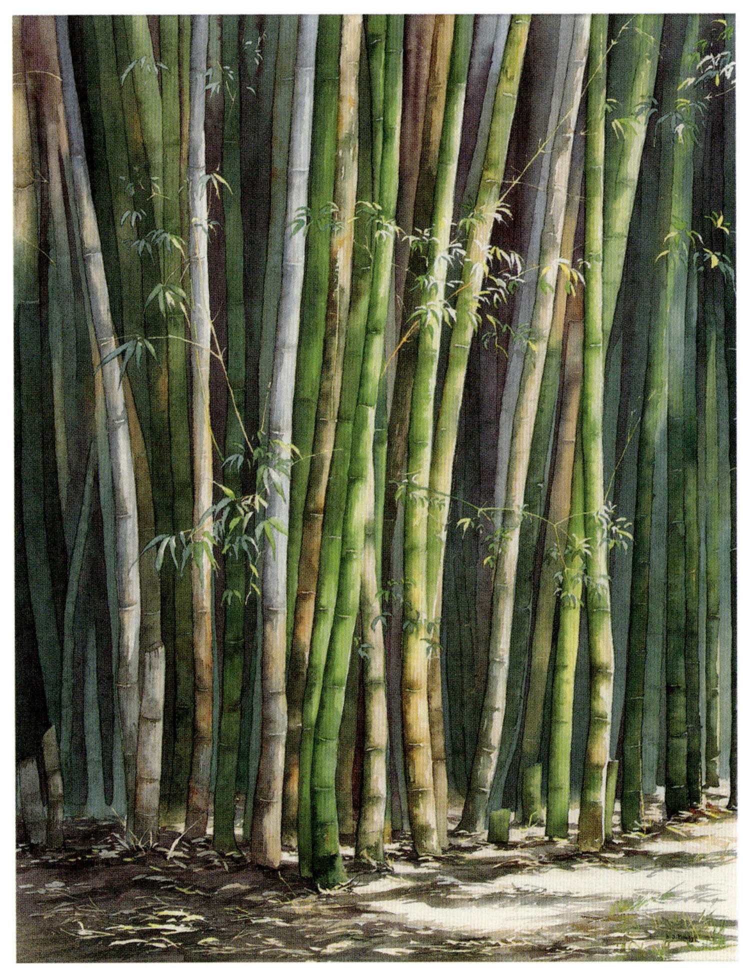

Greater Reedmace in Winter

ALISON PROCTER | Oil on canvas

In this painting Alison set out to capture not only the botanical features of the plant but also the atmosphere of the Somerset Levels in the south-west of England. Where the reedmace grows at the sides of the rhynes (pronounced reens), the local name for the drainage ditches that criss-cross the Levels, it creates an amazing pattern of straight lines and sharp angles, which she also wanted to show. Alison took a set of photographs that she printed in colour and in black and white too, which enabled her to fully appreciate the growth pattern and interlocking stems as they fell over.

Taking a small section at a time, she drew on the canvas, first in pencil then with a fine pen, until she was happy with the composition. The monochrome image helped to establish the dark areas which served to emphasize the stems caught in the light. For this reason it had been important to take the photographs in strong sunlight. Working in oil, Alison needed to build up each area with layers of thin paint, making sure the stems followed through in the right direction. Finally, she turned her attention to the water with its many reflections and the distant Malvern Hills. This is the first of several scenes of the area that she has painted over the years.

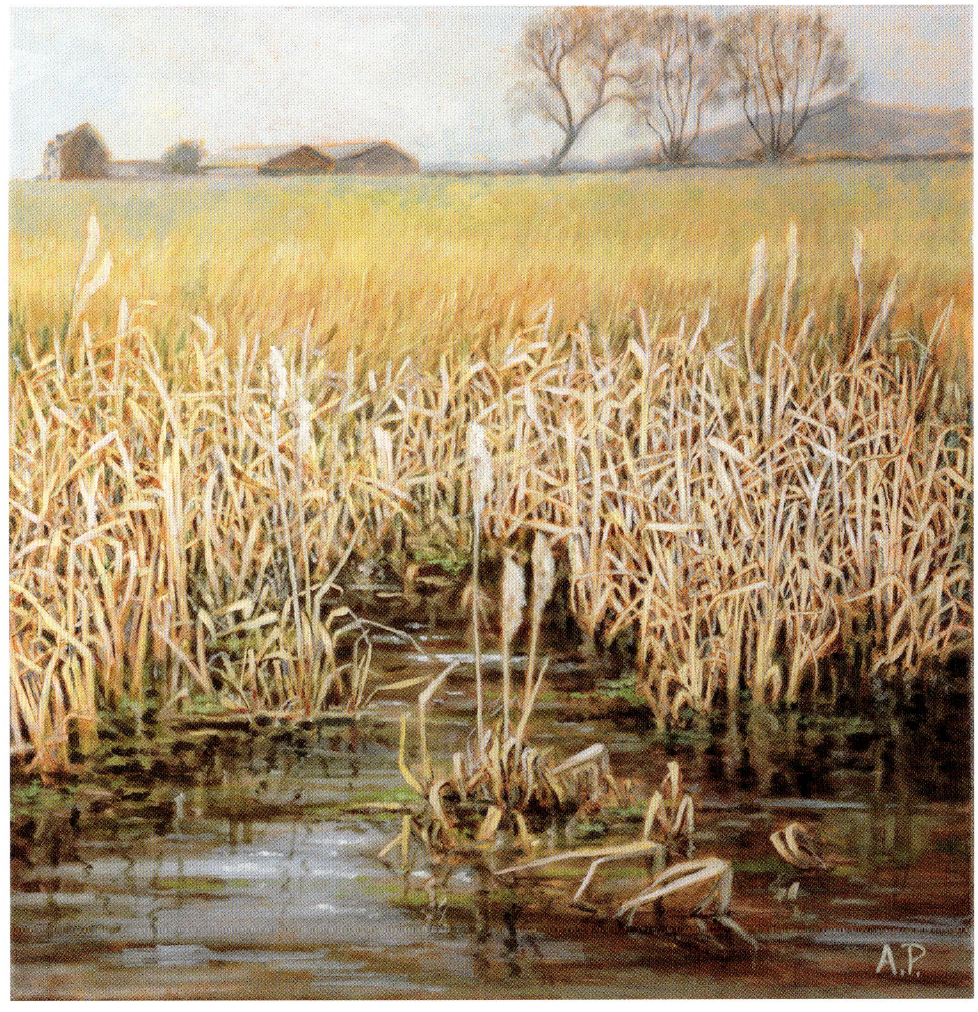

Bluebell Wood

IAN PETHERS | Ink and watercolour on paper

Ian's interest in art began at the age of 11, when he was given a set of oil paints that encouraged him to paint river and canal scenes in the Thames Valley. On leaving school he became a relief lock-keeper, which fuelled his interest further and led to many paintings along the river from source to estuary. Joining the SBA in 1989, he worked as an illustrator for a publishing house for some years and gradually became more interested in miniature painting, later joining the Royal Miniature Society. Now living on the Cornish border, Ian finds it a rich source of inspiration from countryside to coast.

For Bluebell Wood, Ian used a 0.1 waterproof fibre-tip drawing pen followed by washes of artists' quality watercolour. From his photographic reference material he pencilled a rough outline of horizon and main tree positions without going into too much detail. He tackled the lighter leaves first, using a gentle random scribble, then added the darker areas deeper in the forest, becoming darkest on the horizon to give contrast to the floral floor. He drew the bluebells in a repeat scribble 'language' which suggests individual blooms and foliage. He applied various greens in thin washes for the foliage and to get the right shade of blue for the flowers he blended ultramarine with a dash of violet.

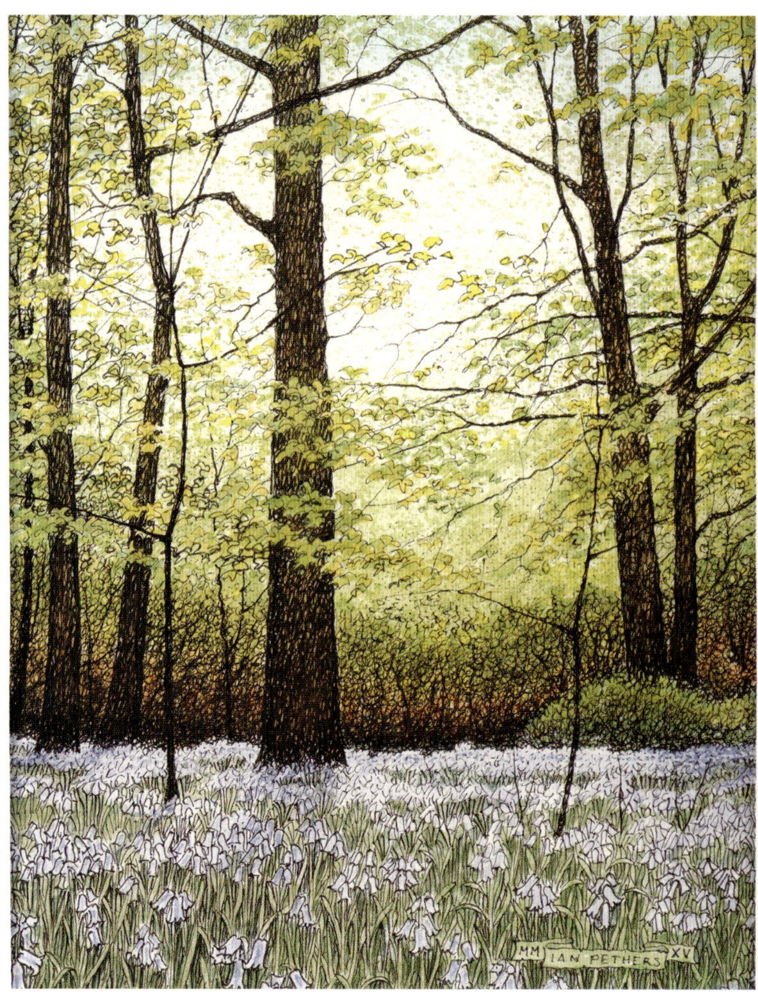

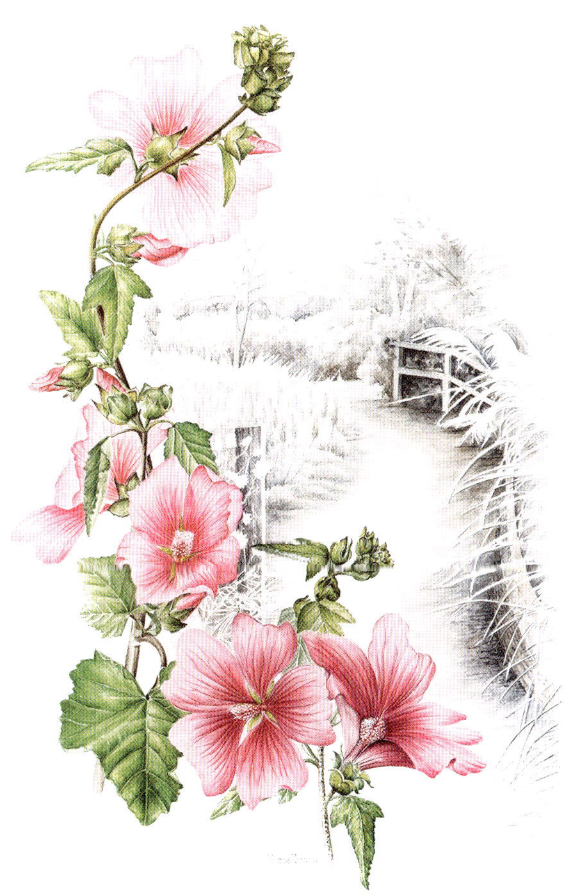

Lavatera

HAZEL RUSH | Watercolour on paper

Hazel submitted this as one of her DLDC assignments. As a landscape painter she was keen to find a way to combine this with her new-found interest in botanical painting, and here she merged the lavatera growing in her garden with a vignette from a study previously made at Pensthorpe Nature Park near Fakenham, Norfolk. This was a full-colour painting of part of the park's Millennium Garden, but in this piece she produced a monochrome or grisaille study as a foil for the colourful flowers, with the composition aided by her computer – a perfect blend of old and new technologies. The size is 45 x 60cm (17¾ x 23½in).

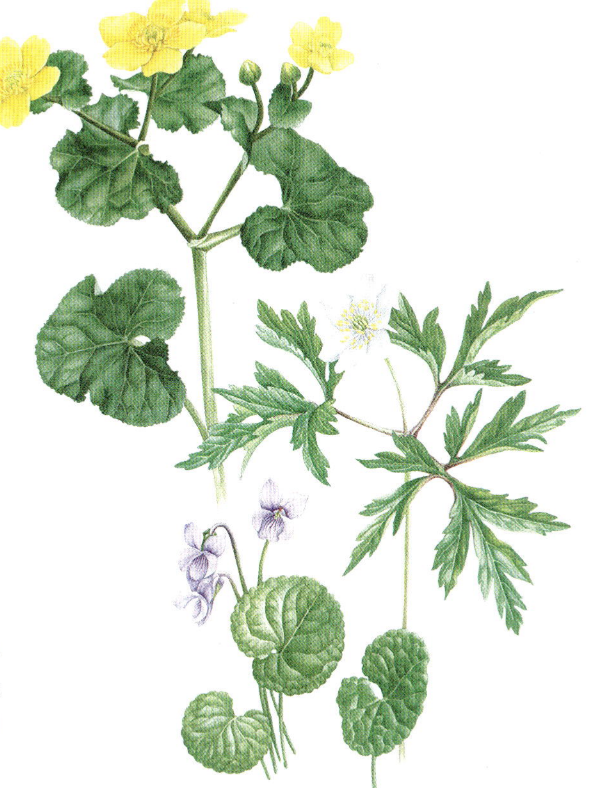

Wild Flowers from the Gulf of Finland – Wood Anemone, Marsh Marigold and Sand Violet (*Viola rupestris*)

MARINA PROTSENKO | Watercolour on paper

Green is always the colour that causes the most heartache, as there are so many shades in nature and many of them are very elusive when the artist tries to mix them. Viridian does not occur in nature but is a useful base when one is attempting to show bloom on a purple plum or grape. Climate and light undoubtedly affect the way we see colour and over the years I have realized that in Britain we often err towards a colour I call 'boiled cabbage green'. The clean, crisp light of the Baltic would no doubt encourage more of our students not to play it safe and to use stronger pigments – not necessarily right but understandable. Here Marina has painted some lovely venation, albeit rather vividly, and she has also captured the differing textures from the leathery marsh marigolds to the quilted viola leaves. Both the marigold and anemone flowers have exquisitely painted centres, in neither case an easy task but achievable with patience.

CHAPTER 10

Design and Inspiration

Towards the end of a course, students are asked to use their botanical skills in a more practical way. Some choose to produce something suitable for a greetings card, while others think of advertising material for a poster or tourist leaflet. It is always exciting to see examples of work which indicate that the student is not a 'one-trick pony', which is sadly often the label hung around the necks of botanical artists. So this section starts with examples of work by students and goes on to some thought-provoking work by members. I hope it will give the reader pause for thought in a positive way and perhaps lead to some exciting new paintings.

RIGHT A Mixed Posy | Kay Leeves | Watercolour on paper

This design – ideal for a greetings card – is composed of *Mathiasella bupleuroides* 'Green Dream', an unknown variety of *Delphinium*, *Astrantia* 'Buckland', *Nigella damascena*, *Dianthus carthusianorum*, *Erigeron* 'Charity', *Knautia macedonica* and *Argyranthemum* 'Aramis Red'. Reminiscent of the tussy-mussies of old, the flowers are in a seemingly carefree grouping, which is deceptive. Note the way the rosy-edged green flowers at the bottom flow through to link with the nigella seedheads, forming a ribbon of similar colour. The strongest rosy shades are more restricted to the centre of the composition, which helps to maintain the balance.

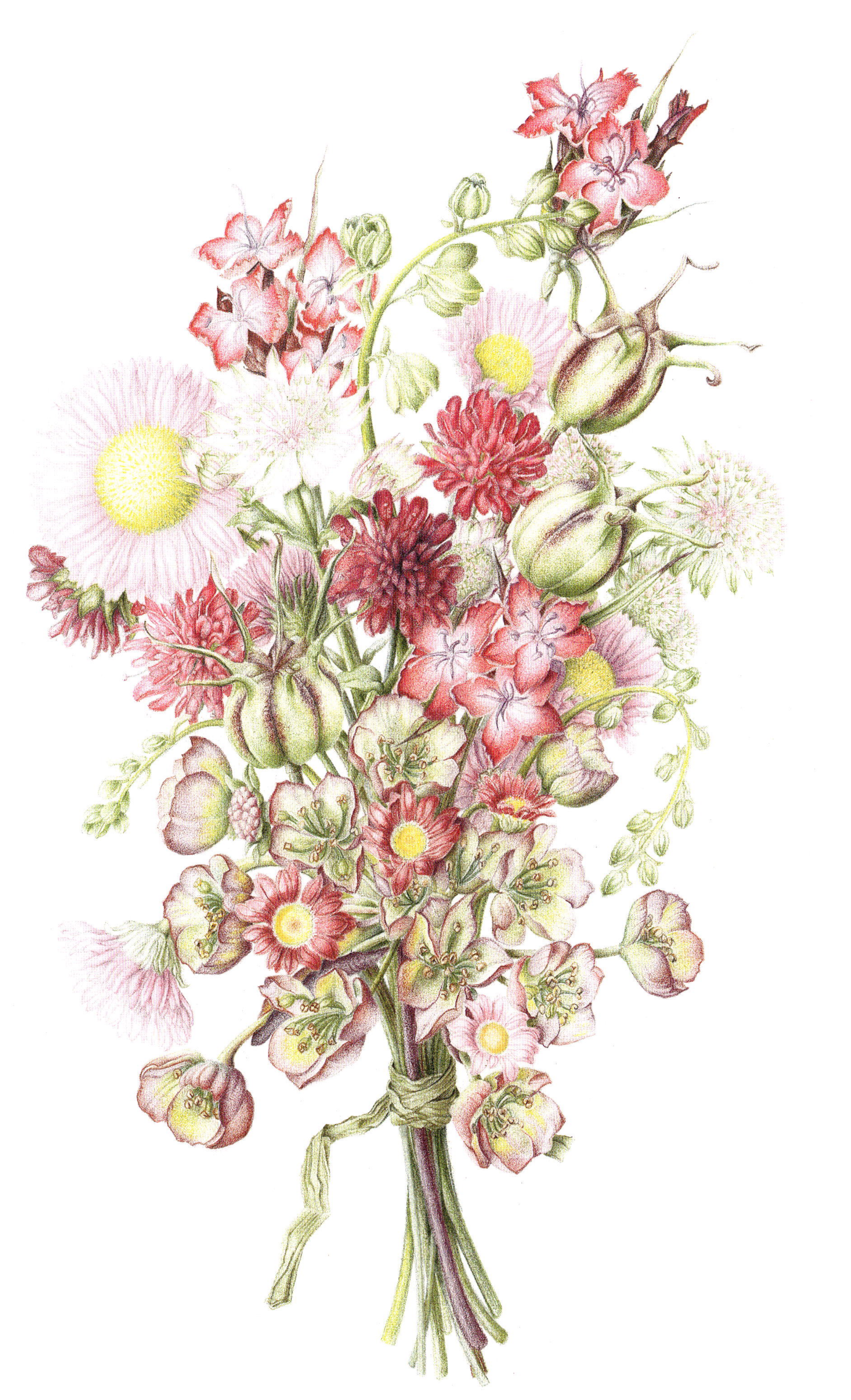

Sussex by the Sea

SUE FLYNN | Watercolour on paper

Sue chose to advertise somewhere she loves and to show the native flowers that thrive on the shingle beach. We ask that wording is given separately, just to give an idea of what the artist has in mind. Here Sue has shown *Echium vulgare* (viper's bugloss) *Glaucium flavum* (yellow horned poppy), *Erigeron glaucus* (beach aster), *Malva sylvestris* (common mallow) and *Crambe maritima* (sea kale). The bugloss was particularly well painted with the most delicate hairs on the stem, fine filaments against the blue flowers and some really detailed buds. The all-important bee and seagulls added life to an otherwise static scene.

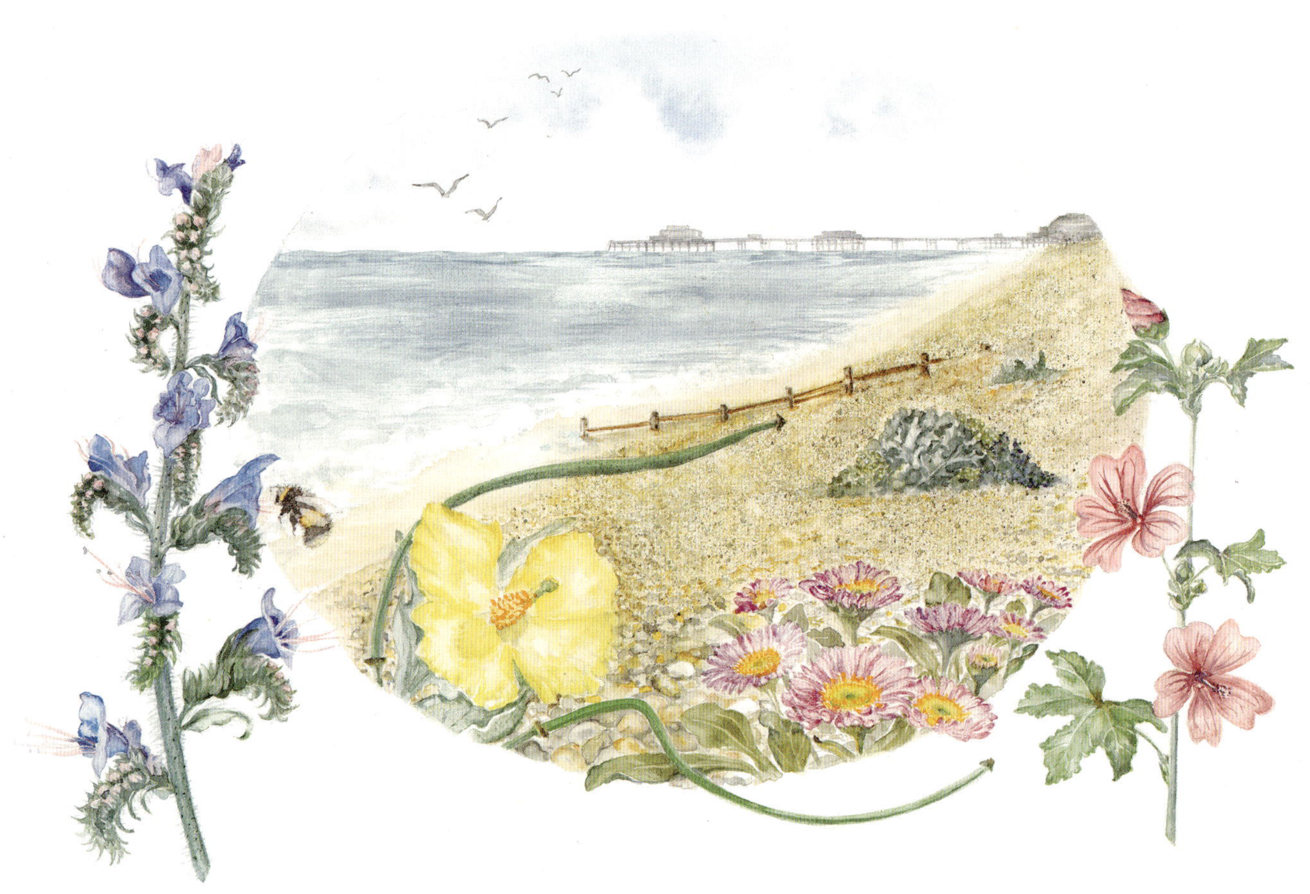

SOMERSET

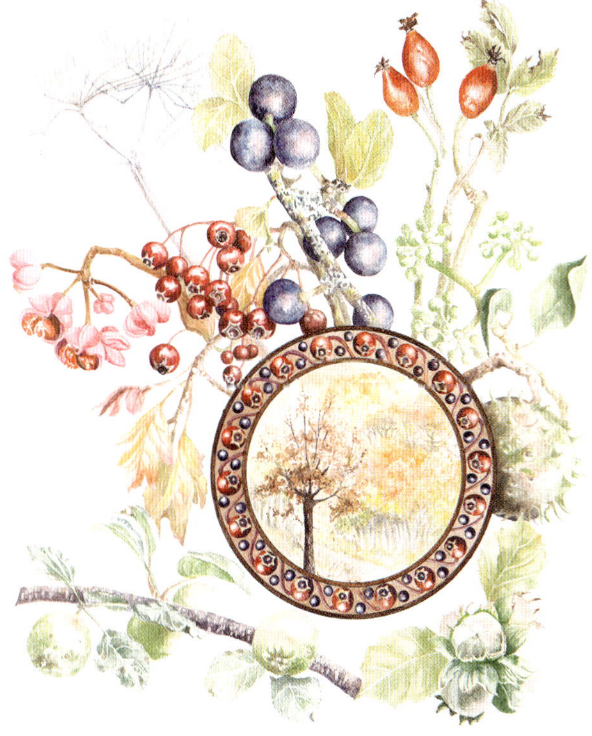

Somerset

SUE SYMONDS | Watercolour on paper

This is a poster design for a tourist board wanting to extend the holiday season. The warm colours and autumn foliage suggest walks through the woods, with the promise of a good meal and a comfortable bed at the end of the day. This time the lettering is shown – straightforward and colour-blended to suit the theme of mixed fruit and nuts.

Napier Art Deco City

GILLIAN RECEVEUR |
Watercolour and ink on paper

Gillian is from New Zealand and she chose to advertise her city, which is noted for its Art Deco architecture. She shows a line of *Araucaria heterophylla* (Norfolk Island pine) leading to one of the iconic buildings. At the top left is *Sophora microphylla* (weeping kowhai), while *Metrosideros excelsa* (pohutakawa) fills the lower corner. Gillian has kept to the linear, pared-down style suitable for the era and has wisely chosen not to fill every bit of paper, thus leaving room for other information such as a date, venue or time.

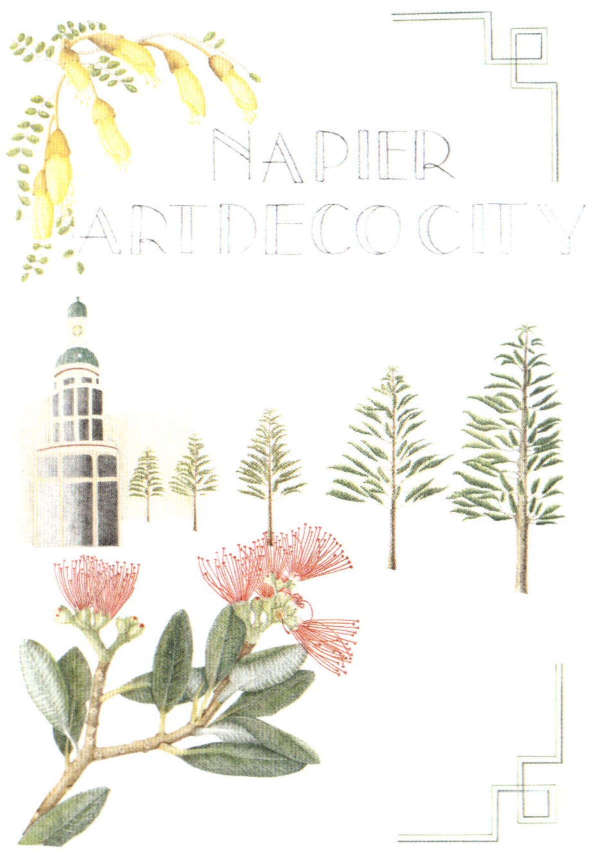

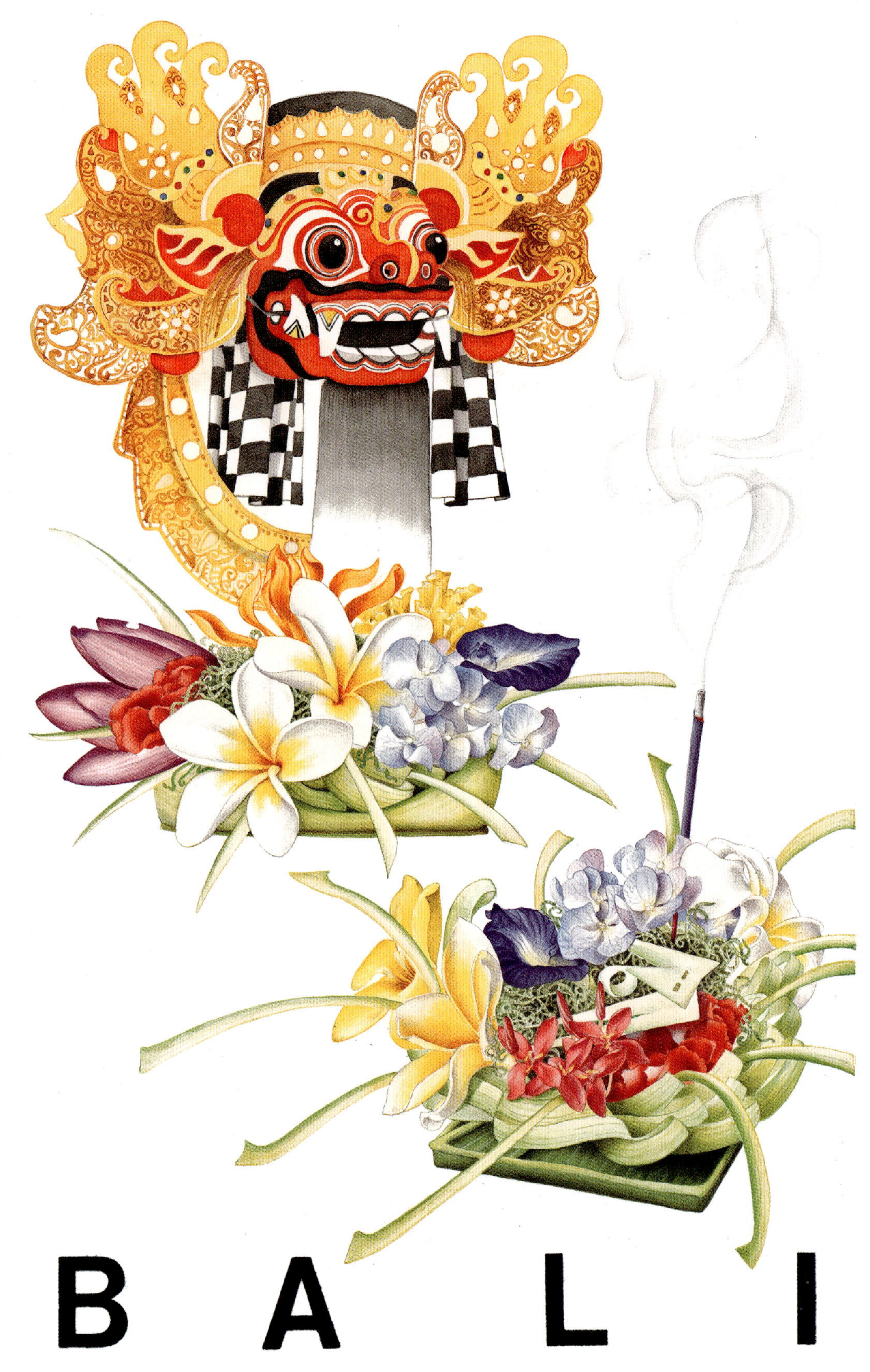

BALI

Bali

SUNANDA WIDEL | Watercolour on paper

This vibrant poster design entices the visitor to the holiday paradise of Bali. It shows examples of the typical offerings of flowers, palm and incense which are made daily to the Hindu gods. Sunanda planned the word BALI in heavy block lettering at the base of the poster, leaving the image to speak for itself.

Summer Selection

ALISTER MATHEWS | Watercolour on paper

This beautiful selection of found objects is an excellent example of how to compose a painting of this description. The diagonal line of blue flowers focuses the eye after being first drawn to the crimson rosehips, then to the left where the shaggy nigella seedpod mimics the form of the *Eryngium bourgatii* (on the right). The ivory shade of the little bird's skull that reminds us of the vanitas paintings of yesteryear is picked up in the eggshell and *Lunaria annua* (honesty) seedhead. The green gingko leaf provides a bright counterpoint to the hips, while the scattered seeds echo the markings on the shell. It is altogether a perfect composition which has been lovingly put together.

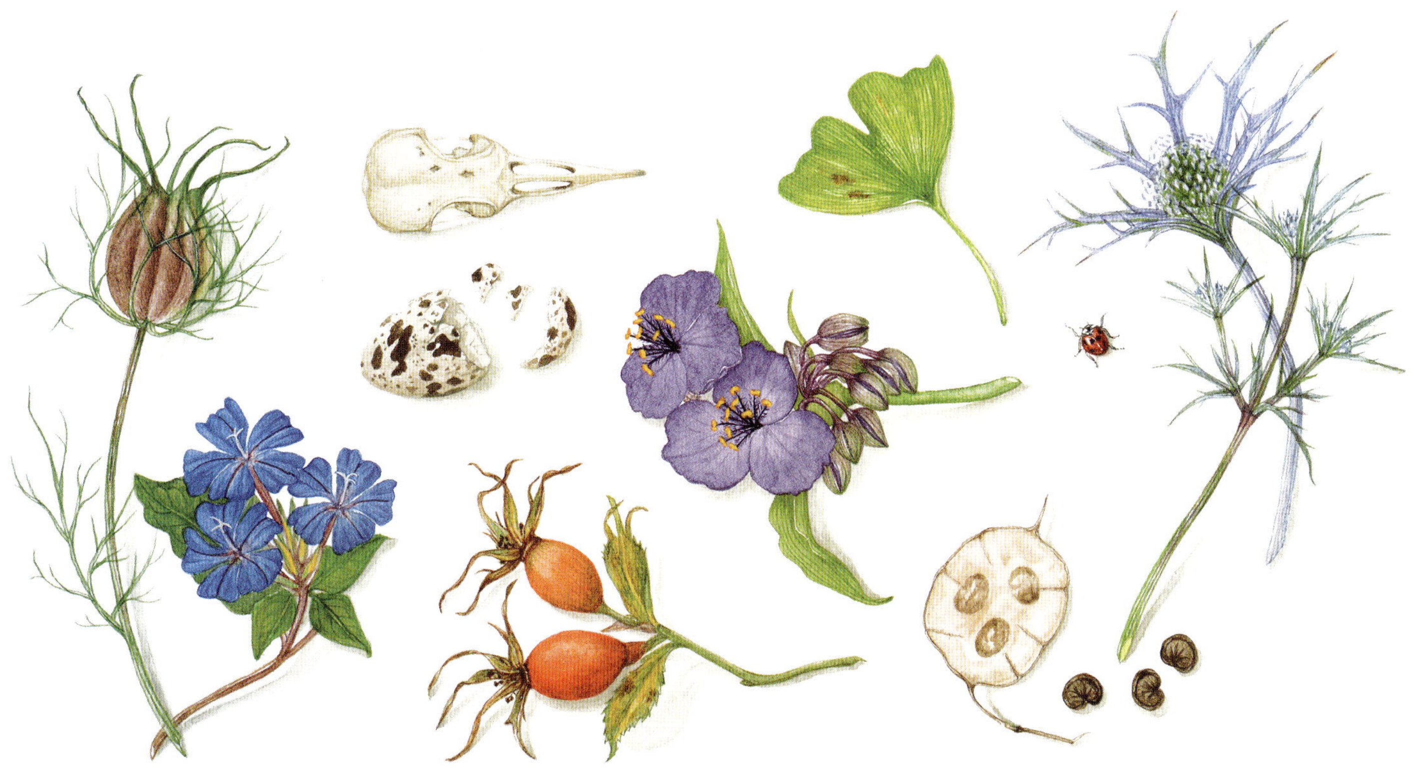

Tulip and Peony Shoe

This is the first of what may be more controversial applications of botanical art. I believe it has a place in our time and, as Billy pointed out, the Victorians often included a shoe in a floral design. I encouraged Billy to exhibit her shoe paintings – if a melting watch is acceptable from Salvador Dali then Billy should be allowed her flights of fancy. In her own words, 'Each shoe is a new creation and unites my fashion illustration past with botanical illustration present. Each design is a challenge – how to combine the flowers and leaves, how to trick the eye to create the form, and how to fill the space, balancing the image in the frame; also painting the flowers in intricate detail in all the positions the shoe design demands.' Her tulip leaves are still perfectly furled and the peony buds resemble marbled paper so no fault can be found with botanical accuracy. Maybe an upmarket shoe designer might like to consider this for a future collection.

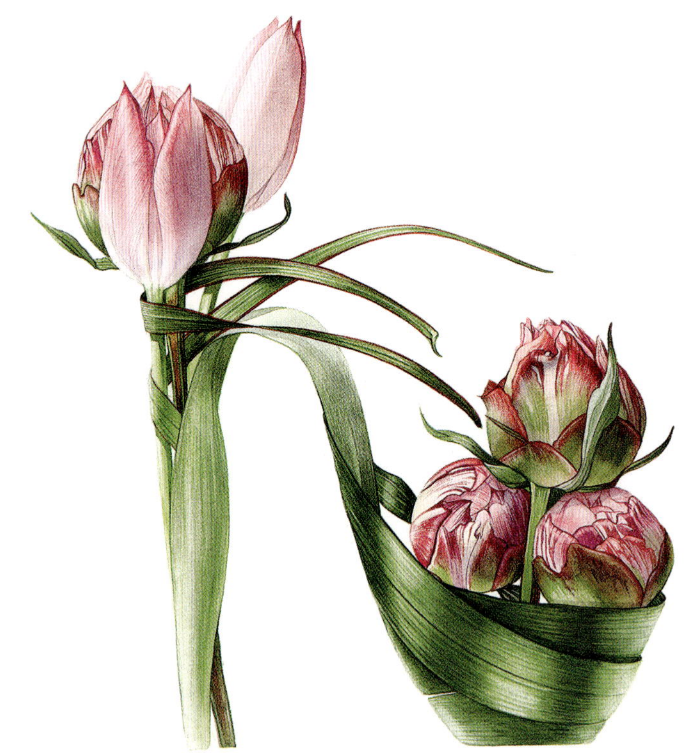

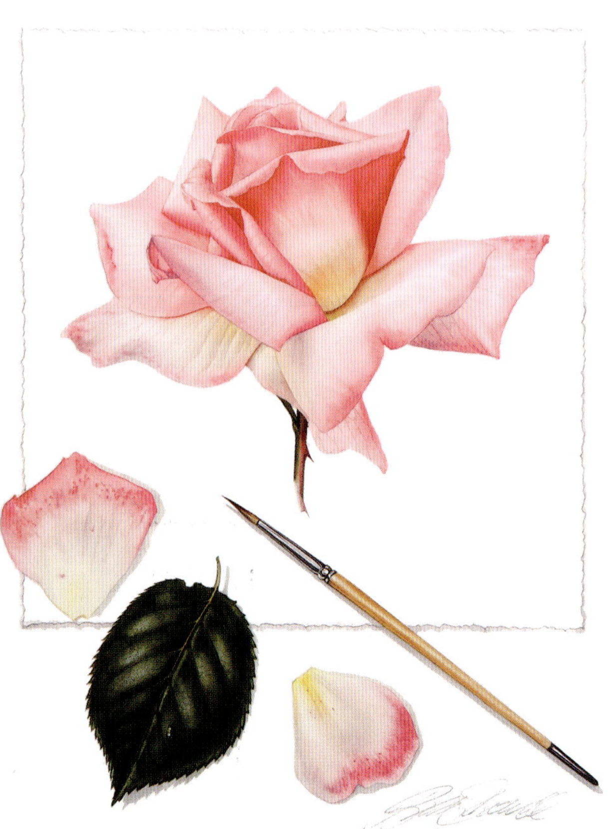

Perfect Happiness

BILLY SHOWELL | Watercolour on paper

Painting from her daydreams is important to Billy and for her a pink rose on the desk is calling to be painted. In spite of its simplicity the rose is a demanding subject, requiring a speedy wet-on-wet technique. When a flower is familiar there is no place to hide; anyone looking at this painting will know the structure of a rose, so painting from life demands a sure touch and confidence, both exhibited here tenfold.

Alstroemerias – Tiempo y Vida

MARTA CHIRINO | Mixed media on paper

This large work (98 x 99cm/38½ x 39in) combines watercolour, coloured pencils and graphite on Okawara paper (a Japanese paper for engraving) and vellum paper. Marta explains: 'In Christianity the circle is a perfect geometrical figure symbolic of eternity, lacking a beginning and end. In Zen Buddhism the circle is opened to infinity and a master sometimes expresses his spirit through a single stroke, painting an open circle, and occasionally a closed one. He considers the imperfection an essential and inherent aspect of existence. I have tried to express in this circle of life the individual's effort to survive, always trying to escape from the inevitable passage of time. The drawing shows a broken and imperfect circle in which two cuts simulate the clockwise motion. Some alstroemerias flee the circle, revolving around it and ignoring their destination.

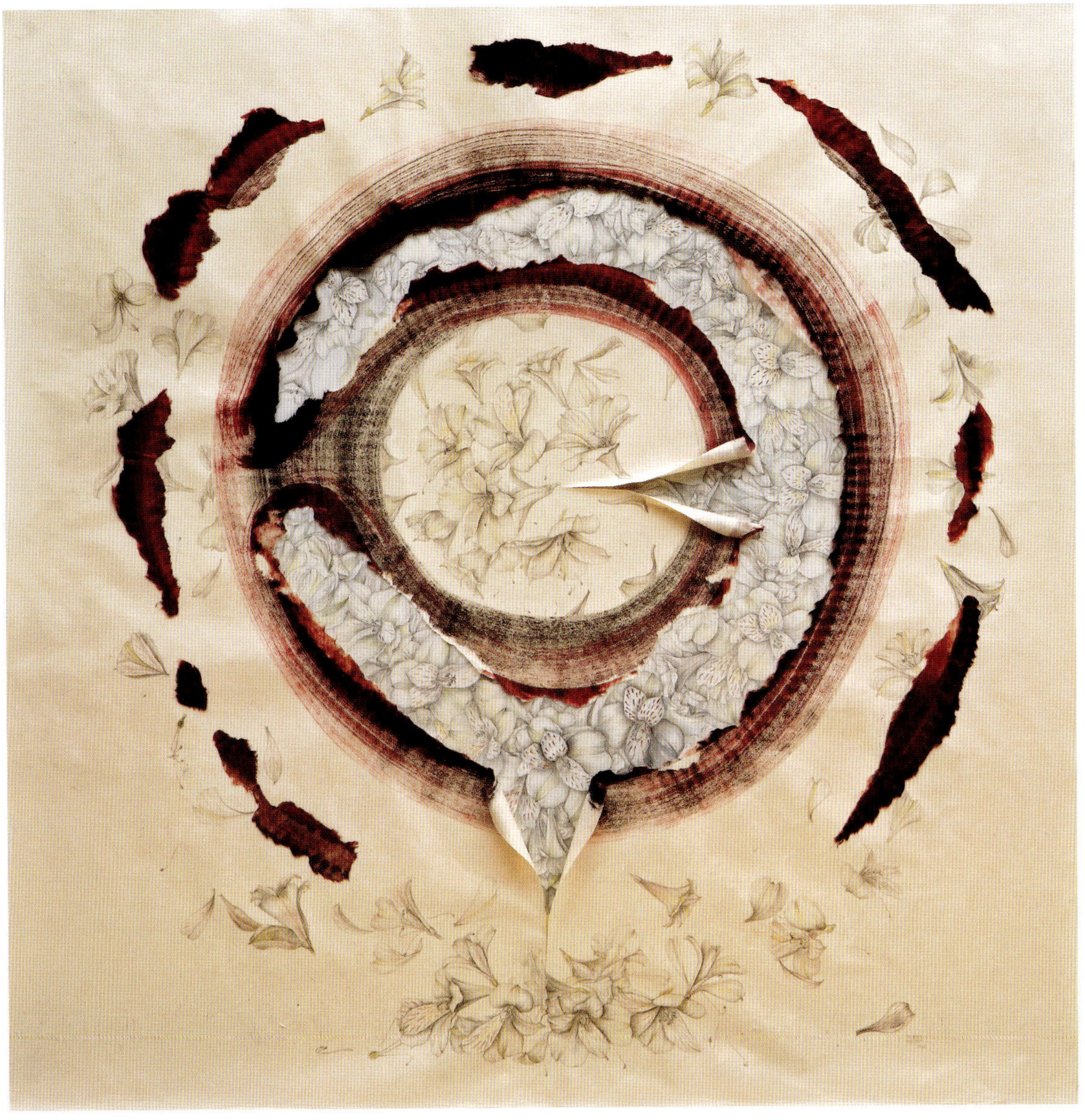

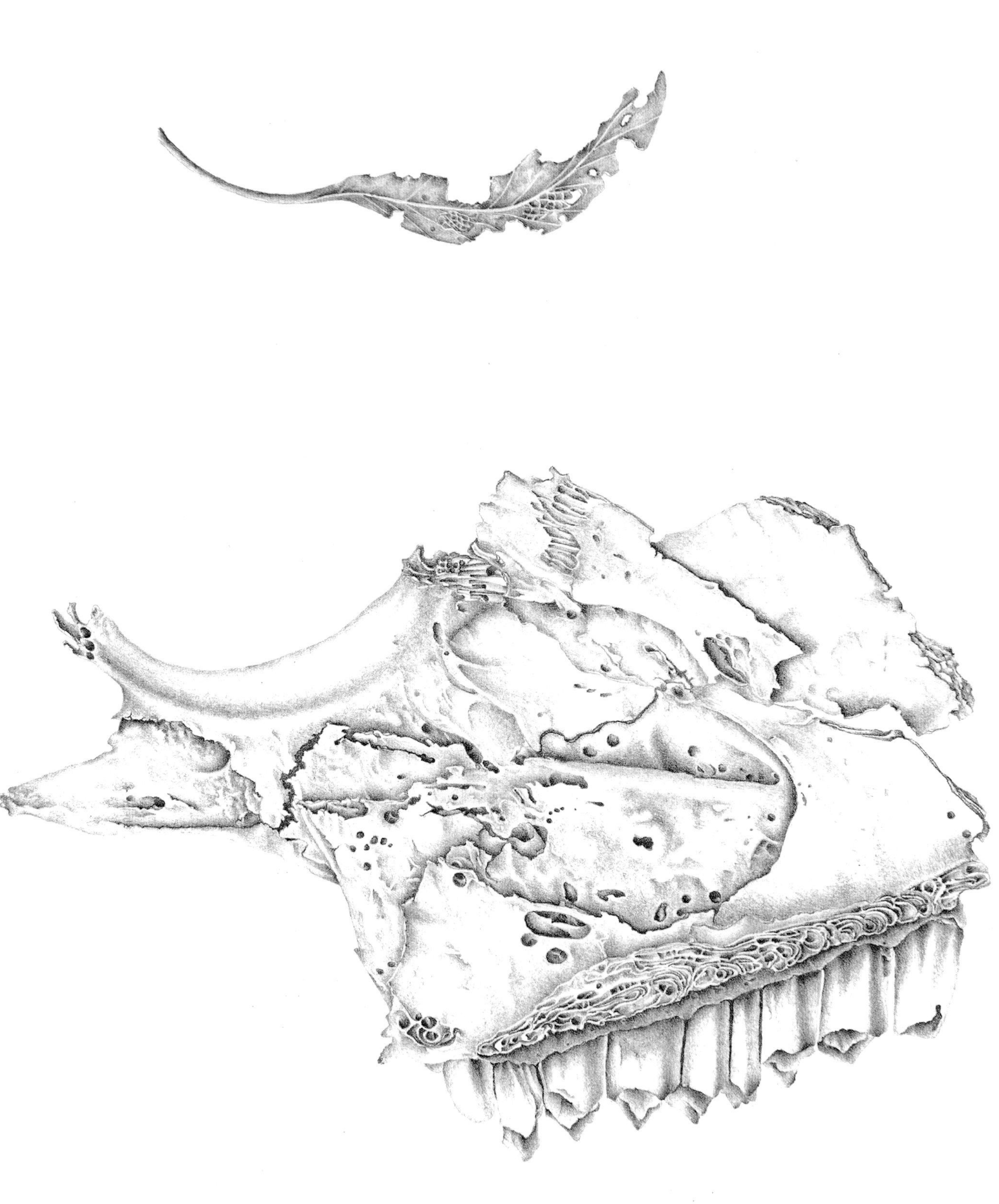

God Works in Mysterious Ways

SHARON FIELD | Graphite on paper

After careers in teaching and the civil service, working in various countries in the Pacific and Africa, Sharon Field embarked on a new career as a botanical artist in 2008. Today, she combines painting with her roles as captain of a volunteer fire-fighting brigade with the Rural Fire Service in New South Wales and a guide with the National Gallery of Australia. Not only has she participated in many group exhibitions in Australia and overseas, she has had two highly successful solo exhibitions and three joint exhibitions with sculptors and ceramicists. A finalist in the prestigious Waterhouse Natural Art Prize, she has won numerous awards, including the Award for Excellence with the SBA Diploma Course. Her work is pushing the boundaries of traditional botanical art and she seeks plants which display the character and the scars of a life well lived, of a purpose achieved. People are always drawn to look at a plant in full bloom. Few people look at the spent bloom, the broken leaf, the decaying stick, the patterns across species. In this piece measuring 16 x 19cm (6¼ x 7½in) she has combined a sheep's jaw bone and eucalyptus leaf

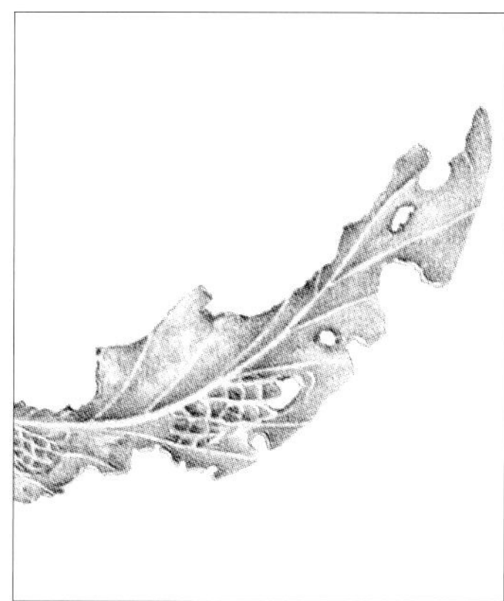

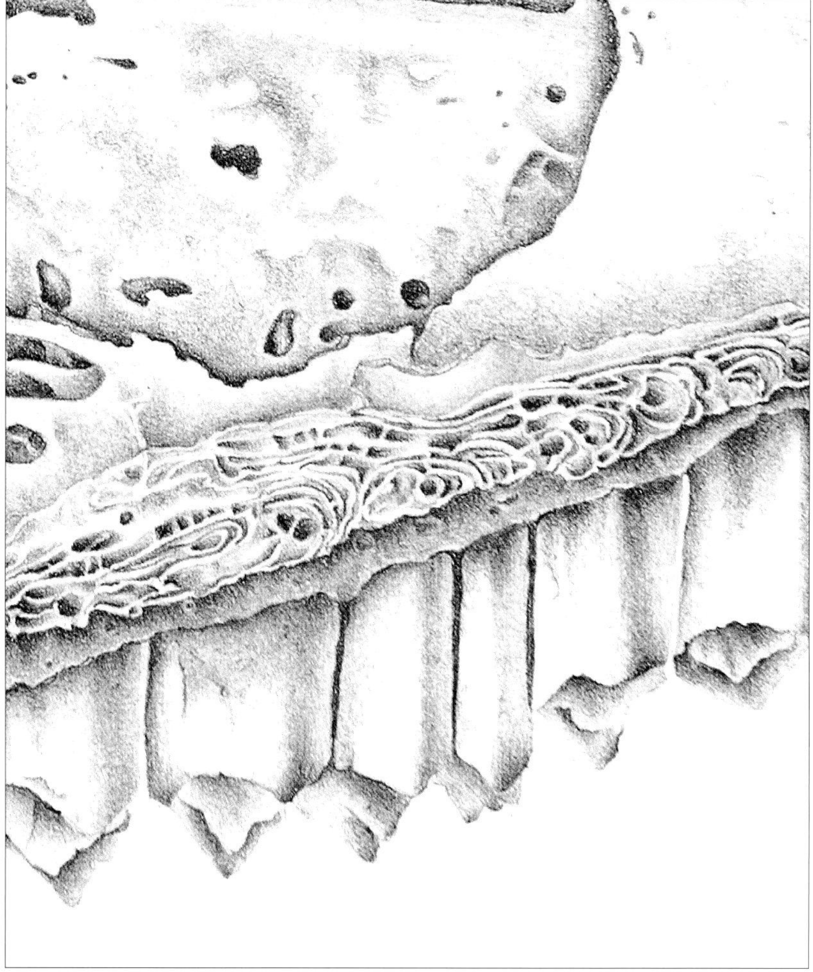

Gallery

Black Worcester Pears | Dianne Frank | Coloured pencil on paper
Sometimes history or curiosity value add interest to the subject.
Probably brought to England by the Romans, the Black Worcester
pear has featured in heraldry for many centuries and was displayed
on the banners of the Worcestershire bowmen at the Battle
of Agincourt in 1415. It has now been adopted on the City of
Worcester's Coat of Arms. Dianne has captured the texture of this
dark-skinned fruit to perfection.

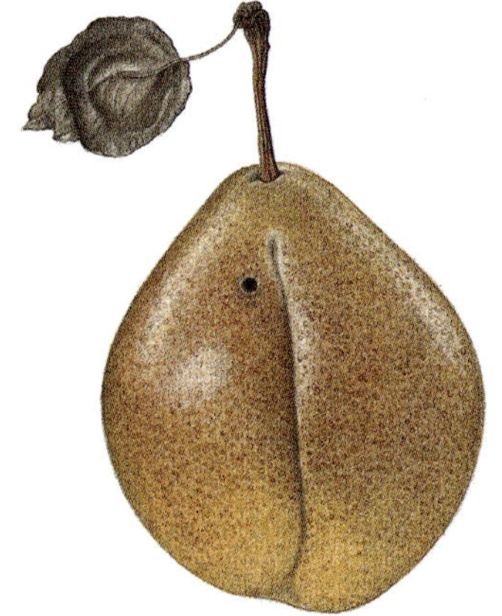

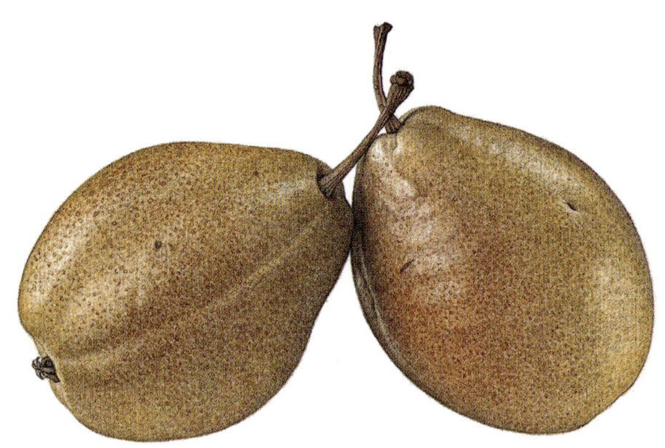

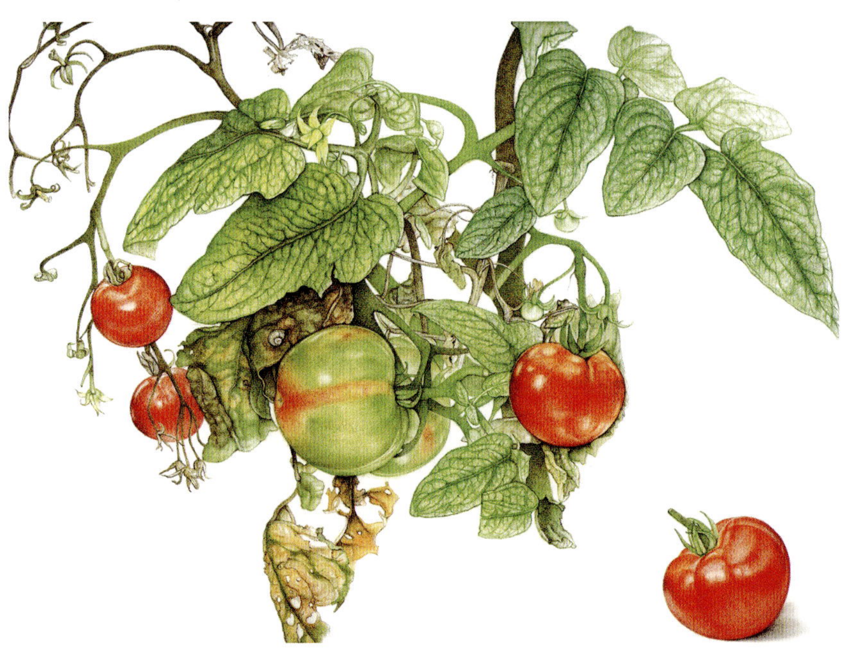

Tomatoes | Dianne Frank | Coloured pencil on paper
Dianne has adopted a very illustrative style for this lively study straight
from the greenhouse. The strong outlines display her excellent drawing
skills and the fruit entice the viewer to pick from the vine; highlights are
particularly well depicted. The mix of decaying leaves adds realism as
well as creating depth behind the ripening fruit.

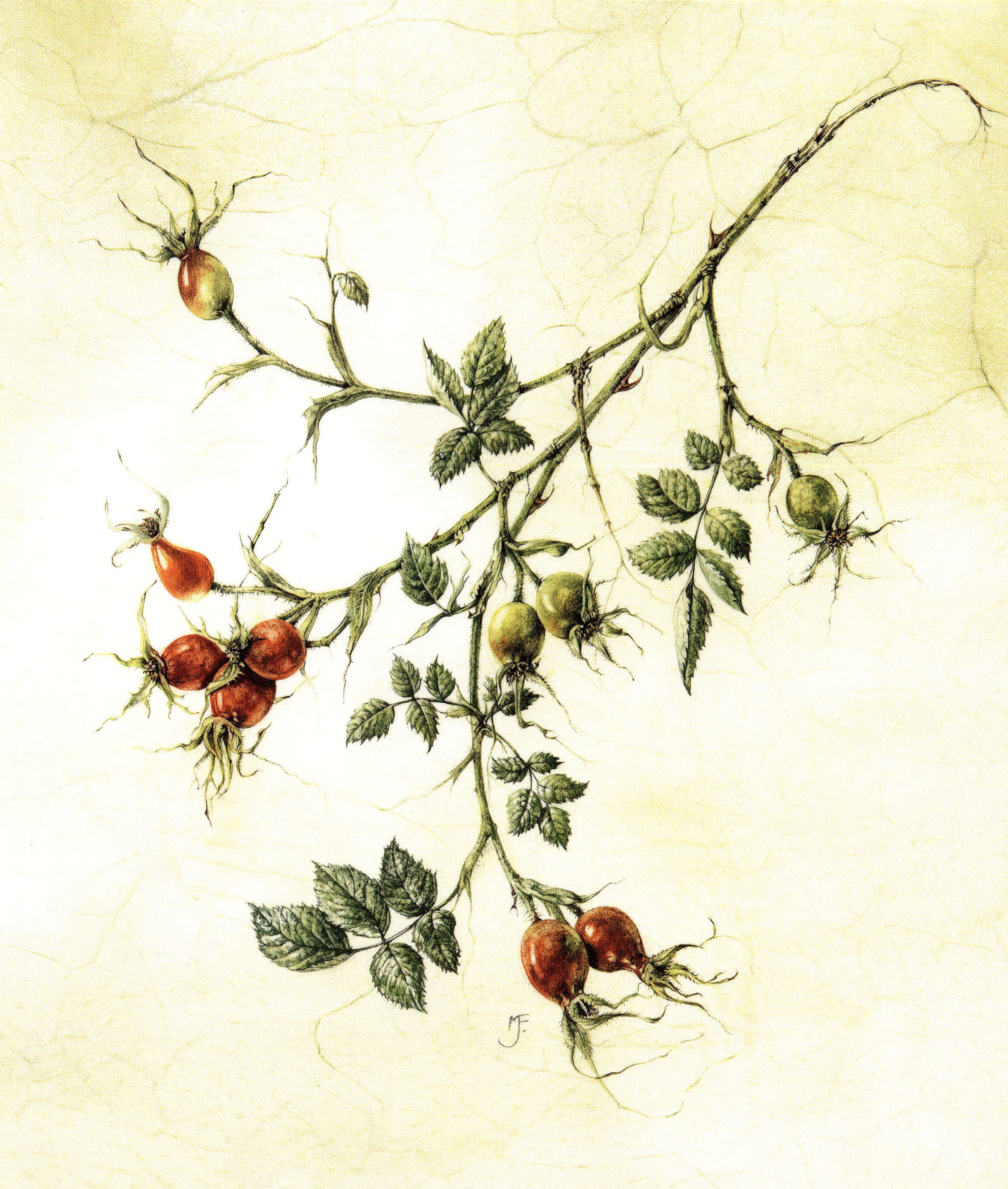

Rosehips | Margaret Fitzpatrick | Watercolour on vellum
In this deceptively simple study the colour and natural markings of the
vellum enhance the subject matter.

Phalaenopsis | Grazia Gianella | Gouache on paper
This gained a nearly perfect mark when Grazia submitted
it for her coursework, with only the lack of shading on
parts of the stems subject to criticism. The texture of the
leaves and the fleshy aerial roots are worthy of special
mention, while the complex reproductive central sections
of the flowers have been well mastered.

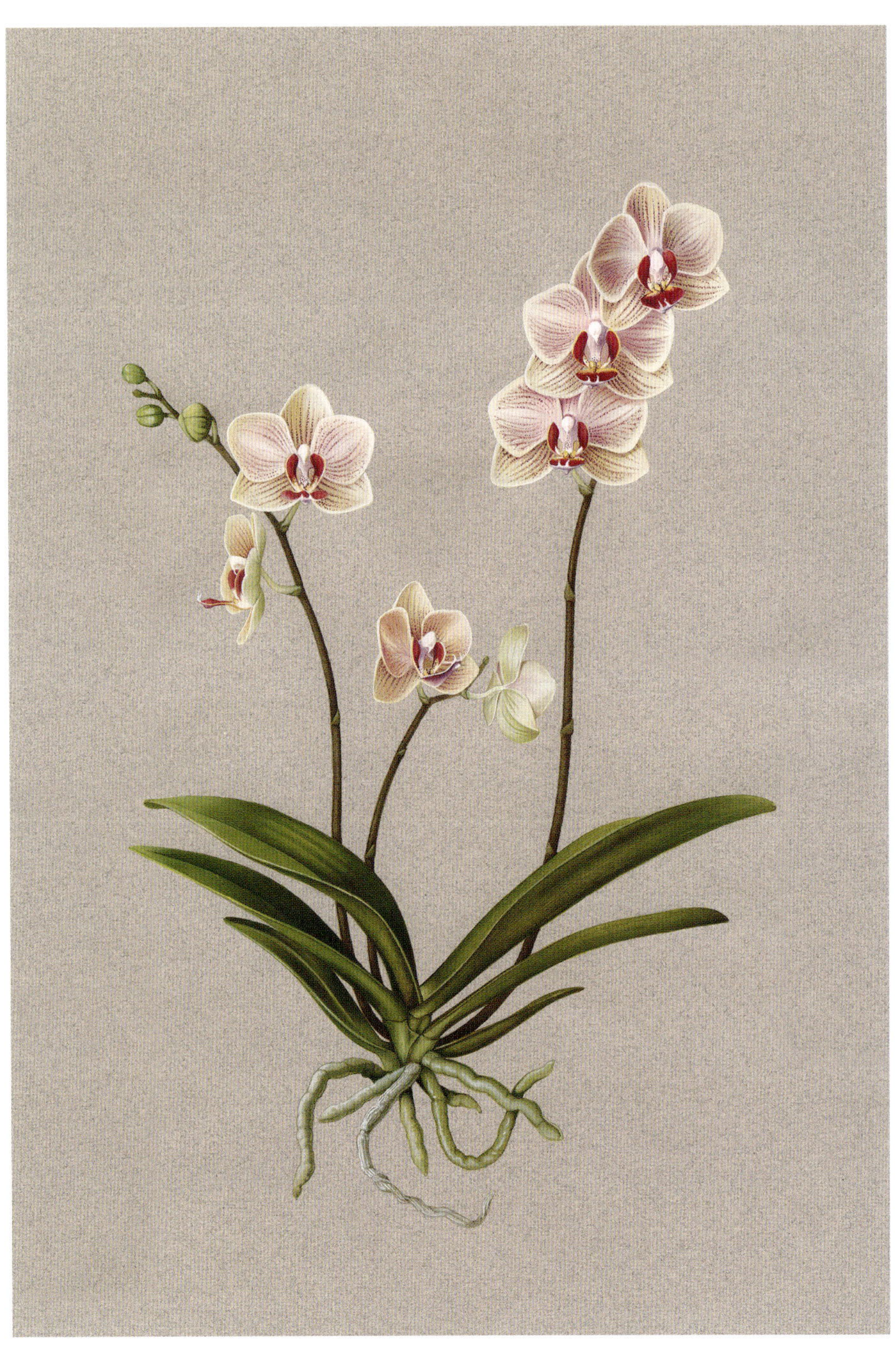

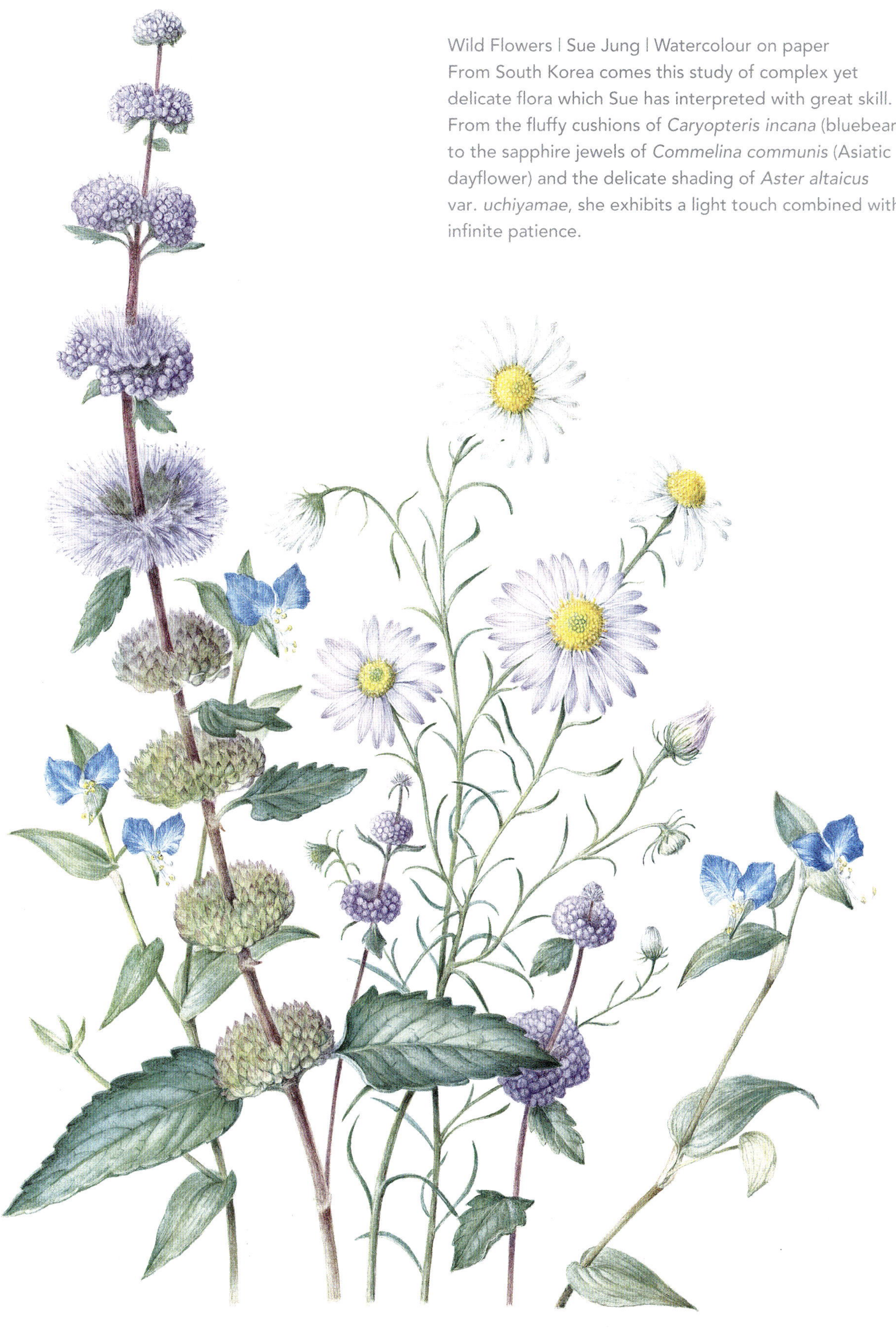

Wild Flowers | Sue Jung | Watercolour on paper
From South Korea comes this study of complex yet delicate flora which Sue has interpreted with great skill. From the fluffy cushions of *Caryopteris incana* (bluebeard) to the sapphire jewels of *Commelina communis* (Asiatic dayflower) and the delicate shading of *Aster altaicus* var. *uchiyamae*, she exhibits a light touch combined with infinite patience.

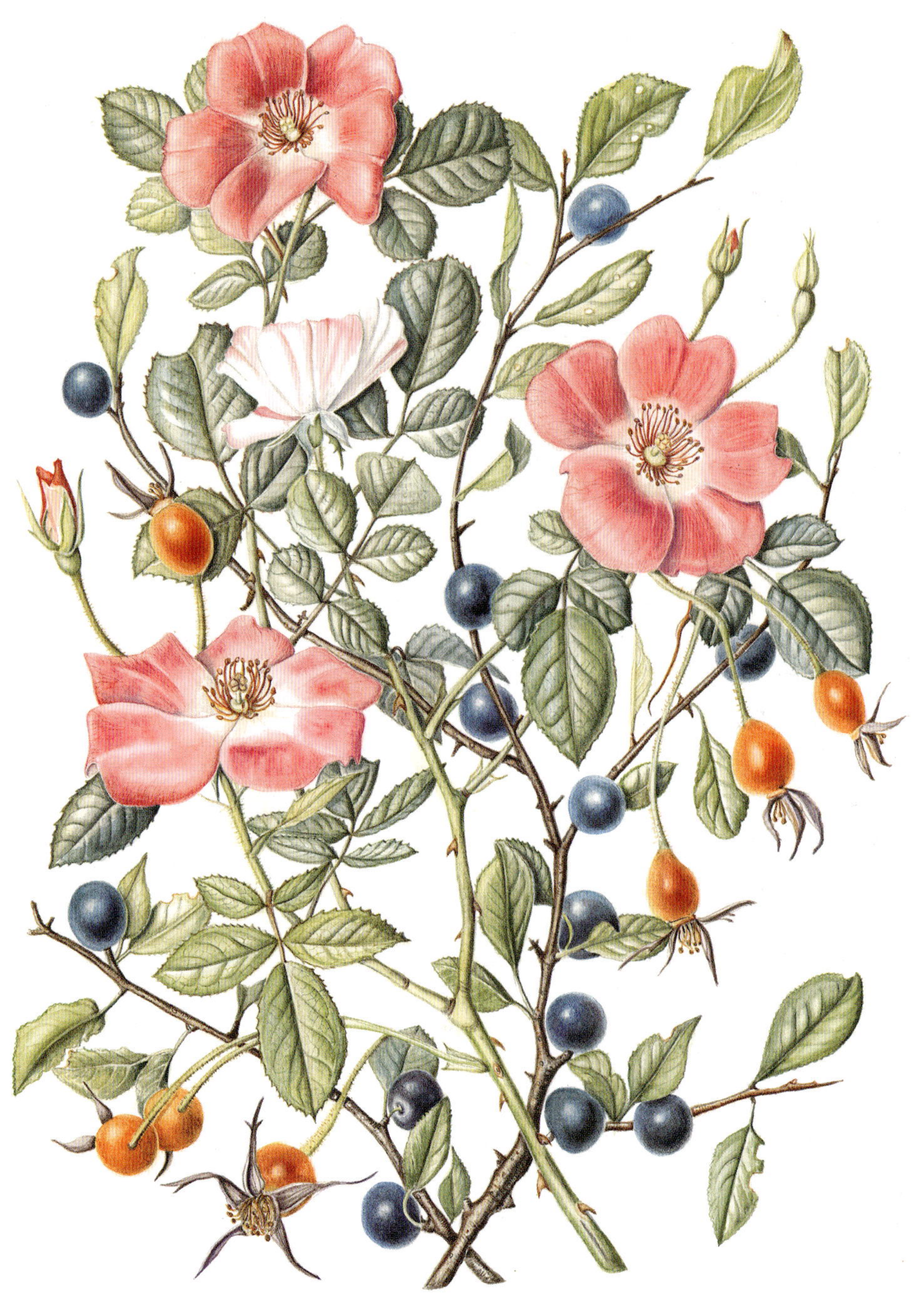

Rosa sp. and *Prunus spinosa* | Dona Leonardi | Watercolour on paper
Dona's beautiful, natural study looks as if the contents have been freshly picked from a hedge, which perhaps was the case. She has taken great care to ensure that stems follow through correctly and nothing appears to grow in the wrong place, which is a common error in student work and so easily avoided. If a stem 'disappears' behind a leaf or bloom it must re-emerge to continue its travels, connect up with another stem or be finished off neatly.

Verbascum | Vickie Marsh | Watercolour on paper
After Vickie painted the many green subjects that formed
the Liverpool project (see page 84) she needed colour
in her life and this was the result – a lively explosion of
stems like a floral firework display, each flower given the
attention it deserves.

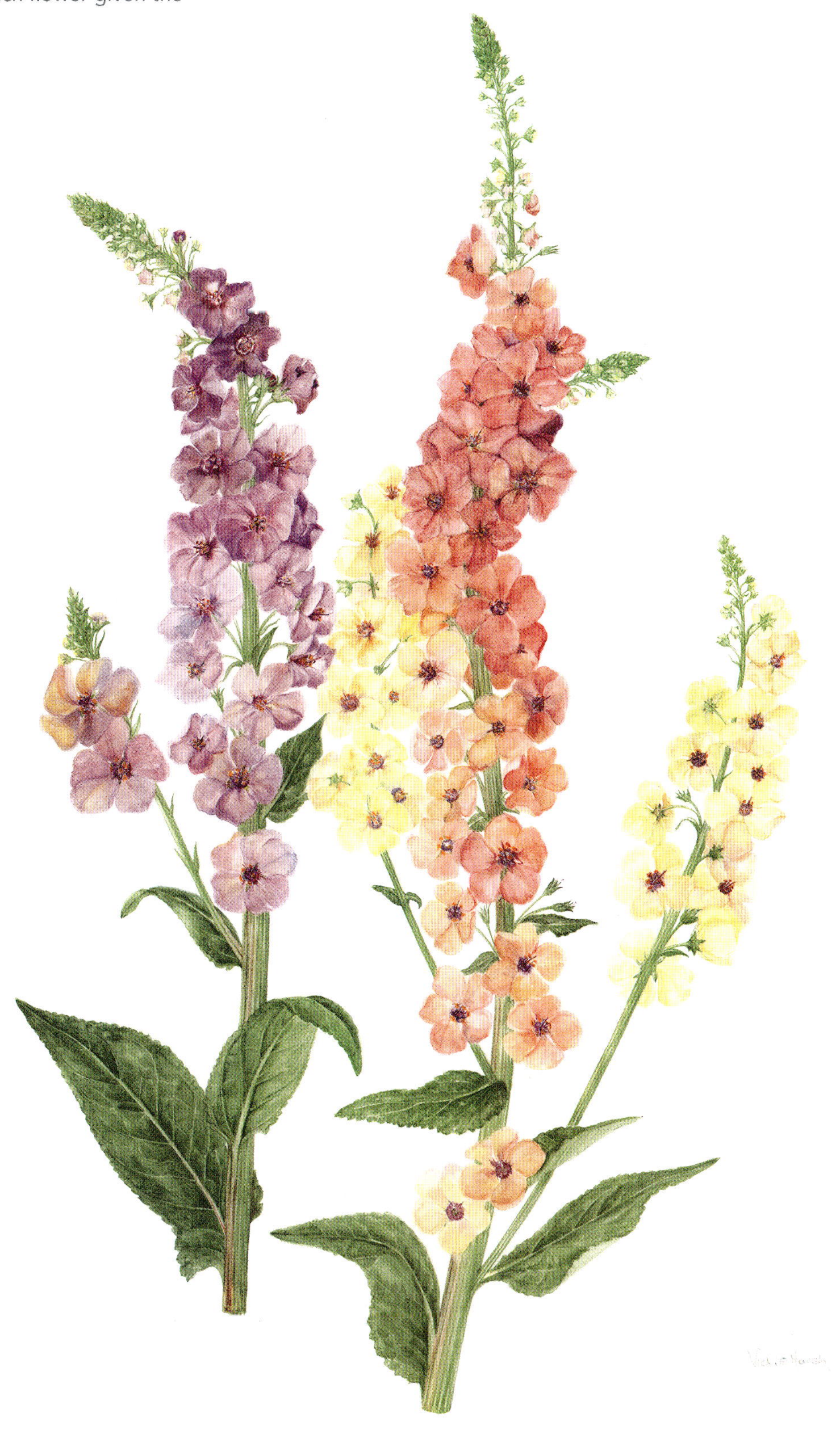

Wisteria | Vickie Marsh | Watercolour on paper
In this delicate subject, the graceful racemes and almost
translucent leaves are perfectly captured. Each fine
pedicle has been attached to the main stem and it has
all been shaded with great care so that nothing looks
hurried, even although the shelf life of the subject would
have been limited.

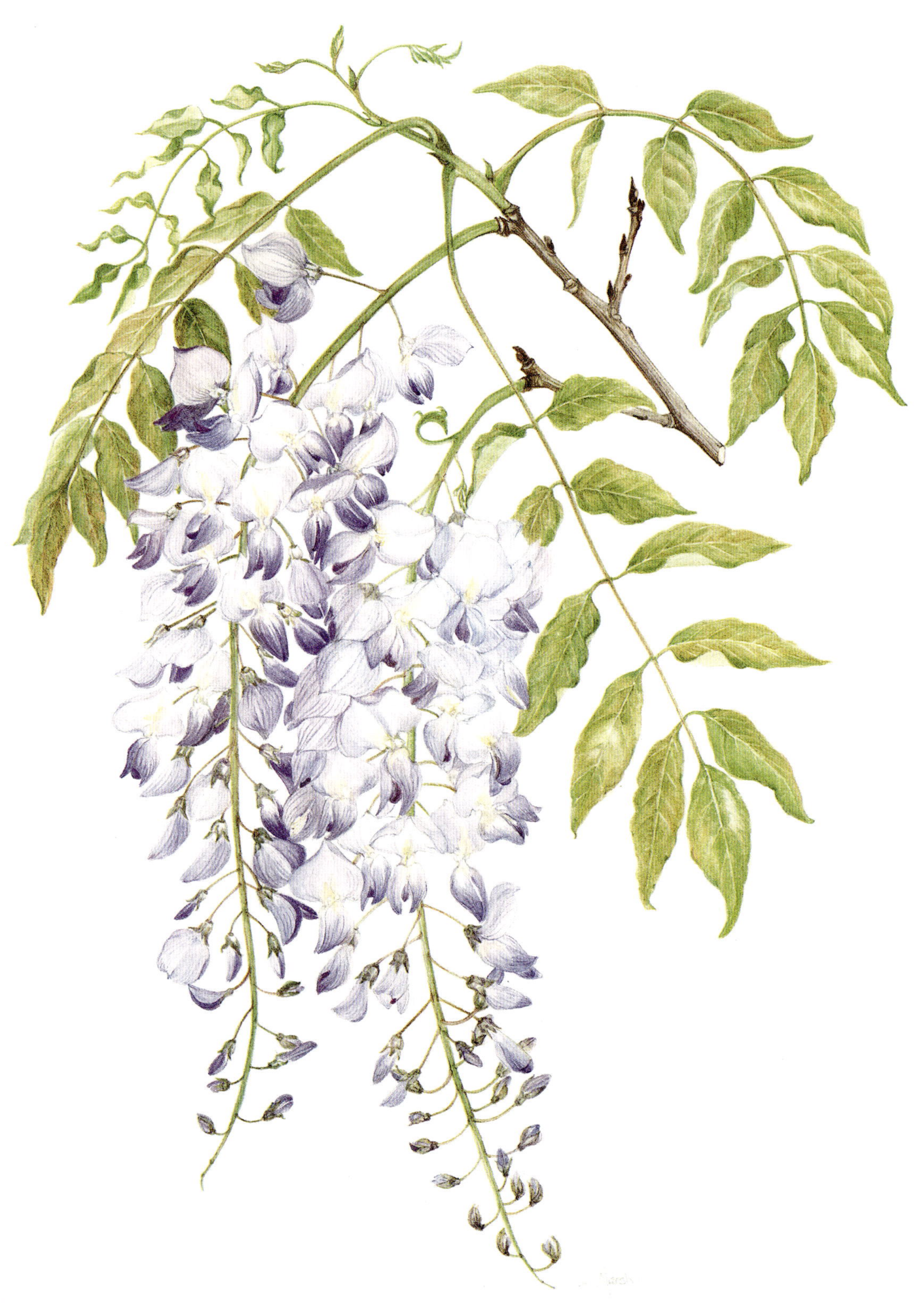

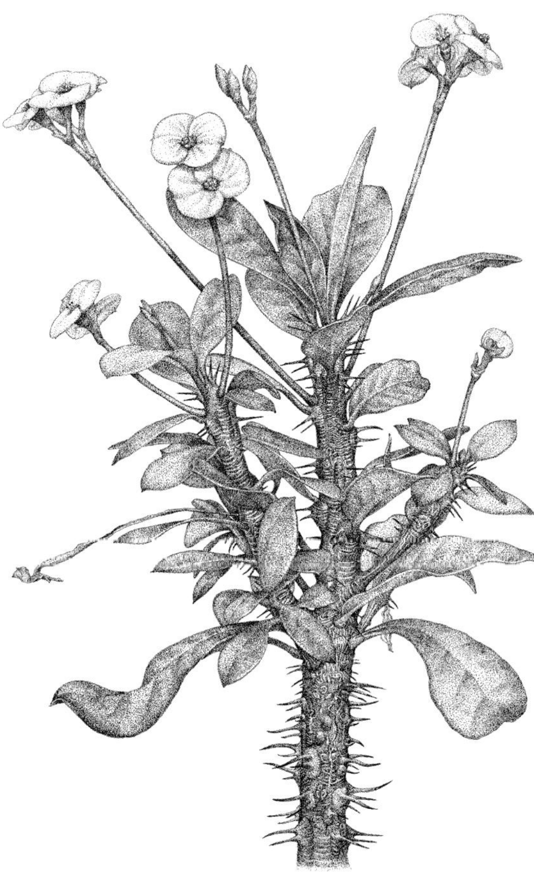

Crown of Thorns | Jae Young Min | Ink on paper
This stippled ink study shows incredible skill way beyond anything usually produced by a student. Jae Young has captured form, tone and texture with consummate ease, demonstrating how an illustrator's technique can be used to create a fine art study.

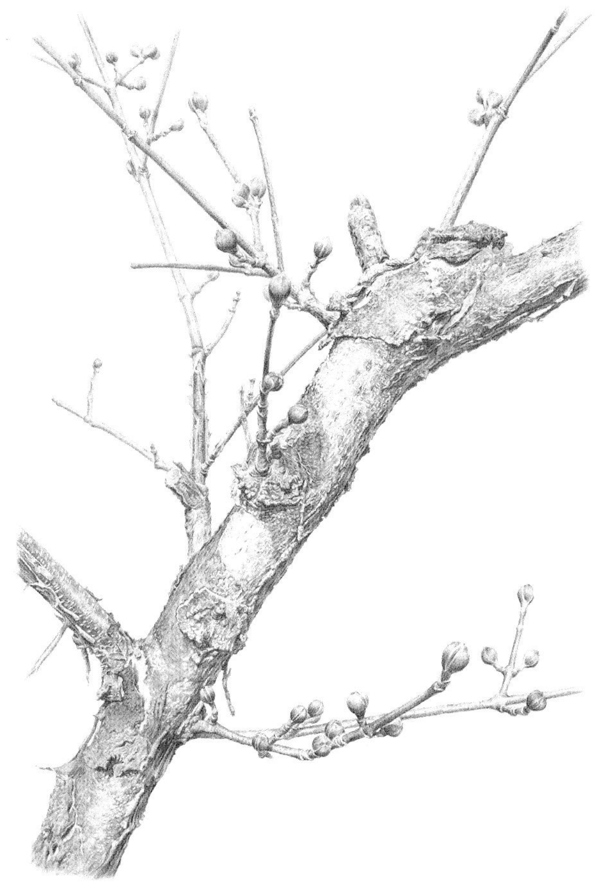

Tonal Study in Graphite | Jae Young Min | Graphite on paper
Here a tree branch with emerging buds has captured Jae Young's interest and she has displayed her talent for observation of chiaroscuro to the full. The texture of the peeling bark, rough to the touch in some places but smooth as silk where it is highlighted, adds to the beauty of the piece.

Primroses in Cornwall | Marion Perkins | Egg tempera on paper
Proving once again the versatility of the medium, Marion uses it to show us this delightful early spring landscape. From the detailed clump of primroses the eye travels back across the field then pauses to take in the church and bare tangled branches before continuing up to the distant woods. It is altogether a beautiful example of how flowers can be brought naturally into the landscape. As a West Country woman I have encountered this kind of scene many times in days gone by: primroses, snowdrops, Lent lilies, bluebells – all at home in Betjeman country.

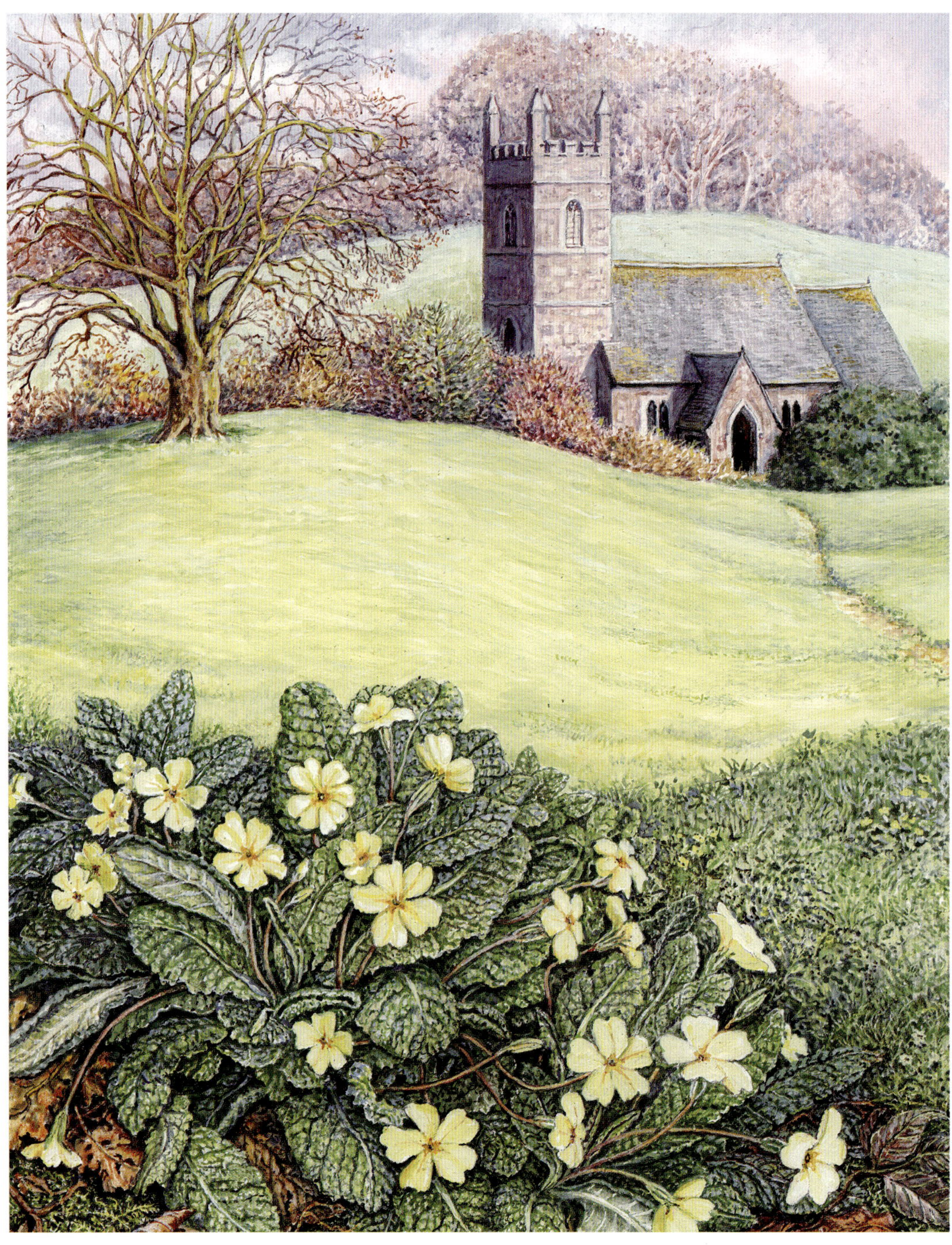

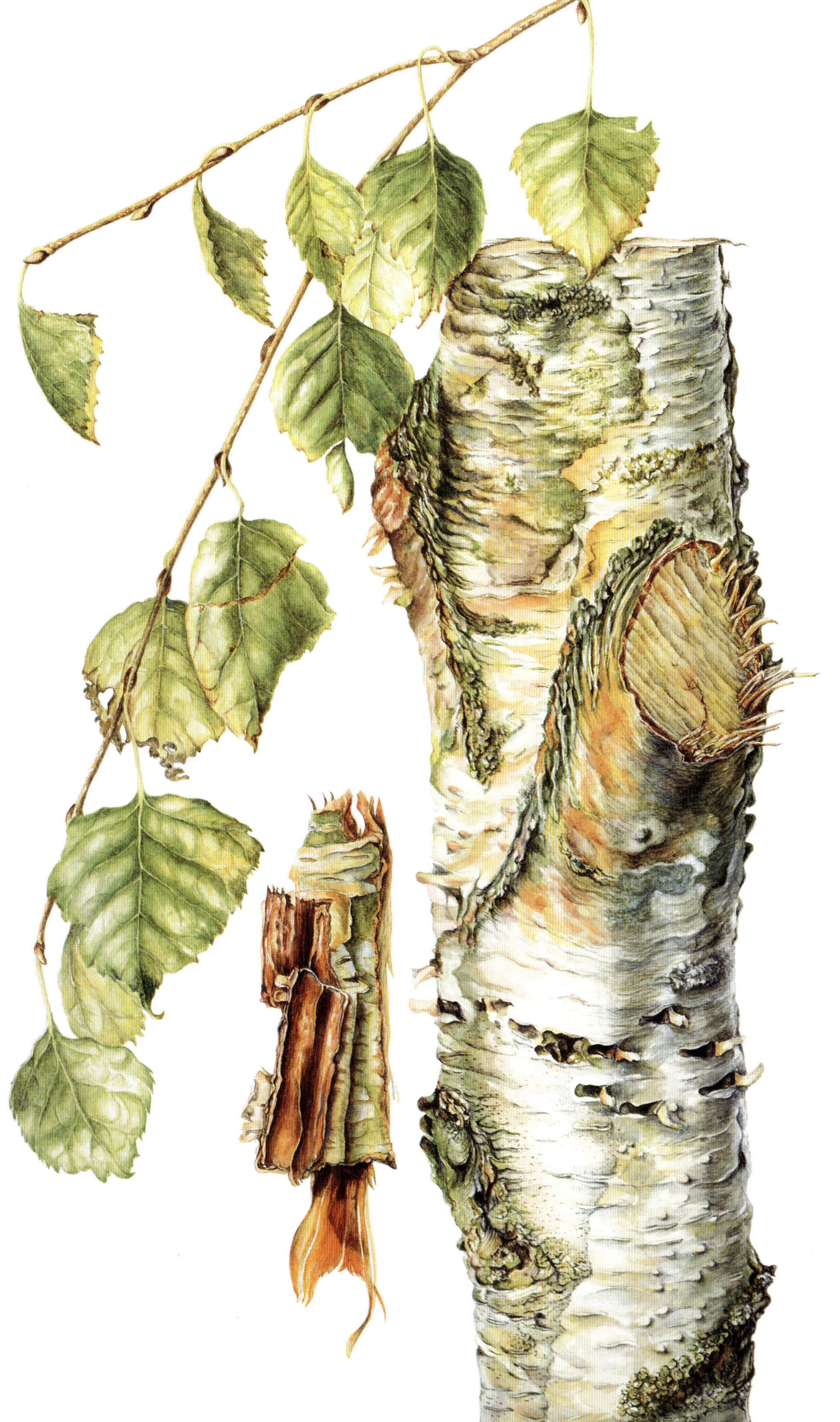

PREVIOUS PAGE Medicinal
Bark Study (*Betula pendula*) |
Janet Pope | Watercolour
on paper
Not only do the leaves, sap
and bark all have medicinal
uses, the silver birch is always
attractive. Janet shows us the
delicate leaves, from which a
tea can be infused, and the
peeling bark, almost cinnamon
red on the inside in contrast to
its pale outer surface.

Dahlia 'Twyning's After Eight' |
Heidi Venamore |
Watercolour on paper
This plant, from HRH The
Prince of Wales's garden at
Highgrove, was eye-catching
with its near-black leaves. It
took Heidi around 15 hours
to collect specimens, draw,
colour match and work out the
composition as she wanted to
show the large growth habit
of this busy plant and only A2
paper would do it justice.
Heidi found that Perylene
Violet made a perfect base
colour for the leaves, with
French Ultramarine to darken
it. She used light washes of
Permanent Rose, Perylene
Green and/or Sap Green to
convey their stage of growth
and location on the plant.
Less detail is apparent on the
younger leaves. White flowers
are always challenging and one
has to be aware that it is easy
to go in too dark. The whole
painting took around 80 hours
to complete.

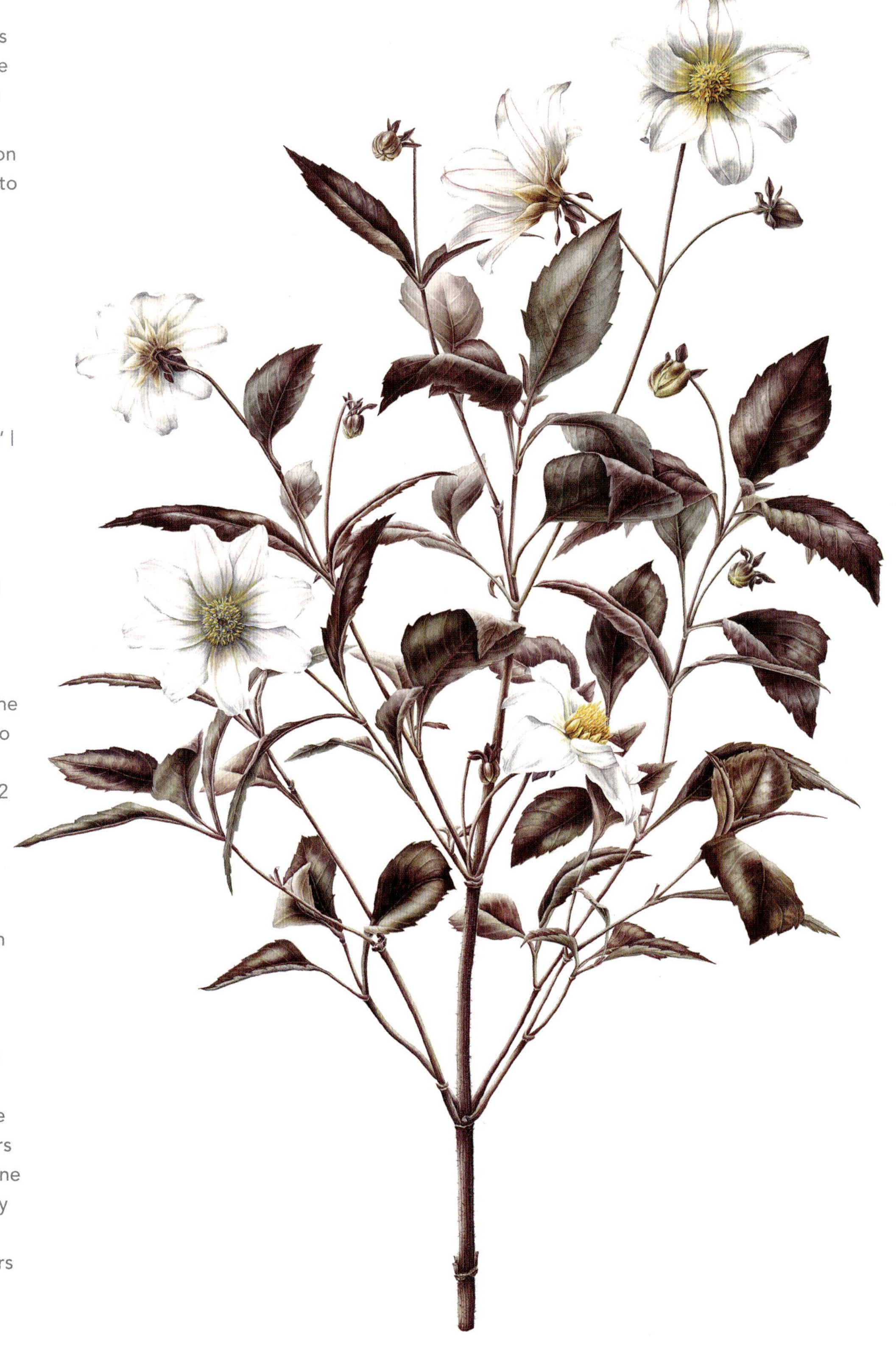

Pointed Cabbage | Billy Showell | Watercolour on paper
Billy has once again excelled herself with this everyday
vegetable, turning it into something resembling a modern
sculpture. There is a metallic quality to the smooth,
shiny leaves and it's easy to imagine breaking off the
other leaves with a crack and slicing through the heart
with the crisp swish of a sharp knife. As always she has
demonstrated her skill in handling washes. Note the
frontal lighting which certainly works best here, rather
than the light from the top left that has become the norm
for much botanical work.

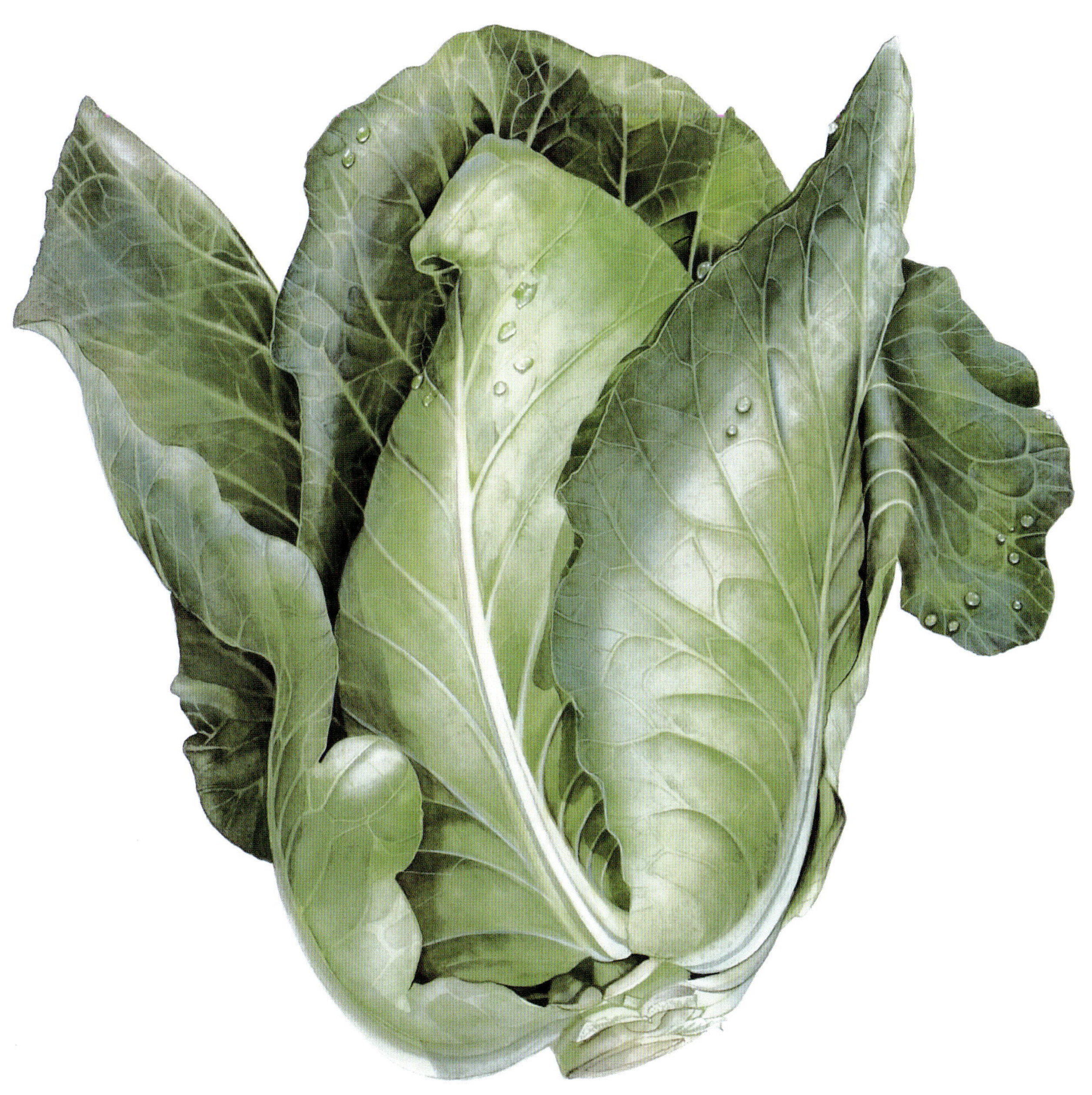

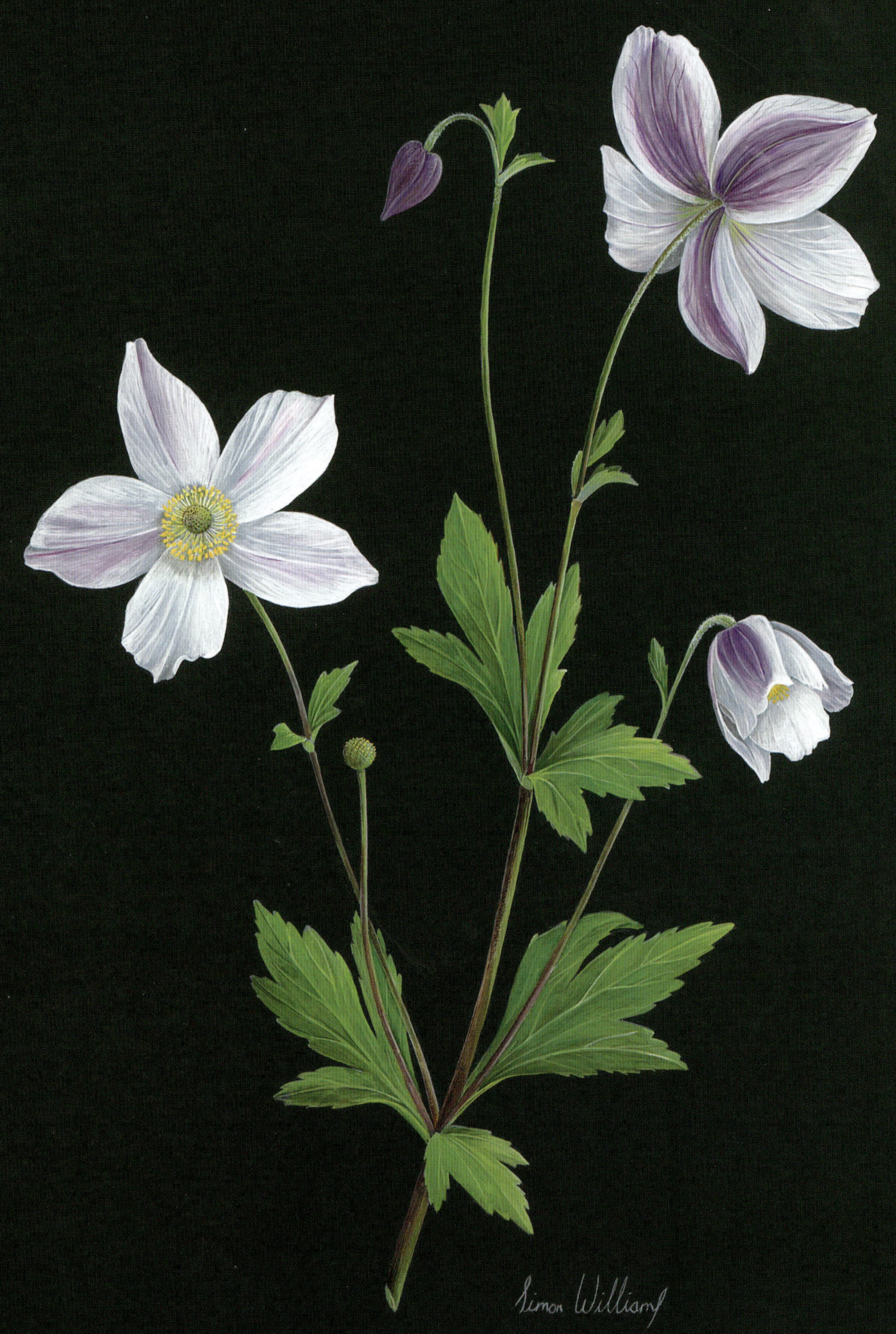

Simon Williams

OPPOSITE Anemones | Simon Williams | Gouache on
mount board
Simon has chosen a deceptively simple subject in these
anemones. Too often gouache is associated with heavy
painting techniques, but here it is used to portray a very
delicate flower with softly shaded petals and stems. Look in
particular at the flower centre, through a magnifying glass if
necessary, and see the minute filaments, not to mention the
pollen-dusted seedhead. This is work worthy of the master
miniaturists of old.

BELOW Fungi | Simon Williams | Watercolour and gouache
on paper
A poisonous top row and an edible bottom row of fungi gives
us an example of botanical art as an educational tool. It shows
a very well-balanced composition both of form and colour as
well as a highly accomplished technique.

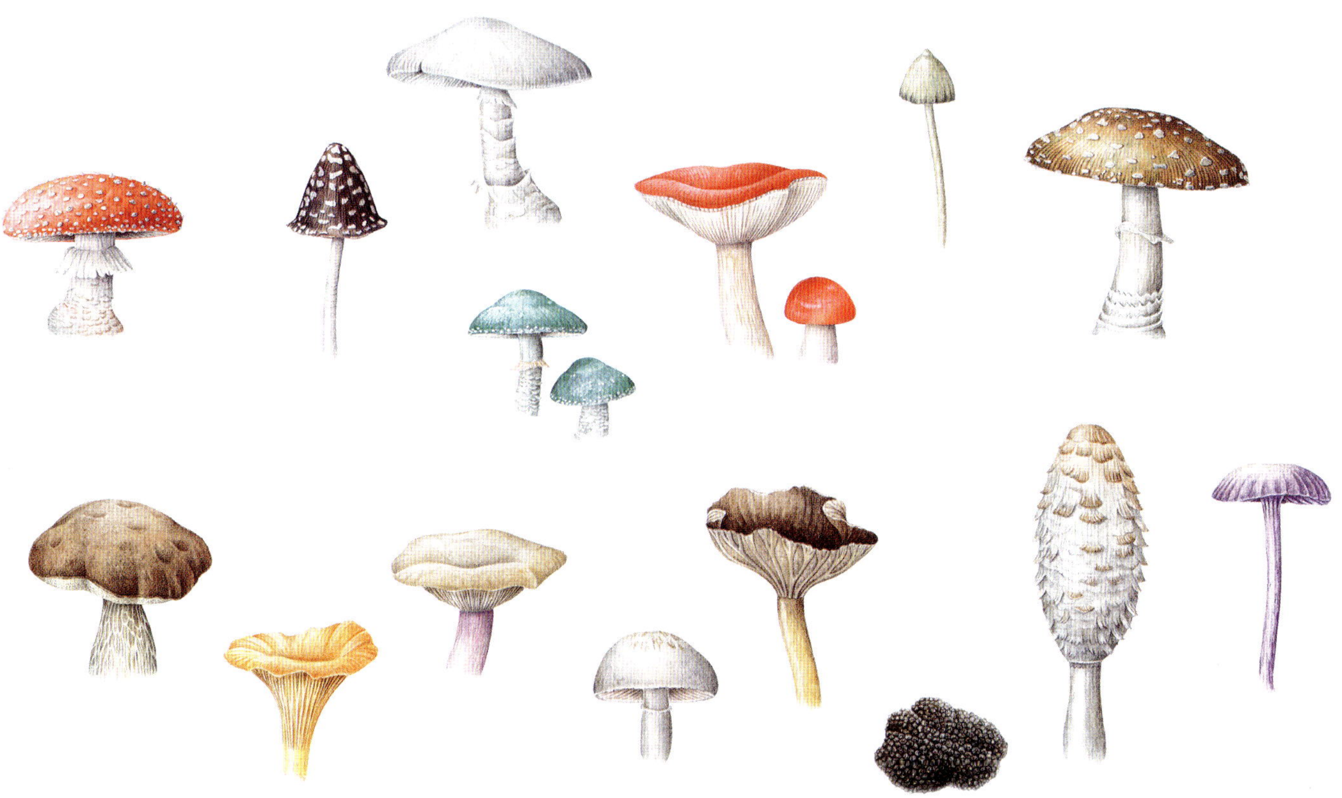

Tips From the Artists

Complementary colours: Jan Harbon

The high contrast of using two complementary colours next to each other can create vibrancy, but it can be tricky to avoid unpleasant jarring of the senses. To overcome this, and to express the soft and flowing translucency of petals, I use a blending technique. I also apply this to bi-coloured flowers such as pansies.

1   Dampen the paper with clean water, sufficient to ensure the paint will run slowly.
2   Apply one colour, the pigment thicker than the water, to just short of the point where it will join the next colour. Generally use the lighter colour first, as boundaries are not always exact and you may have an occasional tiny overlap you can overlook.
3   Apply the second colour, exactly the same consistency as the first, leaving a gap between the colours.
4   The pigments will attract one another, although a little encouragement with a nearly dry brush may be necessary. Do not drag the brush across the two colours. Leave to dry. It does not always turn out the way you expect, to so make this the first stage of painting in case adjustments (or abandonment) are necessary – and practise first!

Preserving your plant: Vickie Marsh

When faced with a challenging dandelion seedhead, or something similarly fragile, make sure it does not blow away before you complete it by giving it a gentle puff of hairspray.

Colour matching: DLDC tutor Yvonne Glenister Hammond

Take a small piece of paper – say 12 x 8cm (5 x 3in) – and use an ordinary stationery punch to make holes along each side, roughly an inch apart. It is best to use the same paper that you intend to paint on. Mix your pigment, for example green for a leaf, and paint an area of about 2.5cm (1in) around one of the holes. When it is dry, hold the paper over a leaf and you should be able to judge how good a match you have achieved.

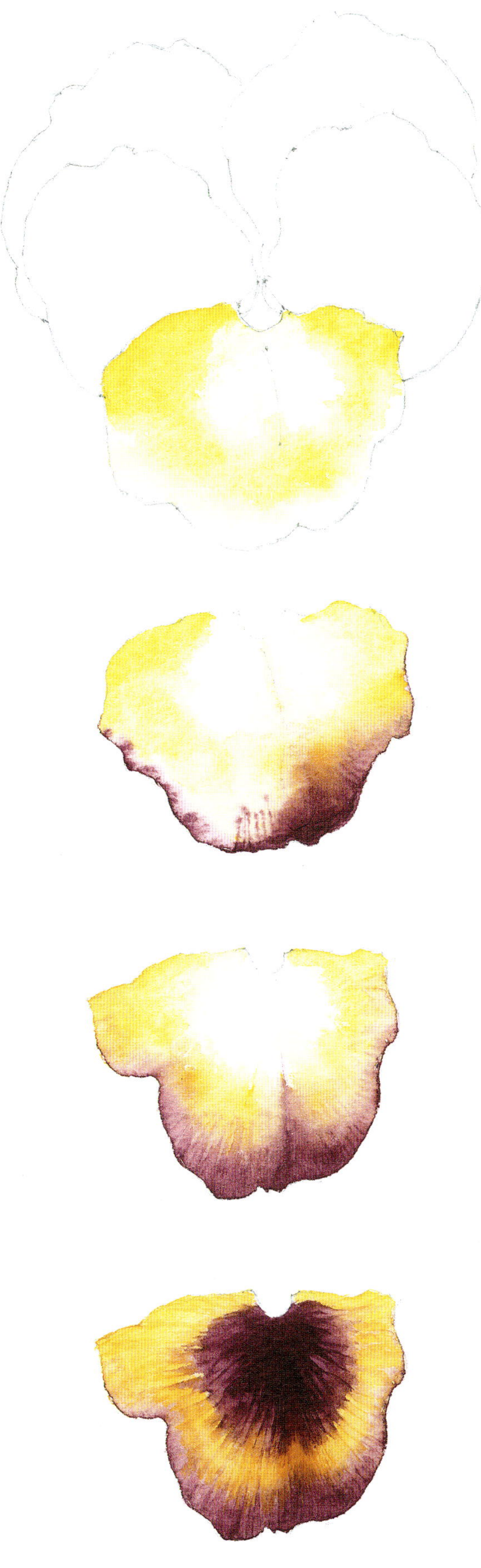

Contributing Artists

Sandra Wall Armitage SBA President 2013–18
Valerie Baines SBA (Hon Ret'd)
Vivien Burgess SBA
Sarah Caswell SBA
Marta Chirino SBA (Spain)
Danielle Choi DLDC Course 13 (S. Korea)
Elizabeth Sherras Clark SBA (Ret'd)
Joanna Craig McFeely SBA
Shevaun Doherty Dip SBA (Dist) SBA (Eire)
Margaret Eggleton SBA
Sheila Etchingham SBA
Guy William Eves SBA
Sharon Field Dip SBA (Dist) (Australia)
Margaret Fitzpatrick Dip SBA (Dist) SBA
Sue Flynn Dip SBA (Credit)
Dianne Frank SBA
Karen Gavin Dip SBA (Dist)
Grazia Gianella DLDC Course 14 (Italy)
Yvonne Glenister Hammond SBA
Kate Green SBA
Jan Harbon SBA
Erika Hargesheimer Dip SBA (Dist) (Canada)
Denise Heywood SBA
Rachel Hughes SBA
Jenny Jowett FSBA
Sue Jung Dip SBA (Credit) (S. Korea)
Jiyoung Kim DLDC Course 14 (S. Korea)
Mary Lasserson SBA
Kay Leeves Dip SBA (Dist)
Dona Leonardi DLDC Course 13 (Italy)

Vickie Marsh SBA President 2010–13
Diane Marshall Dip SBA (Credit)
Alister Mathews SBA
Jae Young Min DLDC Course 14 (S. Korea)
Maria Moldavsky DLDC Course 13
Barbara Munro Dip SBA (Dist)
Dorothy Pavey SBA
Marion Perkins SBA
Sally Jane Perrin SBA
Ian Pethers SBA
Janie Pirie SBA
Janet Pope SBA
Alison Procter SBA (Hon Ret'd)
Marina Protsenko DLDC Course 12 (Russia)
Ros Purkis DLDC Course 13
Gillian Receveur Dip SBA (Credit) (New Zealand)
Kay Rees-Davies SBA
Hazel Rush Dip SBA (Dist) SBA
Billy Showell SBA President 2018–
Margaret Stevens FSBA President 2005–10
Sue Symonds Dip SBA (Higher Pass)
Choon-Ying Tan DLDC Course 13 (Singapore)
Heidi Venamore Dip SBA (Dist)
Sunanda Widel DLDC Course 13 (Singapore)
Simon Williams SBA DLDC Director
Sarah Wood SBA

Index